KATHARINE DREXEL

Nihil Obstat: Rev. Msgr. Daniel H. Mueggenborg, S.T.L.

Pastor of Christ the King Parish, Tulsa, Oklahoma

May 7, 2014

Imprimatur: Most Rev. Edward J. Slattery, D.D.

Bishop of the Diocese of Tulsa

May 9, 2014

In accordance with Canon 824, permission to publish was granted on May 9, 2014, by His Eminence, the Most Rev. Edward J. Slattery, D.D., Bishop of the Diocese of Tulsa. Permission to publish is an official declaration of ecclesiastical authority that the material is free from doctrinal and moral error. No legal responsibility is assumed by the grant of this permission.

Katharine Drexel

The Riches-to-Rags Story of an
American Catholic Saint

Cheryl C. D. Hughes

WILLIAM B. EERDMANS PUBLISHING COMPANY
GRAND RAPIDS, MICHIGAN / CAMBRIDGE, U.K.

Published 2014 by
Wm. B. Eerdmans Publishing Co.
2140 Oak Industrial Drive N.E., Grand Rapids, Michigan 49505 /
P.O. Box 163, Cambridge CB3 9PU U.K.

Printed in the United States of America

20 19 18 17 16 15 14   7 6 5 4 3 2 1

Library of Congress Cataloging-in-Publication Data

Hughes, Cheryl C. D., 1945-
Katharine Drexel: the riches-to-rags story of an American Catholic saint /
Cheryl C. D. Hughes.
pages   cm
Includes bibliographical references and index.
ISBN 978-0-8028-6992-0 (pbk.: alk. paper)
1. Drexel, Katharine Mary, Saint, 1858-1955.
2. Christian saints — United States — Biography.
I. Title.

BX4700.D77H84   2014
271'.97 — dc23
[B]

2014012174

www.eerdmans.com

Contents

Abbreviations

ASBS	Annals of the Sisters of the Blessed Sacrament
EBD	Emma Bouvier Drexel
ELD	Elizabeth Langstroth Drexel
FAD	Francis Anthony Drexel
LBD	Louise Bouvier Drexel
MKD	Mary Katharine Drexel (before entering the convent), born Catherine Mary Drexel. Mother Mary Katharine Drexel (after entering the convent)
NA	Nocturnal Adoration
OASBS	Old Annals of the Sisters of the Blessed Sacrament
Positio	*Canonizationis Servae Dei Catherinae Drexel, Fundatricis Congregationis Sororum A SS. Sacramento Pro Indis et Colrata Gente, (1858-1955): Positio super virtutibus*
SBS	Sisters of the Blessed Sacrament
SJ	Society of Jesus (The Jesuits)

Introduction to the Mystery of Katharine Drexel

On October 1, 2000, Pope John Paul II proclaimed Katharine Drexel a saint of the Roman Catholic Church. She became the second American-born saint of the Catholic Church and its answer to the relative social, political, and economic disadvantages of African American and Native American people.[1] Katharine Drexel lived a life of virtue, of even the heroic virtue required for sainthood, and through her inspiration and effort she improved the lives of untold numbers of Native Americans and African Americans; her life, work, and example are appropriate mirrors for Catholic Christians at the beginning of the twenty-first century.

Everyone's life is a mystery of sorts. My project with St. Katharine Drexel was to uncover, as much as possible, her mystery, those personal, intellectual, and religious motivations that helped her to become a saint. Not all philanthropists or workers in the field of social justice are considered saints, but Katharine became a saint, in her own terms and in her own time, and her canonization illuminates her importance as saintly exemplar early in this third millennium. I will explore what I believe Pope John Paul II wished to teach by canonizing this particular American woman. It will become apparent that she was a worthy candidate for sainthood, but many worthy people never become saints of the Church. John Paul II was able to look at Katharine and see a woman who was necessary to his pastoral project, particularly in what he referred to as the superdeveloped countries, like the United States.

---

1. St. Elizabeth Ann Seton was the first native-born American saint. The founder of the American Sisters of Charity was canonized in 1975. St. Kateri Tekakwitha, an Algonquin-Mohawk Native American, was canonized in 2012.

Most people are naturally inquisitive sorts who enjoy hearing about the lives of the rich and famous. The case of Katharine Drexel (1858-1955), who turned away from a wealthy and socially elite family background to embrace the poverty and hardship of the veil, the habit, and the convent, is perplexing. Her chosen life, in style and substance, runs counter to everything most people hold dear. She turned her back on marriage, family, and society. To flout all that was opposed to the American ideal of womanhood in the late nineteenth century. It was not modern. It did not seem natural. However, if by "American," "modern," and "natural" one means living a life of individuality and action with great practical ability, then Katharine perfectly exemplifies it. True, her interests did not bend toward mammon; her goals were of both this world and the next. She became a mystic with a kenotic, or self-emptying, and deeply eucharistic spirituality that called her to a very difficult vocation. In the midst of ease and plenty and wealth, it is most singular to flee to poverty. It is, however, natural — and modern — to follow one's inner voice.

Moved by her Catholic Christianity to see the face of Christ in each person, she took up the causes of Native Americans and African Americans. She founded the order of the Sisters of the Blessed Sacrament for Indians and Colored People, the only order so dedicated.[2] She formed and supported almost sixty missions and schools, mostly in the American West and South, as well as in and around her own Philadelphia. Her first mission was opened in 1894 in Santa Fe, New Mexico, for the Pueblo Indians, who were at the time completely unschooled. She met with their chiefs, and bearing gifts of friendship, she won their confidence and support for St. Catherine's School and Mission. Later, in 1917, outside of New Orleans, she founded Xavier University to train young African Americans to teach in the segregated black schools of the day. The university was, and remains, the only Catholic institution of higher education in America founded to educate predominantly African American Catholic young men and women.[3]

For over forty years, while she was physically able, Katharine paid an-

2. There was at the time another order called the Sisters of the Blessed Sacrament, so to distinguish her order and avoid confusion she added "for Indians and Colored People," since they constituted her specific mission. The mission of the order has not changed, but its title has been shortened in common usage to the Sisters of the Blessed Sacrament. It is abbreviated in this book as SBS.

3. Primarily established for Catholic African American men and women, Xavier has never had a policy of racial segregation or a policy of religious exclusivity.

nual visits to all her missions. She traveled six months out of each year, not only to check on the health and progress of the missions, but also to succor her sisters and to lead them in retreats to refresh their souls and renew their enthusiasm. Personally, she engaged in mortification of the flesh and spent hours prostrate on her face with arms outstretched in prayer before the consecrated Host of the eucharistic Sacrament. She kept a daily journal for most of her life and kept separate prayer journals, which are especially poignant at the end of her life, when the Sacrament was exposed to her at all times. Within forty-five years of her death, she was credited with the miraculous cures of a child deaf from birth and a young man who had lost his hearing through illness.

St. Katharine's eucharistic spirituality and mysticism came together to make her an American ideal, in the best sense of the word. Orson Welles once said, "The ideal American type is perfectly expressed in the Protestant, individualistic, anti-conformist."[4] This type was portrayed in classic films by Bette Davis and Katharine Hepburn in the golden age of Hollywood; they were self-confident, forthright, and smart. The nonconformist Katharine Drexel got it right, except for the "Protestant" part. She was a loyal Catholic in a very Protestant country. In the great democratic poem "Song of Myself," Walt Whitman wrote,

> And I know that the hand of God is the promise of my own,
> And I know that the spirit of God is the brother of my own,
> And that all the men ever born are also my brothers, and the women my
> sisters and lovers.[5]

To Katharine Drexel, all were her brothers and sisters.

Her individuality and action were turned from seeking personal fame and wealth to benefiting others less fortunate. And while she is not the only member of her class to devote her life to this cause, she is, to date, the only canonized saint and mystic from among America's socially prominent families. It is this, as well as her relative obscurity, that makes her such a compelling subject. How ironic that she, who eschewed the transitory fame of social privilege, is remembered and celebrated on her feast day by a church of a billion people. In canonizing Katharine Drexel, the Catholic Church is

---

4. Orson Welles, quoted in *Hollywood Voices: Interviews with Film Directors,* comp. Andrew Sarris (London: Secker and Warburg, 1971).

5. Walt Whitman, "Song of Myself," online.

not merely honoring her memory as a saintly person; it is holding her up as a role model for others to emulate.

I have known about Katharine Drexel since the 1960s. I learned that she had come from a very wealthy and socially prominent family and that she had become a nun, but that was all I knew until I started looking into her life. Everyone I had ever encountered had seen money and prestige as the only routes to personal happiness. But in Katharine I found a compelling and fascinating countercultural example. She did not fit into any of my known categories. Initially, it was her rejection of wealth and social position that drew me toward her; what kept me interested in her was what she did with her life after she gave up her ball gowns and put on a habit, and, more importantly, why she chose the life she led and what sustained her throughout. Her inner beliefs and spirituality moved to the foreground to illuminate what she did over her long and productive life. Hers was a life of contemplation in action, the results of which are still being felt today. In my adopted hometown of Tulsa, Oklahoma, Katharine financed the building of the first Catholic school and church. The school, St. Theresa's for Creek Girls, was opened in September 1899, the day after the first mass was said in the new church. Today they are known as Holy Family Cathedral School and Holy Family Cathedral. As an inner-city parish school and church, they still serve a multiethnic population, including a large percentage of African Americans and Native Americans.

Each chapter of this book elucidates a different aspect of Katharine's story, beginning with her family life. It was within the family that she began to develop her understanding of not only what it means to be a Catholic Christian, but also how to be a Catholic Christian, how to put her Catholic Christianity into action. Chapter 1, "Simply Katie: Katharine Drexel's Family Life," is mainly historical in nature, rather than psychological or even theological, and addresses the origins of Katharine's spirituality and social concern.

Chapter 2, "'Make Haste Slowly': The Discernment of a Vocation," describes the long and difficult process of her vocational discernment, entered into with ardor in 1883 and not resolved until 1889, when she finally entered the convent. The process involved an internal struggle as well as a struggle with church authority, in the person of her spiritual director, the Reverend James O'Connor, who for a long time discouraged her from entering a convent.

Chapter 3, "Growth of the Order," covers the development, growth, and ultimate decline of her order, the Sisters of the Blessed Sacrament for

Indians and Colored People. A number of missions are investigated as case studies of the challenges faced by Mother Katharine.

The essence of Katharine's spirituality is the topic of the next chapter. It is ultimately not what she did in her lifetime, though that is incredibly interesting, but her motivations that make her so compelling, so unique. What stands out about Katharine is her spirituality, which was profoundly eucharistic and deeply kenotic, that is, self-emptying. By filling herself with the Eucharist and by emptying herself at the same time, Katharine was able to transform herself into a missionary dedicated to the least fortunate in the United States. Her kenotic spirituality was made evident in her ascetic practices and her great poverty, both of which may appear extreme to modern readers. Chapter 4, "The Kenotic and Eucharistic Spirituality of Katharine Drexel," reveals her deep spirituality as essential to nourishing her apostolic works. It was her spirituality, linked to her singular mission, that made her a saint in her own time.

The next chapter demonstrates how well Katharine fit into Pope John Paul II's pastoral program. It establishes the pope's analysis of the late twentieth century as morally threatened by materialism and secularism, thereby elucidating how Katharine served his purpose as an example of one who turned from material wealth to spiritual perfection, making her a viable candidate for sainthood by the Catholic Church. Chapter 5, "The Pope, the Times, and the Saint: Be Not Afraid," interrogates the writings of John Paul to demonstrate why Katharine was deemed worthy of sainthood by the Roman Catholic Church.

The canonization of saints belongs to the pope's teaching authority within the Church. Pope John Paul II was teaching something very specific when he made Katharine a saint. David Tracy argues in *The Analogical Imagination* that individuals can become as classic texts, to be read fruitfully over and over again by people of different times and different places. By recognizing an individual as a classic, "we recognize nothing less than the disclosure of a reality we cannot but name truth."[6] The truth that is Katharine Drexel, by her canonization, is held up for all to read. It is my contention that the canonization of this saint was intended to teach those in the developed countries, particularly Western countries, and especially in the United States, to value spiritual goods over material goods; to develop the spirit, if not the reality, of poverty; to end all forms of discrimination, especially racism; to work for social justice for all peoples; to see Christ in every individual; and,

---

6. David Tracy, *The Analogical Imagination* (New York: Crossroad, 1981), p. 108.

moreover, that the path to these moral goods is found in the imitation of the eucharistic and self-emptying Christ. John Paul II was teaching his flock and, by extension, the entire world not to be afraid in the face of the ills of modern societies, because personal sanctity and social justice are possible, as witnessed by Katharine and her works, and because, despite evidence to the contrary, God is still in charge. If there were indeed more like Katharine Drexel in the world, according to the pope, one need not be afraid. In knowing Katharine Drexel, one would know the truth.

What will not be found in this story are malicious tales of strife between Mother Katharine and various priests and bishops or between Mother Katharine and her sisters. There is no written or even anecdotal evidence that Katharine ever argued with a bishop. Archbishop Joseph McShea said of her, "I never heard of any controversy that she had. . . . Mother Katharine, I never heard of any dissent or any disagreements with bishops."[7] Her sisters were, to her, "my dear daughters," and though mother-daughter relationships can be fraught with conflict, none is recorded in the annals or collected letters. When I asked the Sisters of the Blessed Sacrament for anything controversial about Mother Katharine, the only implied criticism I heard was that she did not challenge her father's will in order to endow the congregation.

An essential primary source for the sanctity of Katharine Drexel is the *positio*,[8] the main legal document presented to the Congregation for the Causes of Saints in support of her canonization. It consists of three volumes. The biographical section of the *positio*, volume 1, was written by Bishop Joseph Martino when he was a young priest; it is by far the longest volume. His authorial job was to sell the canonization of Katharine Drexel to the officials in Rome. Martino's biography is compelling and positive. The second volume contains the transcripts of interviews conducted with thirty-four witnesses to her heroic virtues and life of holiness (the necessary qualifications for sainthood, along with two authenticated miracles). The witnesses were chosen because they were "either collaborators of Mother Katharine, close observers of her work, or among those who benefited from her apostolic zeal."[9] All witnesses responded to the same ninety questions. Many of the

---

7. Kenneth L. Woodward, *Making Saints: How the Catholic Church Determines Who Becomes a Saint, Who Doesn't, and Why* (New York: Simon and Schuster, 1990), p. 239 note.

8. Congregation for the Causes of Saints, *Canonizationis Servae Dei Catherinae Drexel, Fundatricis Congregationis Sororum A SS. Sacramento Pro Indis et Colrata Gente, (1858-1955): Positio super virtutibus*, 3 vols. (Rome, 1986). Vol. 1 written by Rev. Joseph Martino. Hereafter this work will be referenced as *Positio*.

9. *Positio*, 2:ii.

questions would constitute "leading questions" in an American court of law, even though a *positio* is often likened to a legal brief that states the case for or against someone. Some typical questions: "What do you know of the spiritual activities of Katharine Drexel?"[10] "How did Katharine Drexel exhibit her outstanding love of God?"[11] "Do you consider Katharine Drexel a saintly person?"[12] The only question that may have elicited a negative response was "Did Katharine Drexel ever display herself in such a way as to show loss of self-control?" The most damaging example was by Sr. Mary Frances Mc-Cusken, who recalled that Mother Katharine once "tossed a badly shrunken woolen garment at the Sister who had laundered it."[13] The third volume is the shortest. It presents, and often repeats, the most pertinent testimony of the witnesses by way of a summation of the cause for the canonization of Katharine Drexel.

*   *   *

Some background on the social, historical, and political contexts for Katharine's emergence is important for understanding her life's trajectory. As early as the sixteenth century, several orders of missionary priests came to the New World to evangelize the native peoples; the Jesuits, Benedictines, and Franciscans are only the most famous. The priests were aided by the Ursuline and Franciscan women, among others. Over the course of three hundred years, the Catholic missionaries met with varied, but steady, success. Most of the Native American tribes, from the Saint Lawrence River to the Great Lakes to the Mississippi River and across the West to the Pacific Ocean, were evangelized by Catholic missionaries.

After the Civil War (1861-1865), President Ulysses Grant believed that the settlement of the West by white settlers was inevitable. To make the territories safe for white settlers and to accommodate the Native Americans' desires to have areas set aside for their way of life free from the presence of whites, native tribes signed treaties with the federal government providing for their removal from homelands to reservations and territories. From the confines of the reservations, bands of young Indian warriors frequently went on the "warpath" to steal horses or brides, or merely to assert their manhood.

---

10. *Positio,* 2:iv.
11. *Positio,* 2:v.
12. *Positio,* 2:vii.
13. *Positio,* 2:24.

Native uprisings were ruthlessly put down by the United States cavalry, and whole tribes suffered greatly for the actions of a few. Grant believed that the best means to pacify the native tribes and to save them from extinction was to educate and Christianize them. To this end, he promulgated in 1870 what is known as Grant's Peace Policy. He said to a joint meeting of the United States Congress: "Indian agencies being civil offices, I determined to give all the agencies to such religious denominations as had hitherto established missioners among the Indians and perhaps to some other denominations who would undertake the work on the same terms — i.e. missionary work."[14]

Agency heads, though civil servants, were to be appointed by the religious denominations. As Sr. Consuela Duffy, SBS, points out, at the date of the proclamation "there were seventy-two Indian agencies; in thirty-eight of these, Catholic missionaries were the first to establish themselves." However, only eight agencies were assigned to the Catholic Church. The Protestant churches in the United States were so much better organized politically than the Catholic Church that the U.S. Board of Indian Commissioners was made up exclusively of Protestant men. As a result, "some eighty thousand Catholic baptized Indians were put under Protestant Control."[15] Amazingly, railroad tracks served as boundaries by which tribes were assigned to denominations.

Naturally, this parceling out of the Indian tribes met with a great deal of protest from Catholic leaders, as well as from various Indian tribes. After over two years of trying to deal with the government's intransigence, the United States Catholic bishops in 1874 created the Catholic Commission for Indian Affairs. In 1879 the Bureau of Catholic Indian Missions was formed to replace the commission. Its purpose was to secure, if possible, the remainder of those agencies to which Catholic missionaries were justly entitled under the terms of Grant's Peace Policy and to direct the agencies assigned to Catholic missionaries, as well as to establish and staff schools for the Indians.[16]

Although the government assigned various tribes to various denominations, it was up to the denominations to support the missions financially. The burden on them to fund their missions and their missionaries was tremendous. And for the Catholic Church, this was at a time of immense foreign-born Catholic immigration into the cities of the Atlantic seaboard. Most eastern dioceses were completely overwhelmed just seeing to the spiritual

14. William H. Ketchum, "Bureau of Catholic Indian Missions," in *Catholic Encyclopedia,* vol. 7 (New York: Robert Appleton, 1912), p. 745.

15. Sr. Consuela Duffy, SBS, *Katharine Drexel: A Biography* (Philadelphia: Reilly Co., 1966), p. 81.

16. ASBS, vol. 1, p. 52.

and material needs of the throngs of Italian, Irish, Polish, and German Catholics who were daily joining them. Mostly due to immigration, the Roman Catholic population of the United States quadrupled from 1860 to 1895.[17] Church societies had great difficulty turning their attention to the desperate needs of Native Americans, or for that matter, African Americans, most of whose ancestors had been forced to come to the continent as slaves. Much of their blindness to the plight of these groups was due to the rampant racism of the nineteenth century. The new European immigrants were copies of themselves, but Native Americans and African Americans were "different" and not high on the list of charitable priorities. This attitude, however, held no sway in the Drexel household. The Drexel family was dedicated to serving the needs of those who could claim to be among the least of Jesus' brothers.

Shortly after the death of their father in 1885, the three Drexel sisters were gathered on the second floor of the Walnut Street, Philadelphia, family home when two visitors requested an interview. For some reason, it fell to Katharine to go down to receive them in the drawing room. Her visitors were Fr. Joseph Stephan, director of the Bureau of Catholic Indian Missions, and Bishop Martin Marty, the vicar apostolic of northern Minnesota. They explained to Katharine the new contract system whereby the federal government would pay some support for native students to attend missionary schools, provided that the schools were built, provided for, and staffed by churches. This contract system was the successor to Grant's Peace Policy, which had failed largely because many of the denominations assigned to mission territories were either unequipped to deal with such a large and expensive undertaking or chose not to accept the challenge. On the other hand, the Catholic Church had a long history of missionary activity in the New World, and some Catholics were keen to extend the Church among the native peoples. However, they lacked the money and people to serve the missions. Fr. Stephan and Bishop Marty came to the right place when they showed up in the Drexel drawing room.

They left there with a $500 check written by Katharine to fund a new boarding school for the Sioux Indians on the Rosebud Reservation. She followed that up with much more financial support for the Rosebud mission, personally engaging and financially supporting the Sisters of St. Francis of Stella Niagara to staff the school. She built a school for the Osages in Indian Territory, which was destroyed by a tornado shortly afterward. She imme-

---

17. Sydney E. Ahlstrom, *A Religious History of the American People* (New Haven: Yale University Press, 1973), p. 827.

diately rebuilt it with a stronger design and sturdier materials. Eventually, her own Sisters of the Blessed Sacrament would staff both missions. Later in 1885, Fr. Stephan wrote to her to thank her for her financial support: "You and your sisters are the only ones who take a lively interest in the Catholic Indian question. True friends of the Indian are hard to find, says Bishop Marty, and we thank you with the blessings from Heaven. May the Lord be your reward."[18]

Despite General Philip Sheridan's famous 1869 dictum that the only good Indian is a dead Indian, the romantic sentiment of Jean-Jacques Rousseau's noble savage still influenced the attitude of many Americans toward Native Americans.[19] This attitude could prevail because most European Americans never came in contact with the native population. This was not true for African Americans, who mixed freely in commerce, if not socially and politically, with European Americans. In several southern states the African American ex-slave population outnumbered Americans of European descent.

The white citizens of the southern states of the former Confederacy felt they were humiliated in their defeat by the Union army during the Civil War and the subsequent presidential Reconstruction of the southern states from 1865 to 1877. Reconstruction swept white politicians out of office in the South and filled the state legislatures with former slaves.

In reaction to Reconstruction and in support of white supremacy, the Ku Klux Klan was founded in Pulaski, Tennessee, in 1866. It employed tactics of intimidation, whipping, and lynching in its attempts to control the behavior and deny the voting of the newly enfranchised former slave men. Southern whites also passed a number of state bills, called "Jim Crow laws," that imposed literacy tests, poll taxes, property requirements for voting, and other measures that controlled the behavior of African American citizens. The 1886 U.S. Supreme Court decision of *Plessy v. Ferguson* legalized "sep-

18. Quoted in Katherine Burton, *The Golden Door: The Life of Katharine Drexel* (New York: P. J. Kenedy and Sons, 1957), p. 75.

19. In January 1869, General Sheridan held a conference with fifty Indian chiefs at Fort Cobb in Indian Territory (later part of Oklahoma). Comanche chief Toch-a-way introduced himself to the general by saying, "Me Toch-a-way, me good Indian." To which Sheridan is reported to have replied, "The only good Indians I ever saw were dead." The story may be apocryphal, but the saying eventually became widely repeated as "The only good Indian is a dead Indian." Dee Brown reports this and similar stories in *Bury My Heart at Wounded Knee: An Indian History of the American West* (New York: Henry Holt, 1990; 1st ed. 1970), pp. 147-74.

arate but equal" treatment of and facilities for African American citizens.[20] Racial segregation was legal until the 1954 Supreme Court decision *Brown v. Board of Education of Topeka,* which stated, "We conclude that, in the field of public education, the doctrine of 'separate but equal' has no place. Separate educational facilities are inherently unequal."[21]

A second incarnation of the Ku Klux Klan in 1917 not only infected the southern states but also succeeded as far west as California and as far north as Pennsylvania. It turned its wrath and violence against Jews, Catholics, and especially African Americans and those who sympathized with them. The Klan once burned a cross on the grounds of the motherhouse of the Sisters of the Blessed Sacrament in Bensalem, Pennsylvania, to protest the mission of Katharine Drexel and her sisters to aid Native Americans and African Americans. It was not the only threat by the Klan to the Sisters of the Blessed Sacrament.

When the sisters marched in the civil rights demonstrations in the 1950s and 1960s, they were spat upon and called "nigger sisters." When the members of the group complained to their founder, she urged them to pray for their tormentors. The Klan was not the only oppressive organization opposed to African Americans, Jews, Catholics, and foreigners (meaning Chinese, Polish, and other eastern Europeans), but it was the worst. As a symbol, the Klan stood for the same feelings shared by many Americans of western European ancestry.

When Katharine Drexel undertook to form an order of sisters to attend to the needs of Native Americans and African Americans, she was willingly taking on an almost insurmountable task. The majority of the population was mainly apathetic or even hostile to the plight of these peoples.

To add to her burden, she was female and Catholic. Nineteenth-century women were considered under the protection of their fathers or husbands. Women could not vote in federal elections until 1920. In many states, married women had no right to their own property or wages; they could not enter into contracts on their own. They had no control over their bodies or even their children. Children belonged to their fathers. To be a woman was to be second-class. Women were marginalized from public life and subjugated in the home. While working-class women could flout social con-

20. *Plessy v. Ferguson,* Judgement, Decided May 18, 1886, *Records of the Supreme Court of the United States.* Record Group 267, 163, #15248, National Archives, Washington, D.C.. The phrase "separate but equal" does not actually appear in the decision.

21. *Brown v. The Board of Education,* Judgment, Decided May 17, 1954, *Records of the Supreme Court of the United States.*

ventions and many laws, the lives of middle- and upper-class women were severely circumscribed by customs and laws. Katharine Drexel's velvet-lined circle was very tight.

Adding to her marginalization was her Catholicism. Protestants distrusted the Catholic minority in the United States. They believed that to be Catholic was not to be truly American, and feared that Catholics gave their political allegiance to the pope in Rome, not to the president in Washington. As recently as 1844, a mere fourteen years before Katharine's birth, there had been anti-Catholic riots in Philadelphia, her hometown, during which several churches, schools, and homes were burned; twenty had been killed and hundreds left homeless. In 1856, the anti-Catholic Committee of Vigilance took over the city government of San Francisco and "proceeded to execute four people and sought to banish from the city close to one hundred more."[22] In the presidential campaign of 1884, the slogan "Rum, Romanism, and Rebellion" was used by the Republicans as a rallying cry against the Democratic candidate, Grover Cleveland. This period of vehement anti-Catholicism not surprisingly coincided with the period of Catholicism's greatest growth, largely due to increased immigration. The period from 1850 to 1906 saw Catholics in the United States grow from 5 percent to 17 percent of the population. By 1906, the fourteen million Catholics in the United States constituted the single largest Christian denomination. Yet despite their numbers, Catholics remained marginalized socially and economically. "No Irish need apply" was a sign my father recalled seeing in Pennsylvania storefronts. Historian Arthur Schlesinger Sr. once commented, "I regard the prejudice against your [Catholic] Church as the deepest bias in the history of the American people."[23] Such prejudice became law with the enactment of quota systems that all but halted immigration from Catholic countries by 1924.[24]

Becoming a nun added further to the marginalization of Katharine Drexel. If Protestants thought that to be Catholic was to be un-American, they believed that for a woman to become a nun was positively unnatural. Even the inimitable Henry James, writing in his novel *The American* about Madame de Cintre's escape into a Carmelite convent, described the convent

22. Jay P. Dolan, *The American Catholic Experience: A History from Colonial Times to the Present* (Garden City, N.Y.: Doubleday, 1985), p. 202.

23. John Tracy Ellis, *American Catholicism,* 2nd ed. rev. (Chicago: University of Chicago Press, 1969), p. 151.

24. Julie Byrne, "Roman Catholics and Immigration in Nineteenth-Century America," National Humanities Council, online, n.d.

alternately as a tomb or a prison.[25] Nineteenth-century American literature of a more popular sort was replete with lurid, indeed pornographic, tales of women forced into convents, especially convents with tunnels connecting them to priests' rectories or monasteries, convenient for burying within the walls the babies born of lustful unions. The most famous of these anti-Catholic diatribes was *The Awful Disclosures by Maria Monk of the Hotel Dieu Nunnery of Montreal,* by the eponymous, and apocryphal, Miss Monk.[26] Works such as this helped to fuel the anti-immigration, anti-Catholic, antinun, nativist political party, the Know Nothing, or American, Party, which was formed as a national political party in the 1850s. While the party dissolved after the 1856 election, its sentiments persisted to some degree until the 1960 election of John F. Kennedy as the country's first Catholic president, when it was widely and preposterously rumored that the pope was preparing to resettle from Rome to the Mississippi Valley.

To be a woman, a Catholic, and a nun in nineteenth-century America was to be thrice marginalized. However, Katharine Drexel was more than prepared for what might be termed her white martyrdom. Her preparation for life, and death, began, as it does for all of us, at home in the embrace of family; that beginning is the subject of the first chapter.

C.C.D.H.
Tulsa, Oklahoma
March 3, 2013
The Feast Day of St. Katharine Drexel

25. Henry James, *The American* (New York: Library of America, 1983), pp. 867-69.

26. A reproduction of the 1836 book is available from Kessinger Publishing of Whitefish, Montana (July 1, 2003).

CHAPTER 1

Simply Katie: Katharine Drexel's Family Life

The family has been called the first school for virtue; indeed, Pope John Paul II called the family the "first seminary," "the domestic church," and "the nursery of vocations."[1] Catholic Christian families teach their young what it means to be Catholic and how, practically, to live one's life as a Christian. Katharine Drexel's parents fostered in her and her sisters a love of virtue carried out for the benefit of others less fortunate. This chapter will demonstrate that what she learned from her parents, who through word, deed, and example set in motion the development of personal sanctity and benevolent actions that ultimately made Katharine Drexel a saint.

Katharine Drexel was not born a saint. She worked toward sanctity her entire life and, in her own estimation, fell miserably short of her goal. Her sainthood was the result of a lifelong pursuit of the perfection commanded by Jesus of his disciples. She came into this world with many of its blessings — a large, loving family and great material wealth. She was a debutante and an heiress, but these are not what one thinks about when contemplating the essence of a saint. In fact, wealth is more often than not a stumbling block to sanctity. After the encounter with the rich young man who had kept all the commandments but could not give up all his possessions to follow Jesus, Jesus remarked to his disciples, "How hard it will be for those who have wealth to enter the kingdom of God!" (Mark 10:23).

Yet Katharine Drexel is recognized by the Catholic Church as a saint in that very kingdom. She became a saint not because of her wealth, but because of the spirit of poverty and stewardship with which she grew in

1. Message for the XXXI World Day of Prayer for Vocations, 1994, 1 and 3, online at the Vatican Web site, www.vatican.va.

perfection, judiciously dispensing her wealth for the specific spiritual and educational benefit of Native Americans and African Americans, the least of Jesus' brothers in America. She lived into her ninety-seventh year. For the last sixty-seven of them, she was known as Mother Mary Katharine Drexel, founder of the congregation of the Sisters of the Blessed Sacrament for Indians and Colored People, but until she was thirty she was simply Katie Drexel. The love and charity she would later channel through her religious order were extensions and amplifications of the lessons she learned from her family.

This chapter will consider Katharine's early life within the circle of her family until that circle was broken, indeed shattered, by the death, first, of her mother and, then, of her father. It will reveal a close family that thoroughly enjoyed its wealth and social position, but will also reveal a family life tempered by the spirituality of its wife and mother, who wrote to her eldest daughter, Elizabeth, then aged eleven: "Chère Petite, Read the beautiful device above [*Aidez vous et Dieu vous aidera* (Help yourself and God will help you)] and resolve to try for yourself that you may have the grace of God in all your undertakings, particularly in your studies, that one day by the cultivation of your mind and the elegance of your deportment . . . you may become my jewel, my crown, my glory."[2] It became the goal of each of her three daughters to become, by the grace of God, their mother's jewel, crown, and glory.

Family Background

Katharine Drexel was born on November 26, 1858, the second daughter of Francis Anthony Drexel and Hannah Langstroth Drexel, in Philadelphia, Pennsylvania.[3] Her father was a well-known businessman whose banking empire maintained firms in Philadelphia, New York, San Francisco, London, and Paris. He had entered the banking business at the age of thirteen as a clerk and night watchman for his father's Drexel & Company. His father, Francis Martin Drexel, was a native of Dornbirn, Austria, born on an Easter Sunday, who left his homeland twice to escape military conscription and

2. EBD to ELD, February 26, 1867. Unless otherwise noted, all quoted Drexel letters are in the Archives of the Sisters of the Blessed Sacrament at the motherhouse in Bensalem, Pennsylvania.

3. The woman known today as St. Katharine Drexel was baptized Catherine Mary Drexel. She signed various legal papers as Catherine or Catharine. As an adult she spelled her name Katharine. When she became a novice, her religious name became Mary Katharine.

again later in search of commissions as a painter of portraits. Francis Martin Drexel was educated in Austria and then sent to Italy to learn painting before being apprenticed to an Austrian painter. Like many young men of his generation, he decided to try the opportunities available in the United States. He was willing to give America a six-month trial, but he did not intend to stay indefinitely. He left Amsterdam on May 16, 1817, aboard *John of Baltimore* and arrived in Philadelphia on July 28. In short order, Francis Martin opened a studio at 131 South Front Street and became employed as an art instructor at Bazeley's Female Seminary. He was immediately popular as a portrait painter and teacher. He painted three portraits in the first month he was in Philadelphia. The following year he exhibited nine oil paintings and three drawings at the Philadelphia Academy of Fine Arts. The annual exhibition of the Academy showed his work for six consecutive years.

In 1821 he married Catherine Hookey of Philadelphia, giving up on his vow to return to Austria and not make the United States his permanent home. His work as a painter and art teacher continued to prosper until he became the victim of libel and slander by Bernard Gallagher, Catherine's brother-in-law.[4] Francis Martin sued Gallagher, and even though Gallagher admitted his falsehoods and the case was settled out of court, the taint of a lawsuit caused the drop-off of Drexel's commissions among his high-class clientele and the loss of his art students. He was released from Bazeley's Seminary. Without other employment prospects, he was forced to leave his wife and two sons in Philadelphia to make two long trips to South America and Mexico in search of commissions.

He painted copies of portraits of Simon Bolívar and other liberators and undertook personal commissions from the socially elite. Between 1826 and 1837, Francis Martin was gone from Philadelphia for a total of six years. He earned approximately $22,000 in commissions during his South American sojourn. He sent $14,000 home to Catherine and the children; of the rest he was either robbed or refused payment, or he spent it on expenses, paints, and travel. While on his travels, he learned from the men and women with

---

4. Sr. Mary Dolores Letterhouse, SBS, *The Francis A. Drexel Family* (Cornwells Heights, Pa.: Sisters of the Blessed Sacrament, 1939), p. 5. None of the Drexel family's personal papers discusses the lawsuit. The libelous action may have arisen out of a dispute among the trustees of Holy Trinity Church, the bishop of the diocese, and the parish priest over control of the parish. Catholic churches were sometimes built and paid for by a lay board of trustees, who often expected to control the staffing and the business of the parish, much like the Congregationalist churches were controlled by the laity. Issues of control caused conflicts among all concerned, as happened at Holy Trinity.

whom he had contact about the world of finance and currency. He returned to the United States on the eve of the 1837 financial panic precipitated by the end of the charter for the Bank of the United States and by President Andrew Jackson's manipulations and decision to accept only gold or silver species for federal land transactions. Seizing what he saw as an opportunity, Francis Martin opened a small currency brokerage firm in Louisville, Kentucky, doing business in state currencies and in gold. He did well but decided that because Nicholas Biddle's Second Bank of the United States (1816-1836) was in Philadelphia, that city was a more likely banking capital than Louisville. Accordingly, he moved his operations to Philadelphia and took his sons Francis Anthony and Anthony, then thirteen and eleven, into the business of Drexel & Company. Ten years later, Drexel & Company was in a position to lend money to the federal government for the war against Mexico. When gold was discovered in California in 1849, Francis Martin was off to San Francisco to establish the firm there, leaving his young sons in charge in Philadelphia. The boys proved to be talented and hardworking bankers who complemented one another's style and inclination and increased the family fortunes. Drexel & Company raised large sums of money for the federal government during the Civil War (1861-1865). So important were the Drexel brothers to President Ulysses Grant, that Grant offered Katharine's uncle Anthony Drexel a position in his cabinet as secretary of the treasury. He declined the honor, though he and the president remained friends for life. The Drexel brothers, according to historian Dan Rottenberg, maintained a straitlaced life out of the public eye, "unsullied by financial or sexual scandal, unlike, say, the lives of . . . more colorful Wall Street contemporaries Jay Gould and Jim Fisk."[5]

On September 28, 1854, Francis Anthony Drexel married Hannah Jane Langstroth at the Assumption Church. The Langstroth family belonged to a sect of German Baptist pietists called Dunkards because of their practice of adult baptism, which prescribed total immersion three times during the sacrament, once for each person of the Trinity. The Dunkards stressed high moral standards, plain living, and what we would today call social justice as the road to heaven.[6] Even as the wife of one of Philadelphia's richest men, Hannah Langstroth Drexel followed the plain-living Dunkard precepts of her girlhood. When she died, all her personal property was put into a small

5. Dan Rottenberg, *The Man Who Made Wall Street: Anthony J. Drexel and the Rise of Modern Finance* (Philadelphia: University of Pennsylvania Press, 2001), p. xiv. See also p. 104 on Grant's offer of public office.

6. Sydney E. Ahlstrom, *A Religious History of the American People,* vol. 1 (Garden City, N.Y.: Image Books, 1975), p. 301.

box, locked away in a vault at Drexel & Company, and forgotten for several decades. When the box was opened, it contained only a brooch, a jeweled barrette, a few ornamented hair combs, a gold thimble, a gold lorgnette, and a few calling cards. Hannah was the mother Katharine was never to know because she died five weeks after Katharine's birth. However, Hannah's mother, Elizabeth Lehman Langstroth, was a loving and influential grandmother to Katharine and her older sister, Elizabeth.

Francis Anthony Drexel met the death of his young wife with Christian stoicism. After her passing he wrote, "If I know myself I am resigned to this dispensation of the Almighty. His will in all things be done, for he ordereth all things wisely and well. He has not left me comfortless for I have been received into the Mother Church wherein is my consolation. I have every assurance that my beloved one has gone to her heavenly father."[7] Although he was born a Catholic, Drexel may have lapsed somewhat during his marriage to the Protestant Hannah, only to be received again into the Church, "wherein is my consolation," after her death.[8] Nearly two years later, he married again. His second wife was the daughter of a prominent Philadelphia Catholic family of French origin. Emma Mary Bouvier turned out to be a fortuitous choice for Francis Anthony and his two small daughters, Elizabeth and Katharine. She was a devoted wife and stepmother who did not differentiate among her children, and, though she encouraged her daughters to enjoy a social life, she personally preferred the simplicity of family life to that of society. This is a fact that takes on greater meaning over the next twenty years as the girls matured into young adults. Two successive New Year letters from Francis Anthony to Emma give a glimpse into their personal lives.

My dear and affectionate wife:

It is well at the beginning of another year to give expression to the thoughts that have been active in the mind during the one just gone by, as well as to form resolutions which may govern us in the one to come.

Many various blessings have been conferred upon us the time we have been united — a special Providence it has been that brought us together, and if we operate according to its designs it will be the means of amending much in us that needs correction.

7. Letterhouse, *Francis A. Drexel Family,* p. 11; FAD to his cousin, Anthony J. Drexel, December 30, 1858. All quoted materials retain their original spellings, punctuations, and emphases.

8. His brother married an Episcopalian woman and joined her church.

A similarity in feeling and disposition unless regulated by mutual love and forbearance, does not in general produce perfect accord — what each of us offends in we are less liable to forgive in the other — mutual forbearance is necessary for both of us and for my part I feel that you have shown it toward me in a greater degree than I have returned it. Had I performed my religious duties with more seriousness and attention I should probably not now stand self-convicted.

We have received many and various blessings. Let us not be forgetful of them but in the time to come may we show by our punctuality in approaching the Blessed Sacrament and the attention and devotion that we manifest in preparing for it, that we appreciate the means of salvation which have been designed to sustain our spiritual live. May our hearts be continually directed towards Him who suffered and died for us and gave us his flesh for our life — when tempted let us instantly call on our Blessed Mother — she is our friend and helps us. God has bestowed on us abundance. Continue your charities in His name. Be the dispenser of His gifts and let us also extend the charity of thought to those who offend us.

In conclusion, my dear, dear one, let me wish you a happy New Year indeed, and strength to bear all the little trials that may befall you. May your warm, tender, loving heart beat more tenderly toward your loving and affectionate husband, pardoning him his faults and sustaining him in trials, and thus make home a heaven here below.

Affectionately your own,
Frank[9]

Not only does this letter show the intimate connection between husband and wife, but it also demonstrates their connection to Christ, the sacraments, and the Virgin Mary; the writer also recognizes that their abundant goods are but gifts from God in their stewardship intended to be shared with others in need. Remove the references to husband and wife, and this letter could well have been written by Frank Drexel to his daughter Katie, who would in time take his very instructions to heart.

In the following year's letter Frank makes note of the birth of Louise and of the death of his father, Francis Martin Drexel. The elder Drexel died after falling under the wheels of a train.

---

9. Letterhouse, *Francis A. Drexel Family,* pp. 42-43; FAD to EBD, January 1, 1863.

My own darling,

Another circle has been added to those gone by, and during it God has been very bountiful to us, giving us an abundance of both spiritual and temporal blessings, not the least of which is that sweet pledge of our affections — Louise. Having followed His divine order may she, if she be preserved to us, be a means of strengthening and increasing our affection.

The tender cares of a mother have kept us much apart and thrown additional responsibilities on you, but may we not expect increased blessings on both mother and father and also as the child increases in age, our alleviation.

This past year has separated me from my dearly beloved father — He has gone before me and needs all our prayers for his soul — Remember him as you would me.

I have to thank you for your kind forbearance and gentle love which you have bestowed upon me. You have overcome yourself, I have retrograded. I will try to do better and will pray to Him from whom Only help can come.

With most tender affection,
Your husband,
F. A. Drexel[10]

This letter again emphasizes the importance of God and things of the spirit in the Drexel family home. Exactly why Frank needed Emma's forbearance is never made clear, but the mention of it indicates the level of introspection and self-discernment that was the norm in the Drexel household.

When Emma gave birth to Louise, the family was rounded out to three daughters. It is clear from reading their family letters that the Francis Anthony Drexel family was particularly close and loving. In later years, the sisters would refer to themselves as "We Three" and the "All Three." As the sister in the middle, Katharine, or Katie as she was called, was emotionally closer to both Elizabeth and Louise than they were to each other. They each were devoted to their parents. So close were they that Katharine did not know until she was thirteen that Emma was her stepmother, not her birth mother. Almost unbelievably, it did not seem to occur to young Katharine that three sets of grandparents was one set too many. Emma would always be "Dear Mama" or "Darling Mama" to Katharine. Six-year-old Katharine wrote a note to her mother on her birthday.

---

10. Letterhouse, *Francis A. Drexel Family,* p. 43; FAD to EBD, January 1, 1864.

Dear Mama:

Happy Birthday. I hope you will be pleased with Grandpa's likeness and present. May the Blessed Mother send you a kiss from Heaven.

Your affectionate little daughter,
Katie[11]

Both Emma and the Virgin Mary would be Katharine's role models of the perfect mother and servant to others.

Academic and Religious Education

Emma supervised the education of her three daughters. She sent Elizabeth to the sisters of the Sacred Heart at Eden Hall to be educated, where she herself had gone to school. Emma's own sister, Madame Louise Bouvier, was a member of this French order and in residence as the superior at Eden Hall, near the Drexel home. Emma set aside and decorated a room in their home as a classroom and engaged tutors when it was time for Katharine and Louise to begin their formal education. Katharine fondly recalled and described her classroom as "our bright, cozy little school-room, with its bay window, convenient map rack, picture covered walls, study table piled high with interesting books and its jardinière of green ferns."[12] Emma Drexel insisted on a classical education for all three of her daughters. They read Cicero, Horace, and Livy in Latin; English classics by Chaucer, Shakespeare, and Pope; French literature, German philosophy, world geography, ancient and modern history, and church history; and they studied mathematics. Many of their well-thumbed and annotated schoolbooks are in the archives at the motherhouse in Cornwells Heights, outside of Philadelphia. The girls also studied music, played the piano, and sang as required of young ladies of their era and social standing.

They had specific teachers for Latin, French, and music, but their mother hired Miss Mary Bernice "Bern" Cassidy to oversee all the other elements of the girls' academic education. Miss Cassidy came to the Drexels

11. November 1864.

12. Miscellaneous writings of Mother Mary Katharine Drexel, including those before she became a religious, are found in the Archives of the Sisters of the Blessed Sacrament, #3202.

via Madame Bouvier, who recommended her as a governess for her nieces. Miss Cassidy was a well-educated Irishwoman who had immigrated to the United States with her family. Her father died almost immediately upon their arrival, leaving Miss Cassidy in need of a position to support her mother and younger brother. She became an important and intimate member of the Drexel family until her death in 1902. Fortunately for future Drexel biographers, one of the main avenues for teaching the girls grammar, punctuation, vocabulary, and style was Miss Cassidy's insistence on original compositions in prose, poetry, and letter writing. Miss Cassidy wrote an initial assessment of her pupils for their mother shortly after she took over as their governess. Of Katharine she noted, "And Kate will make a good steady, constantly advancing scholar — opening the valves of her mind slowly, but keeping them closed securely on what she has once admitted."[13]

Not only did Emma Drexel oversee the academic education of her daughters, she also took their religious education in hand. On Sunday evenings, the family would gather in the parlor for a religion seminar of sorts. They took turns reading and reporting on the lives of saints. As young children, the girls would make up little dramas and plays about their favorite saints. Katie took as her patron saint Catherine of Siena. She was also particularly fond of St. Francis of Assisi because of his simple piety and his poverty. But she was open to all the saints. She prayed to St. Joseph to teach her how to speak French, and she asked her mother to keep all her French correspondence so she could see how she was improving. Katharine's mastery of French was due to her own diligence rather than to the intervention of St. Joseph, but even in something as small as this, Katharine was willing to see the fruits of her labors as the result of God or the saints working through her.

Most important for the girls' religious and spiritual development was the example set by their parents. Emma Drexel had an oratory built in their home, where the entire family said nightly prayers together before the girls went to bed. Francis Drexel spent a half hour in personal prayer immediately after arriving home from the bank every evening. He would then relax by playing the organ for an hour before dinner. As a young man, he had made about $150 a year playing the organ for St. John's Church in Manayunk, Pennsylvania, so he was an excellent musician. He played a mixture of secular and religious classical compositions, which could be heard all over the house. Johann Sebastian Bach was a favorite composer.

13. Letterhouse, *Francis A. Drexel Family*, p. 72.

My father would come home from the office and go right up to his room and kneel down beside a chair — one of those chairs that I think are now in our sacristy, the round ones, you know — and there he would pray — the oratory would have been too public — there he would have been seen — but in his room he would not have been seen by the help. Then he would go to the organ and play — oh, he would play so beautifully. . . .

Prayer was like breathing . . . there was no compulsion, no obligation . . . it was natural to pray. . . .

Night prayers were always said together. We were usually in bed by eight o'clock when we were children. Then in our little night dresses we would go to the top of the stairs and call down, "Mama! Papa!"

Then Papa (we did not call him "Dad") would leave his organ or his paper and Mama her writing, and both at the call of the children would come up and kneel for night prayers in the little oratory.[14]

Francis Drexel sat on a number of charitable boards and gave regularly and generously to a variety of mostly, but not exclusively, Catholic enterprises. His charities would often be the topic of discussion at the family dinner table. When he died, his philanthropy, covered by both the Catholic and secular press, became the topic of conversation for millions of Americans who were amazed at its extent. Emma Drexel approached charity in a far more personal manner — personal to herself and personal to the recipients of her charity. Three days a week she would open her doors to Philadelphia's poor, who would come to ask her for shoes, clothes, medicine, or rent money. Hundreds of people would gather at her back door and wait for an opportunity to ask Mrs. Drexel for help. "The front door and the back door was [*sic*] besieged by a crowd of beggars, who at last became so clamorous that Mama had to scare them off with the face of a policeman. The poor man was at wit's end as to how the crowd was to be diminished."[15] However, Emma Drexel did not simply hand out money arbitrarily. She employed Mary Bilger as her assistant. Miss Bilger would visit the tenements looking for those who truly needed help. She would give the person a card to present to Mrs. Drexel on an appointed day. Mrs. Drexel would listen to the individual's story and give what she thought appropriate. Katharine wrote, "It is amazing how humble the old people are when arriving in Mama's presence." Katharine went on to tell a charming story of one very persistent woman.

14. Katharine Drexel, Oral Memoir, November 29, 1935, ASBS.
15. ASBS, vol. 1, p. 117.

The woman began, "I have none but auld shoes on me feet." Emma gave her new shoes. Next she asked for shoes for her five children and got them. Then she asked for coal, and then for flannels, then for the rent money to keep her family from being evicted — then "a bit of food for Jimmy, he's so sick." Lastly she begged, "Little Mary needs a dress." Even though the woman asked for so much, Emma Drexel filled all her requests. But she kept meticulous records and would know if the woman were to return too soon and that her charitable funds and her kindness had been abused.[16]

About my mother . . . , she employed someone to go around and visit the poor and she made a report to my mother. If the report were favorable and the woman had given the person a ticket, the ticket could be presented to my mother in person.

About three times a week, my mother would go to the back room, and people would come to her. They would crowd around the entrance on Moravian St. As soon as my mother opened the door, there would be a grand rush to be the first one in.

I often think my mother had no human respect. She never seemed to wonder what the neighbors would think or say when they saw the crowd gathered day after day during the winter months. My mother remained in this room, and each one who came and presented a ticket was received and given all the time she wanted to tell her story. My mother knew the details beforehand, from the woman [Miss Bilger] who had reported it. My mother would try to devise means of giving the needed help right then and there — a grocery order or an order for coal or rent, or shoes — poor things, they mostly needed shoes. But all according to their needs. Sometimes when the crowd was large and the weather extremely cold or bad, those who had tickets would be told to wait in the out-building, which was warm, and those who had no ticket would gradually disperse. The great need was for shoes. I remember . . . Mrs. Smith, Elizabeth, often helped them — she graduated before I did, and then she could help Mama.

Everything given out was noted down in a book, so Mama knew if the same need was brought to her again very soon it was because the right use had not been made of the thing given before, or they might have sold or traded it for drink, or something else, and then Mama would be able to inquire and the records gave her the information she needed. In this way Mama took a personal interest in them. And they knew it and she was

16. ASBS, vol. 1, p. 117.

able to direct them. She got to know them and know their needs. And her sympathy was unwearying.[17]

Katharine Drexel and her sisters learned a great deal from working with their mother in her direct and personal approach to charity. Within the family, Emma Drexel's personal charity was called the Dorcas, after Dorcas (or Tabitha), the woman in Acts 9 who ministered to the poor. As soon as her daughters were old enough, they helped their mother by meeting with the poor and sorting out the needs that could be helped by the Dorcas. They also helped her keep records. Emma taught the girls not to let themselves be taken advantage of by the unscrupulous, because that would be to the disadvantage of the truly needy. After a gravedigger tried to overcharge her for a five-dollar job, thinking that a rich lady would not know any better, Emma sent him away. Later she reflected on this in her journal.

> Because a man is poor he need not necessarily be mean, nor is it true charity to encourage him in his meanness by indolently or good naturedly permitting him to compromise his manhood. If a man is poor and despite his poverty, is above temptation of littleness, he is nobler than a monarch. . . . Look not then, foolish man, upon the benevolent lady as an imbecile whose soft heart receives every impression, but rather regard her as one who in the exercise of her vocation calls forth all the powers of her mind as well as heart and who possess[es] the "keenness of a knave, the kindness of a fool, and the judgment of a philosopher."[18]

Emma Drexel paid the annual rent for over 150 families and spent up to $30,000 a year through the Dorcas. This is the charitable activity Francis Drexel referred to in his New Year's letter to Emma in 1863. "God has bestowed on us abundance. Continue your charities in His name. Be the dispenser of His gifts."[19] Katharine absorbed these early lessons in charity and how to manage it.

No one would ever take Katharine or her sisters for fools or imbeciles. They learned at their mother's knee to be keen, kind, and clear in judgment, lessons that were amply reinforced by their father. Charity and good business practices went hand in hand. Katharine would put these early lessons

---

17. MKD, Oral Memoir, November 29, 1935.
18. Emma Bouvier Drexel, Journal, July 29, 1877.
19. See above, n. 9.

to work in even greater magnitude than that envisioned by either of her parents, yet all was not dullness and duty in the Drexel household.

Perhaps inspired by the travels and adventures of Martin Drexel, Francis Drexel took his family on annual tours of the United States. When the girls were old enough, the family went on a grand tour of Europe. He believed that his daughters should learn their geography firsthand. He took them hiking in the mountains and bathing at the seashore. When a very young Katie was frightened by the waves, her father carried her in his arms into the spray, holding on to her tightly. His laughter and his strength calmed her until she actually enjoyed the experience. The incident had a profound influence on the little girl. "When he brought me back to shore, my fear was gone. Many times in life after, that incident has given me courage, for I felt my Heavenly Father's Arms were as protectingly around me as had been dear Papa's."[20] The spiritual presence of God seemed to be a constant reality for Katharine.

Girlhood

At a time when most American Catholics took Communion no more than once a month and went to Mass only on Sundays, the senior Drexels took Communion weekly and went to Mass almost daily. While young Katie went to Mass with her parents, the custom of waiting until the age of twelve to receive first Communion galled her. She begged to be admitted to the Communion table: "Dear Mama, I am going to make my first Communion and you will see how I shall try to be good. Let me make it in May, the most beautiful of all months."[21]

Later, when she was nine, she wrote to her mother a Christmas letter in French: "I am going to make the Stations of the Cross for you, my darling Mama, and for Papa and Louise, too. I am trying to study hard so that I may make my first Communion this year. Mama dear, my letter is nearly finished. A thousand thanks, my dear Mama, for all of the Christmas presents you will give me. Nothing in the world could please me more than if you like this letter. I am hoping it will please you as much as your presents will please me." In true childish fashion, even as Katharine was longing for Communion, she was at the same time longing for sweets. Mrs. Drexel

---

20. Letterhouse, *Francis A. Drexel Family,* p. 44.
21. MKD to EBD, 1864.

did not allow the children candy except at Christmas, and when they were very young they did not get candy even then. In the same 1867 Christmas letter in which Katharine announced that she was studying to make her first Communion, she pleaded for bonbons for herself and for Louise, whom Mrs. Drexel did not believe had ever tasted sweets. "Oh! What fun I shall have enjoying bonbons and receiving so many lovely things. Mama dear, before going any further with this letter, I must ask you to let Louise have some bonbons, too. I assure you that she knows the taste of them very well. Now that she knows almost the whole alphabet, you will let her have some bonbons? She is just a little girl, so intelligent and sweet, you really cannot refuse her some sweets."[22] Katharine loved all kinds of good food. On July 3, 1870, when she was finally allowed to have her first Communion at the age of eleven, a year younger than either of her sisters, she wrote a letter to her aunt at the Sacred Heart convent, Madame Louise Bouvier, telling her about the big day. After the Communion and Confirmation, the Drexels hosted the entire Communion class and their families to an elegant and sumptuous brunch. Katharine was so carried away with her descriptions of the foods that she hardly mentioned the reason for the party. Her aunt quite took her to task: "I am disappointed. I did not want or care to know about the breakfast, but I did want to know your thoughts and feelings as you received our dear Lord."[23]

It was one of those rebukes that a sensitive person could never forget. "I remember my First Communion and my letter that day. Jesus made me shed tears because of His greatness in stooping to me. Truth made me feel the mite I was. I did not realize nor was I ashamed of my sensuality."[24]

Her sensuality for foods extended to sensuality for pretty things. Mrs. Drexel had her underclothes and those of the girls, along with some of their other clothing and clothing to be distributed by the Dorcas, made by the Magdalens at the Convent of the Good Shepherd. In this way she could benefit the Magdalens and the Dorcas recipients at the same time. Emma Drexel specified that the girls' dresses be plain and unornamented. Katie contrarily beseeched the sister taking her measurements, "Please do put lots of lace and ruffles on my dress, just like Mama's."[25] Not satisfied with pretty dresses, young Katharine also craved jewelry.

<hr/>

22. MKD to EBD, December 23, 1867.
23. *Positio,* 1:156.
24. MKD Retreat Notes, vol. 8, pp. 76-77.
25. ASBS, vol. 1, p. 23.

Dear Mama,

I hope this letter will be an improvement on my others, for I am going to take great pains to do it well. Will you have my ears pierced, for I am in such a hurry to have my ears pierced? Everybody loves earrings.

Love, Katie Drexel[26]

Her love of candies, sweets, and pretty things placed young Katharine Drexel in the mainstream of children her age. Even her budding piety was not yet enough to set her apart from other children. Indeed, like other small children, Katharine was not beyond temper tantrums. For some small thwarted desire, she had a temper tantrum on a trolley car with her mother. Once home, Mr. Drexel applied the paternal hand and the young miscreant was denied a place at the dinner table with Mama, Papa, and her sisters. Time, maturity, and greater introspection and discernment would be required for the development of this particular saint.

Katharine and her sisters spent their growing up time in the arms of their extended family. Elizabeth and Katharine were taken every Saturday morning to visit Grandmother Langstroth and their Langstroth and Lehman cousins. Their grandmother Langstroth maintained a duck pond to amuse the children and set aside a playroom stocked with dolls and toys of all sorts for the children. Katie's favorite doll was an African American male doll dressed as a footman in velvet livery. The other cousins rejected this particular doll, but, for whatever reason, Katie adored it.[27]

Though the girls dearly loved their Langstroth relatives, they were confused and worried about them because they were Protestant. Elizabeth once told her grandmother that it was so sad that she, the grandmother, would not go to heaven. It seems that Johanna Ryan, the well loved and militantly Catholic nursemaid of the Drexels, had told the girls that only Catholics go to heaven. Oddly enough, this very Protestant woman would have one granddaughter and two nieces who became Catholic nuns, two of whom would found their own orders and two of whom would be missionary sisters. Her niece Eugenia "entered the Carmelite order at Pamplona, Spain, as Sister Maria Isabel of Jesus. As a cloistered nun, she prayed for the souls of her aristocratic relatives, and, as if in answer to her prayers, her sister, Louisa, the

---

26. MKD to EBD, no date.

27. This doll is in the Visitors' Center at the Shrine of St. Katharine at the motherhouse in Bensalem.

most worldly member of the family, entered religion and founded the Congregation of the Servants of Our Lady of Fatima."[28] Despite the impressive qualities and credentials of her Catholic relatives and their prayers for her conversion, beloved Grandmother Langstroth remained a firm Protestant.

After Sunday morning mass, Elizabeth, Katie, and Louise would visit Grandmother Bouvier, "as stately a dame as ever graced the court of Versailles."[29] There were twelve children in the Bouvier family, so there were always an abundance of aunts, uncles, and cousins to entertain the three Drexel girls. Katharine went almost daily to the Convent of the Sacred Heart while her mother visited her sister, Madame Louise Bouvier. The convent was almost a second home to her and no doubt impressed her greatly.

Sunday afternoons were spent with Grandmother Drexel. There was an implied tension between the senior Mrs. Drexel and Emma Drexel, indicated by the terms of the former's will, in which bequests were left for each of her daughters and grandchildren, except for Louise and any other children born of the union of Emma and Francis Drexel.[30] It seems impossible that Louise had somehow offended her grandmother Drexel, and certainly any children yet unborn could not have, so the most likely explanation is that the rift was between the senior Mrs. Drexel and Emma Drexel. The source of the tension has never been disclosed.

In the summertime, the Drexel family retreated to the countryside. For several years they rented a three-acre farm in Nicetown, Pennsylvania. The girls christened the farm "the Nest." Their life there was far more free, casual, and leisurely. Mr. Drexel took the train into the city each day during the week to conduct his business, while the girls romped in the fields or played with the donkey cart. Elizabeth and Katharine were allowed to drive the donkey cart to the store in town to buy kerosene for the lamps. Mr. Drexel and Emma took the girls for long walks in the countryside in the early evenings. Mr. Drexel believed in walking as a form of exercise important to the health and well-being of women. It was a belief that Katharine would carry over into her later life with the Sisters of the Blessed Sacrament when she had her postulants and novices walking for an hour a day.

After spending several enjoyable summers in their "Nest" at Nicetown, the Drexels purchased a large summer estate near Torresdale, Pennsylvania.

28. Lou Baldwin, *A Call to Sanctity: The Formation and Life of Mother Katharine Drexel* (Philadelphia: Catholic Standard and Times, 1987), p. 15.

29. Ellen Tarry, *Katharine Drexel: Friend of the Neglected* (Nashville: Winston-Derek Publishers, 1990), p. 3.

30. Will of Mrs. Francis Martin Drexel, SBS Archives.

The old farmhouse and outbuildings had to be remodeled extensively, but it was ready for the family in June of 1871. The family now had a new nest, which they called St. Michel, or St. Michael, after the patron saint of Emma's father, pronounced by the family in the French manner. A stone statue of the saint was imported from France and installed over the lintel of the front door. In this home, too, an oratory was built. In many ways, St. Michel was to become the heart of Drexel family life. They came early in the spring and stayed until the leaves were beginning to flame in the fall. They returned for a lengthy stay during the Christmas season. In due time, St. Michel would also become the first novitiate and convent of the Sisters of the Blessed Sacrament, but for years, it was merely the playground of the Drexels, especially the girls.

Yet even there Emma Drexel recognized that young girls, who were becoming young women, needed structure and direction in their lives during the summer months. She assessed the personalities and interests of her daughters and assigned them duties accordingly. Elizabeth, who loved horses, supervised the stables and the kitchen. Katharine, who was good with the servants and accounts, had supervision of the general household. Louise, who loved the outdoors, oversaw the barn and grounds. In this way, Emma prepared her daughters to assume their proper roles as ladies of great households. She saw marriage and children in their futures and set about getting them ready for their adult responsibilities.

She did not overlook the spiritual side of their development. Her idea was brilliant — and practical. Because to teach is to learn, she proposed that her daughters conduct a Sunday school for the children of the servants from their household and from the neighboring households. There was no Catholic church in the immediate neighborhood of St. Michel, but there were many Catholics on the Drexel staff and other staffs nearby. Eventually, fifty children came regularly to the St. Michel Sunday school. Later, Louise would write of their little school:

> St. Michael's was first occupied in 1870. Shortly thereafter our own dear mother proposed to her two eldest daughters, one being about 14 and the other 11 years of age, to establish a Sunday School for the children of the men who worked on the place. The Sunday School was held with the greatest regularity. The older children were taught by Elizabeth, the youngest by Katharine. After the lessons were recited, the children were assembled around the piano in the parlor and hymns were sung. After a few years the number of children increased, so that fifty or more came ev-

ery Sunday. Just before St. Michael's was closed for the winter, prizes were given out for the best lessons and best attendance, and on Christmas Day the children assembled for a celebration when they received useful gifts (such as dresses, knitted jackets, etc.) also cake, candy, etc. This Sunday school was held until 1888.[31]

In a letter to Miss Cassidy written on December 21, 1872, Katharine elaborated on the gifts for the closing of the school and for Christmas.

> We have bought all the presents for our Sunday School children. [For Christmas,] we are to give each girl a dress, or as Johanna would say, the makin's of a dress. The boys are to have scarfs and mittens. . . . [For the end of the Sunday school there are] . . . match safes, Blessed Virgins, Infant Jesus, holy water fonts, & various ornaments — china mandarins, little girls with golden hair and pink dresses, besides a large play tea set & a china menagerie for the children. . . . The "holy" statues are intended for Lise's catechism prizes which are usually distributed in the fall.[32]

Katharine wrote of her own class: "I have a class of 16 young gentlemen, hardly one of which has reached the mature age of seven or eight. It is delightful to listen to them whilst they say 'Hail Mary, full of grace,' we expect however, to go to Holy Communion once a week, and I only hope that the grace received in the wonderful sacrament will impart to me a little of its love."[33] Like the Dorcas charity, the Sunday school had a profound influence on Katharine and her sisters. The school was racially mixed, with white and a handful of African American children. From their experience with the school, the girls learned the essence of charity, the giving of self out of love in a manner that enhances the humanity of both the giver and the receiver, and humility — it was a way of seeing oneself in proper perspective within the divine economy. The gifts they gave to the children indicate a good mix of the practical and the whimsical. They provided the makings of dresses so that the girls would learn how to sew and clothe themselves, and they also gave them dolls. And they passed out religious articles and pictures to reinforce their lessons, the main reason for the entire enterprise. The St. Michel

---

31. ASBS.

32. ASBS, 1872. As Elizabeth Drexel grew older, the family began to call her Lise, deeming it more sophisticated.

33. MKD to Bishop James O'Connor, 1872.

Sunday school also balanced out the Sunday school they held exclusively for black children during the winter at old St. Joseph's in Philadelphia. Between helping their mother with her Dorcas charity, their Sunday schools, their studies, their household duties, and keeping up with the activities of their larger extended family, the Drexel girls were very busy young women. In 1873, Katharine would describe herself as "a hurely-burley [*sic*] girl of about 16, whom everyone loves; always ready for good humored mischief, teasing everyone, even Mamma."[34] This view of herself as good humored and fun-loving was echoed by a letter from Miss Cassidy to Louise Drexel Morrell, shortly before Miss Cassidy's death. "[Katharine's] great delight in your joint childhood was to convulse you with laughter by all sorts of antics; tumbling about, falling down, etc. etc. I can see you now weak with laughing and the tears in your eyes after some performance on the lawn at St. Michel's & hear your 'Oh, Kate . . . you are a funny girl.' "[35]

On the other hand, there was a very serious side to this "hurley-burley," mischievous girl, especially when it came to religion. She complained to Miss Cassidy: "Lou [Louise] calls me scrupulous, etc. . . . Mamma asked me to teach the child for ten minutes daily how to follow the Mass. Well, because the little rogue would insist upon putting Mamma's watch in the middle of the table while I was instructing her and because I wished to keep her about three minutes longer than the allotted time, she immediately bestows upon me the name of scrupulous, pious, praying, etc. etc. and every other religious insult she can think of."[36] It is interesting that she would take umbrage at being called "pious" and "praying," which ought to be religious compliments, even if "scrupulous" is more negative. It is also interesting that her younger sister rebelled at being taught about the Mass. Clearly, while a certain religiosity pervaded the Drexel household, not everyone was always as eager as the next, or at least not everyone at the same time. Naturally, there was also some sibling rivalry going on in this little scene, and while Louise might not have minded being taught how to follow the Mass by her mother, she could understandably object to her older sister as her religious tutor. Yet it is also typical of Katharine to take a directive from her mother very seriously, especially in a religious matter, the protests of her younger sibling notwithstanding.

Louise had clearly touched a nerve in Katharine by calling her scru-

34. MKD, Memoirs, 1873.
35. ASBS, no date.
36. MKD to Miss Cassidy, July 22, 1874, ASBS.

pulous. Her reaction strikes one as a guilty response. Even as a child in her early adolescence, Katharine wrote what she called her accounts. Perhaps it was the banker's daughter in her, but she kept track of all kinds of thoughts, ideas, prayers, and actions. She was extremely conscientious in her attention to detail. In an entry dated November 1873, fifteen-year-old Katharine wrote: "What a long time it has been since I have made my 'accounts,' so long in fact that it has now been four months and I almost forgot how I advanced in virtue. However, I will put down my 'accounts' as far as I am able. I am getting quite scrupulous, and really every scruple as Father Faber says, is mixed up with sin and vanity."[37] Clearly she was including devotional works in her youthful reading. Fr. Frederick William Faber was a Victorian English writer of popular Catholic devotional literature, who was also widely read in the United States. Katharine mentioned him several times in her journals. Together with John Henry Newman, he founded the London Oratory. His books are doctrinally orthodox, only occasionally humorous, and always practical. Katharine took his advice to heart on a certain level, while at the same time remaining a fairly ordinary teenager who loved fun and travel. She would forget for months on end her intentions to take account of her virtues more regularly.

Early Travels

A grand tour of Europe with their parents was a youthful highlight for the Drexel girls, even those who suffered from sin and vanity. They were abroad from September 1874 until May 1875. Katharine was still in her "hurley-burley" stage, but on the cusp of important changes in her life. After visiting a Carthusian monastery outside of Florence, Italy, she wrote to Miss Cassidy: "To see these venerable old monks pacing the cloisters with their white cowls drawn over their heads, or to hear them chanting office in the old walnut choir, just as they did 500 years ago, seemed more like something to be read and wondered about, than to be actually witnessed."[38] She was so inspired by the pervasive peacefulness of the monastery that she announced that, were she a man, she would join the order to spend the rest of her days in the serenity of the cloister. Her family laughed at her at the time. In Vienna, Katharine and Elizabeth spent the better part of a day on a religious esca-

---

37. MKD, Collected Journals, November 1873.
38. MKD to Cassidy, December 8, 1874.

pade to locate an English-speaking confessor. After crisscrossing the city, they finally found a confessor who spoke French, the language with which Katharine had struggled so hard. In Bologna a guide told the family that the patron saint of Katharine was on display at the Church of St. Catherine. He took them into a side chapel where the saint's unembalmed, blackened body sat in a chair ready to receive pilgrims. The saint's lips were still red, according to legend, because there she had been kissed by Christ. The guide told the girls that pilgrims customarily kiss the feet of the saint. Although quite repulsed, the girls did as they were told. In her letter to Miss Cassidy about the affair, Katharine wrote, "The effect of the whole shrine was awful."[39] To make matters worse for her, the shrine turned out to be that of St. Catherine of Bologna, not St. Catherine of Siena, her patron saint. In Rome, the girls enjoyed seeing firsthand the places about which they had studied with Miss Cassidy. And, while they loved the churches, shrines, and museums, their personal audience with Pope Pius IX was undoubtedly the high point of the Drexels' European tour. Louise exchanged a small white cap with the Holy Father, who took off the one he was wearing and gave it to her. Johanna Ryan provided years of family lore and mirth by throwing herself at the pope's feet and exclaiming, "Holy Father, praise God and His Blessed Mother. My eyes have seen the Lord Himself this day."[40] When it was explained that Johanna Ryan was Irish from the "auld sod," the pope understood perfectly her extreme reaction, and the Drexels had a story to tell and retell through the years. The trip home to Philadelphia took the family through Lourdes, where they prayed at the grotto and partook of the waters. Kate wrote to Miss Cassidy: "I attribute to no superstition the spiritual refreshment that I drank from the clear fountain which she herself caused to flow and which has been the channel of so many wonderful blessings."[41] For Katharine, there was superstition, and there was faith. Her negative reaction to the shrine of St. Catherine of Bologna was against the trappings and lore that surrounded the physical body of the saint with its blackened limbs and red lips, all illuminated by hundreds of candles, by which she remained unmoved despite her obedient kiss. Her positive affirmation of the water of Lourdes was one of faith, based on its effect on her.

39. Letterhouse, *Francis A. Drexel Family,* pp. 91-92.

40. Katherine Burton, *The Golden Door: The Life of Katharine Drexel* (New York: P. J. Kenedy and Sons, 1957), p. 35.

41. ASBS, vol. 1, p. 35.

Coming of Age

Katharine Drexel returned home from Europe on the brink of adulthood. On the exterior, she was still the fun-loving sister and dutiful daughter, but on the inside, within her mind, she was wrestling with questions and problems of great import for her future life. She was not alone in her struggle, though, for she turned for help to her parish priest, Fr. James O'Connor.

In 1872, Fr. O'Connor became the pastor of St. Dominic Church, the parish church for St. Michel in Torresdale. When St. Michel was renovated, the bishop of Philadelphia, James F. Wood, a close family friend, came to say Mass for the Drexels in their new oratory. He granted them permission to have Mass said there four times a year, a favor he later expanded to include any occasion when a priest came to call. Fr. O'Connor visited frequently and became a close friend to all the Drexels, but especially to Katharine. He was one of those adults who can enter the life of a young person and have a tremendous influence. He treated her seriously and sensed in her a person of tremendous spiritual possibilities. He did not condescend to her as some adults do when trying to befriend a young person. He became her spiritual director and friend until his death in 1890. Indeed, he was her spiritual father during that time, helping to shape and develop her life's vocation. He was the pastor at St. Dominic for only four more years, but they were four very formative years in the life of a teenaged Katharine Drexel. In 1876, Fr. O'Connor left St. Dominic to become a bishop and the vicar apostolic of the Nebraska Territory, which included parts of the future states of South Dakota, North Dakota, Colorado, Montana, Idaho, and Wyoming. Later, he became the first bishop of Omaha. During the years of his bishopric, the Catholic population of the former Nebraska Territory grew from 30,000 to 300,000.[42] Even the great distance between Philadelphia and Omaha and the great burdens of looking after the spiritual and ecclesiastical needs of a far-flung and fast-growing flock did not lessen the influence of Bishop O'Connor in the life of Katharine Drexel. They maintained a voluminous epistolary friendship. She consulted with him regularly and in depth about her thoughts and spiritual concerns and filled him in on the Drexel family happenings. He wrote fatherly advice, sometimes sternly and sometimes lightheartedly, but always affectionately.

Because the Drexel family had a certain standing in Philadelphia society,

---

42. Lou Baldwin, *St. Katharine Drexel: Apostle to the Oppressed,* ed. Paul S. Quinter, Elena Bucciarelli, and Frank Coyne (Philadelphia: Catholic Standard and Times, 2000), p. 29.

some of the formalities of society had to be observed, and when they were, they were entered into with great gusto. Elizabeth's debut party in January 1876 was one such affair. This coming-out party for her daughter had been on the mind of Emma Drexel during their trip to Europe. In Paris, she dragged Elizabeth from the *corsetiers* to the *cordonniers,* from the *modistes* to the *couturiers.* The girls grew bored with the various delays of the designers and tradesmen, but their mother was on a mission. Elizabeth's debut gown was from the famous Parisian House of Worth in the required debutante white. The fact that Catholic families, no matter how wealthy, were not at the top of the social ladder in Philadelphia did not undermine the festivities of the hour. Philadelphia had experienced the 1844 anti-Catholic riots, the worst in the country. Almost thirty-five years later, although overt anti-Catholicism was well behind those of serious social standing in Philadelphia, still, there would be no invitations to the Catholic Miss Drexels to make their curtsies at the Assembly Ball, the most prestigious of Philadelphia's debutante balls. However, each daughter in her turn had a beautiful, memorable party to mark her official transition into adulthood and, perhaps most importantly, her marital eligibility. Katharine and Louise observed the preparations for Elizabeth's party:

> Louise and I amused ourselves in looking at the men who were draping chandeliers with green smilax vines and pinks. Then after taking one proud look at the table elegantly set with large India dishes and handsome gilt candelabra at each end, we departed to dress ourselves for an afternoon ride. On our return all were edified by the spectacle of two swallow-tailed waiters flying around in search of tumblers and plates. The India dishes were now filled with fancy cakes, meringues, jellied chicken, chicken salad and various other dainties. How I should have liked to take a sly nibble at some of these *friandises,* but the swallow-tails were always sure to appear just as I was taking an innocent walk around the table, intending at their departure from the room to make a grab at some of the goodies.[43]

Katharine had not lost her sensuous desire for foods, but her tastes had become more sophisticated, as becomes a young woman with a European tour under her belt. These were a pleasure for her, and, at this point in her life, not even a guilty pleasure. She was a young woman enjoying her family and her place in the world.

Katharine ended her formal education in the summer of 1878. She found

43. Letterhouse, *Francis A. Drexel Family,* p. 105.

it to be a bit of an anticlimax. "This will be a perpetual vacation for me, and yet strange to say, I do not feel particularly hilarious at the prospect. One looks forward so many years to finishing school, and when at last the time comes, a kind of sadness steals over one whose cause is hard to analyze. Perhaps it comes from this — there was a definite future to look to, up to this time of leaving school. Then the future suddenly looks all vague and uncertain."[44] When asked by Elizabeth what her emotions were on finishing school, Katharine's only response was "I feel very hot." Elizabeth noted that the temperature was in the nineties, and went on to add, "It takes only a very small physical inconvenience to make us callous to momentous events."[45] It is easy to sense the late adolescent ennui and languor in Katharine's "I feel very hot," but soon she would have other things on her mind and other activities to keep her busy.

Katharine made her own debut in 1879, also in a white Worth gown. Thereafter, she and Elizabeth received many invitations for parties and visits. If her future was vague and uncertain, the present proved to be pleasant and amusing. Immediately after her debut party, she wrote a chatty letter to Bishop O'Connor about the plays she had seen with her sisters and her father. "To this list of dissipations can be added dutiful evening calls on aunts and cousins, besides attending a little party the other night where I made my debut."[46] He wrote back a charming letter:

> Perhaps I ought not to "Katie" you any longer. . . . You are no longer a child but a young lady. . . . "My dear child" or "My dear friend" or "My dear Miss Katie" or what? It is better to have a clear understanding on this matter. I only hope it may never be "My dear Condessa" or "My dear Marchesa" or even "My dear Princepessa." God protect you from the fate that would involve such a title! I have known of two and heard of several other young American ladies to whom such titles fell, but hope and pray that you may never be as unfortunate as they.[47]

The bishop had no doubt that the Drexel women would each marry well, raise families in the Church, and carry on the philanthropic and social traditions established by their parents. He encouraged Katharine's social nature, only warning against a certain kind of frivolous society, which might tempt

44. MKD to O'Connor, May 28, 1878.
45. Elizabeth Drexel, St. Michel Journal, May 1878.
46. MKD to O'Connor, January 4, 1879.
47. O'Connor to MKD, January 1879.

her into worldliness. One such possible misalliance would be with an impoverished European nobleman looking for an American heiress.

The Drexel sisters received many invitations to spend lengthy visits at the seaside estates of family and friends during the spring and summer social seasons. There, eligible young men and women would meet and woo within the prescribed social set. Against the explicit directions from their mother not to write home too often, both girls were in constant touch.

On their return home from a brief visit to Cape May, New Jersey, the summer before Kate's debut, Elizabeth made an entry into the St. Michel summer journal that indicates Kate's sociability and also reflects the mother-daughter relationship enjoyed by Emma and her daughters.

> Mother darling came skipping over the fence as lithe as a girl, glad to see us back again, and not too proud to show it. . . .
>
> We met two old friends down there, but much to Kate's chagrin made no new ones — (this I think is the one regret in the mind of my dear sociable little sister).[48]

Because Kate and Elizabeth were of marriageable age, the expectations for each visit ran very high for both the daughters and their parents. It was this expectation that made the Worth gowns de rigueur.

Kate wrote her mother from Cape May while on a visit there two years later:

> My own darling Mamma: —
>
> Now if you were not too impatient and did not skip the above line of address . . . you will call your poor old daughter sentimental. But don't do so, because you can well imagine if you don't close that big heart of yours against all sympathy how very dear you are when, when — I was going to say far away — but here again, were we not the *gens qui s'aiment a demi-mots* [people who love one another without having to say it], you will think that we only loved you when you were far away. But you won't misunderstand me and force me to become a d——— most unpleasant body, will you?
>
> I am glad you made those little visits, for you are now able to understand how one can enjoy oneself to the utmost and yet feel that dear Papa and dear Mamma grow dearer for the separation, and their darling virtues

48. Elizabeth Drexel, St. Michel Journal, August 12, 1878.

which perhaps we might have been fools enough to take as a matter of course when enjoying this sweetness, to present themselves vividly and specially before us, now that we miss them.

It is time to dress for tea. How I wish I could ask you now that oft repeated question, "Mamma, what dress shall I wear?"

So goodbye, Mother darling, and excuse this very poor letter from your own

KMD

How is Prince [her horse]? Information of all kinds gratefully received.[49]

Emma Drexel responded with a lightly chastising letter addressed to both Katharine and Elizabeth:

Remember one principle my children, never be a humbug toward your mother, you are on a visit, you can commit no unfilial act in extracting pure enjoyment from it, do not therefore imagine that you gratify me or flatter me when you pretend to be homesick. . . . Be content with green turtle soup served in a gold spoon, and avoid too much greed of happiness. You cannot possibly enjoy two pleasures at once, put vigor and duty into the visit and on Saturday week return to your usual life with wholesale zest. The real philosopher's stone is the knowledge of how, and the power, to improve the moment.[50]

Katharine immediately responded with a letter to her mother emphasizing the activities of which she and Elizabeth had been a part. In addition to telling her mother about going to the steeplechases and flat races at Monmouth Park the day before, she talked of her dress:

Mother Darling: —

Behold your blooming daughter in a high state of morning dress — the white linen lawn flounced with an abundance of torchon [lace], enlivened on this occasion with violet satin streamers & bows. The effect is "stunning" & was produced by agonizing efforts on the part of Lise and me before the looking glass upstairs.[51]

49. MKD to EBD, August 1880.
50. EBD to MKD and ELD, August 12, 1880.
51. MKD to EBD, August 18, 1880.

This gay letter undoubtedly crossed in the mail one written by Emma to her daughters the day before, the day of their outing to the horse races. Emma's letter perhaps foreshadowed more somber events that were to follow in the fullness of time.

> My own darlings:
>   Last night I had a dream, in which I saw the painting of a door such as we have often remarked in walls of church sanctuaries abroad, the opening of the reliquaries and tabernacles all bedecked and be-jewelled, and it was locked. I inquired for the key and Kate informed me, that the meaning of the painting was, that Jesus held the key, as this was the door of His heart, which He only opened to those who knocked and asked. You, Lizzie, smiled at Kate's pious interpretation, which you denounced a gammon and spinach, and I became alarmed at the thought of your incredulity. At this juncture, I awakened with the entire scene impressed upon my mind, but its meaning and origin I have not yet been able to solve except it is that you both are much in my thoughts either sleeping or waking.[52]

Even Mr. Drexel wrote his daughters and visited them while they were away. Those who were away from home and those who remained behind continued to share their strong familial bonds. Mr. Drexel wrote fatherly advice on August 18, 1880: "I hope you are careful not to get into deep water either with the beaux or the surf. . . . It seems lonely at St. Michael's without you, but life is made up of sacrifices and we willingly bear your absence when we know you are enjoying yourselves."[53] A year later, Mr. Drexel again wrote similar advice to his daughters: "Don't let that blue shirted Englishman steal away your hearts and above all be careful not to go into danger in bathing."[54] For his daughters, Francis Drexel appears to have had an equal fear of men and the ocean. He need not have worried, at least for the time being. Even though their parents encouraged Elizabeth and Katharine to lead fully social lives, which they did within the parameters of their family and social set, both young women were very close to their parents and Louise. Katharine countered an implied criticism of her mother on this account in a letter to Bishop O'Connor:

52. EBD to MKD and ELD, August 17, 1880.
53. FAD to MKD and ELD, August 18, 1880.
54. FAD to MKD and ELD, August 4, 1881.

She plainly saw the *vanitas vanitatis* [alludes to the saying, "Vanity of vanities, all is vanity"], and did not hide the fact from us. She never prevented us from entering society, in fact, she encouraged it, provided us with the means to go into the world abundantly so that our friends marveled at the variety and elegance of our toilets. We loved her dearly, as well we might, and our family union was complete in every respect. Yet we found that if we gave our lives or even a part of them to the world, we could not be in entire accord with her, for she was not "of the world." It was because we appreciated close intimacy with her that we left others for her. I do not wish you to think for a moment that Mama ever advised us to keep from society. Indeed, often I have heard her reproach herself because she had not gone more into the world for our sakes. If, however, she were to devote even a part of her time to visiting, the duties which she must perform at that time must go unfulfilled.[55]

The Deaths of Her Parents

This family circle was not to endure much longer. Emma Drexel had been fatigued and in pain as early as the late autumn of 1879. Her doctor prescribed an operation to which Emma naively and foolishly submitted herself, as long as the doctor would perform the operation at the family home on Walnut Street in Philadelphia, while her husband and daughters were out at Torresdale enjoying St. Michel. Needless to say, neither her husband nor her daughters knew anything about the planned operation. Emma's surgery confirmed a diagnosis of incurable cancer. It is partially her illness that accounts for the particularly loving and solicitous letters she received from her daughters away at the seashore, and Emma's insistence on their going into society. Elizabeth and Katharine were not completely aware of the nature of their mother's disease at first, and Emma hoped to see them married and settled before her death. Had they known of the seriousness of their mother's illness and her impending death, the chances are good that none of the Drexel daughters would have left her side for a minute.

When Emma eventually became bedridden, Elizabeth and Katharine were her nurses. They witnessed their mother suffering the worst sort of pain. Her primary doctor was a homeopathic physician who did not believe

---

55. MKD to O'Connor, January 27, 1884.

in painkilling medicines, but only in "natural" medicines, so she was treated with diet and tonics of various sorts. Emma did not receive narcotic pain medication until very late in her illness, near the end of her life. She told her husband and her daughters that she was offering her pain to Christ that her suffering might take the place of theirs, that they might be spared a painful death since she would have experienced pain enough for all of them. Emma saw her illness as the will of God. She wrote abstrusely to her daughters away at the seashore, "Remember that Obedience is better than Sacrifice."[56] One wonders what Katharine was thinking of, obedience or sacrifice, when she told her sisters during their mother's illness, "If anything happens to Mama I'm going to enter a convent."[57]

Emma Bouvier Drexel died at her home on January 29, 1883. The *Public Ledger* published an editorial praising her:

> The poor, the sick, the unemployed, the dying were the constant objects of her cheering visits. Few women ever secured so many situations for needy but industrious and worthy persons — men, women, boys and girls. The families she has aided can be numbered by the hundreds, some of them supported entirely by her in time of need. And one of the most touching scenes of her funeral was that hundreds who passed through her home for two hours yesterday morning for a mournful farewell were largely composed of those to whom she had been a benefactress in every way in which distress can be alleviated or relieved. Their sorrow was unmistakable.[58]

That of her husband and daughters was similarly evident. The daughters attempted to care for their father. By this time, they were expert at running the household and looking after practical matters. Katharine turned down a marriage proposal from an unnamed suitor. Her biographer, Sr. Consuela Duffy, has suggested in an interview that the young man might have been Walter Smith, whose family's summer estate was in the neighborhood of St. Michel. He was a friend of the family and frequent visitor over the years, who later married Elizabeth Drexel.[59] To Bishop O'Connor, Katharine wrote about the proposal: "I have refused the offered heart. I have every reason to

56. EBD to MKD and ELD, August 9, 1881.

57. Burton, *The Golden Door,* p. 59.

58. Quoted in Sr. Consuela Duffy, SBS, *Katharine Drexel: A Biography* (Philadelphia: Reilly Co., 1966), p. 70.

59. *Positio,* 2:164.

believe that it was not a very ardent one."[60] As a dutiful daughter, Katharine told her father about the proposal and her response. Mr. Drexel for his part was concerned for his daughters and desired their happiness above all. After several months of grieving deeply the inconsolable loss of his wife, Francis Drexel decided to take his family to Europe again.

In the piazza of San Marco in Venice, Kate knelt down facing a statue of the Madonna. In the bright Italian sunlight the face of the Madonna appeared to Katharine to be that of her mother, so she moved closer to the statue to see it more clearly. The statue seemed to address her. In some mysterious manner, the Madonna of San Marco said to her, "Freely have you received; freely give."[61] Katharine kept a holy card of the Madonna of San Marco on which she had written the date of this strange occurrence, November 18, 1883, and she kept it her entire life. "Freely give" was part of the rule of St. Francis of Assisi, and Katharine would vow to make it her own rule. "My mother and His — will help me to find the way" — the way to live the rule is to give.[62] Aspects of her future were beginning to take shape in Katharine's mind, even if she did not yet know the exact direction her life would take her in order to fulfill her vow to "freely give." More insights were yet to come, and they would come from the most unlikely sources.

In Rome, the Drexel family again enjoyed the sights and a meeting with the pope, Leo XIII. While in Rome, they also made the acquaintance of a Belgian missionary to the Native Americans of the Pacific Northwest, Fr. Peter Hylebos. They did some sightseeing with him in the Eternal City, and when parting, received an invitation to visit him at his mission should they ever be "in the neighborhood." While genuine, it was also a somewhat offhand social gesture that no one could have predicted would change the face of the Catholic Church in the United States and positively and inalterably change the lives of hundreds of thousands of African Americans and Native Americans.

The Drexels were not long home from Europe when Francis Drexel needed to go to the Pacific Northwest on business. In addition to his business associates, he invited his daughters and his newly motherless niece, their Bouvier cousin, Mary Dixon, to accompany him. They traveled luxuriously in *The Yellowstone,* a private railcar lent to him by the Northern Pacific Railway Company. Along the way they visited Yellowstone National Park. The

---

60. MKD to O'Connor, May 21, 1883.

61. MKD, Travel Journal, November 18, 1883.

62. MKD, Travel Journal, November 18, 1883.

men were arrested for removing some rocks from their natural sites in the park, a deed actually perpetrated by the young women, who wanted some pretty rocks as mementos. A trial was even held before a justice of the peace who presided over the law from his chair in the local country store. The case ended amicably, if a little humorously, and the group continued detouring here and there on its way to Portland, Oregon.

As was their family practice when traveling, they stopped daily for Mass. *The Yellowstone* would be put off on a sidetrack to be picked up by the next engine going in the right direction. In this way the party had a leisurely trip across the country. One detour for Mass possibly saved their lives and certainly their pocketbooks. They stopped off in Bismarck, North Dakota, to attend church and missed the next train that came through. When they got to their next stop in Gardiner, Wyoming, they were more than twelve hours late. They learned that a gang of robbers had heard of the Drexels' trip and had come into town to relieve the rich folks from the east of their cash and valuables, only to be thwarted by a Mass, a long sermon, and a missed train.

Continuing on the way, *The Yellowstone* stopped in Tacoma, Washington, for the party to attend daily Mass. The young women saw a Catholic chapel and went to inquire about the schedule for services. To the surprise and delight of everyone, they were greeted by Fr. Hylebos, their friend from Rome. He took them to his mission church deep in the forest where he was ministering to the Puyallup Indian tribe. It was a lovely but spare church dedicated to Our Lady of Grace. Kate noticed that there was no statue of the church's patroness and promised to send one to Fr. Hylebos. Francis Drexel wanted his daughters to be modern and independent young women, and one way he facilitated this was by opening a checking account for each with a deposit of $200. The statue that Katharine picked out of the Benziger Brothers' catalogue for the Puyallup chapel in the woods cost $100. She worried about what her banker father would think of her spending half of her allowance on a statue, but she need not have done so. His response was, "I'm glad you did it, Kitty."[63] When the magnificent statue arrived, Fr. Hylebos feared it was too large for the small reservation chapel, but the Puyallup chief told him: "No, this big statue will speak better to our hearts than a little statue, and now we can think better of Our Mother in Heaven. We never before knew how to think of the Blessed Virgin Mary. Now we learn to think. Now we can think that she had a crown and that the little Jesus has the world in

63. Letterhouse, *Francis A. Drexel Family*, p. 223.

His hands with His cross to save us all. We want to pray now."[64] Fr. Hylebos wanted to move the impressive statue to a larger church and replace it with a smaller one, more appropriate to the small reservation chapel, but the chief would not let him. Katharine Drexel had known intuitively what was needed by the mission.

This $100 statue was her first gift to the Native Americans, and her first venture into the mission field. It would not be long before she would support a school for the Puyallup mission of Fr. Hylebos. The picture of Katharine's future was coming more into focus, yet she could still not make it out. The bonds of family affection and duty prevented her from the necessary deep introspection and discernment.

These bonds would be all but sundered by the abrupt death of Francis Drexel on February 15, 1885, of a heart attack brought on by complications of a pleurisy that grew out of a bad cold he had caught a week or two before. His death came two years and two weeks after that of his wife, and her prayer that he be spared a painful death was answered. Kate was with her father when he succumbed. Her sisters may or may not have been home at the time; the records are a little unclear. It is possible that Elizabeth and Louise were on a brief trip to New York when their father passed away.[65]

Archbishop Patrick J. Ryan celebrated the funeral Mass for Francis Drexel. In his homily, the archbishop noted: "Every man may be more or less a philanthropist, but only the religious man can have charity, for charity is the love of neighbor for God's sake. . . . The loss of such a Christian philanthropist to any community is a serious one and no legacies that he may leave can compensate for it, for the daily life of such a man, his personal example to a whole community cannot be estimated by the standard of money."[66] While the loss to the community of the daily example of Francis Drexel as he went about his business as a banker, family man, and Christian philanthropist was incalculable, the conditions of his will and the disposition of his estate were exact. He left an immense estate of $15,500,000, the largest until that time of any probated in Philadelphia.[67] His will immediately distributed

---

64. Baldwin, *St. Katharine Drexel*, p. 50.

65. MKD in a later oral memoir transcribed in the archives said she was alone with her father at his death and that her sisters were away shopping. Contemporary accounts indicate that all three sisters were at home. Considering Katharine's severe reaction, it seems more likely that her memory of the circumstances surrounding her father's death is correct.

66. ASBS, vol. 2, p. 170.

67. According to economist Jim Wadley of Tulsa Community College, this would be worth approximately $218,640,000 in 2002 U.S. dollars.

$1,500,000 to twenty-nine charities; all but one, a Lutheran hospital, were Catholic institutions, and all were within the Archdiocese of Philadelphia. The remainder of his estate was put into a trust for the benefit of his daughters. The annual trust income only, not its principal, was to be distributed equally among his three daughters, then aged twenty-nine, twenty-six, and twenty-one. The principal was to remain untouched in the trust and could not be encumbered in any way by the beneficiaries.[68] Neither, should they marry, would their husbands have any control over the trust; nor could a widowed husband inherit his wife's annual share of the trust income. If one of the trust beneficiaries were to die, her share of the trust income would be equally divided among her surviving children. Should she die childless, her surviving sisters would divide her portion of the trust income equally. Should two sisters die childless, the remaining sister would enjoy the total income of the trust until her death. Upon the death of the last surviving daughter of Francis Drexel, the trust income would devolve onto her children. Should she die childless, the entire trust would be dissolved, and its funds distributed to the original twenty-nine charities specified by Drexel in his will.

Francis Drexel's will was a well-drawn legal document that took into account all the possible contingencies for a father trying to reach beyond the grave to care for three orphaned daughters. They were three attractive and extremely wealthy young women, possibly America's most eligible young women. While they had seen a great deal of the world, they were not worldly women. Their lives had been circumscribed by their close family circle, now unalterably shattered by the deaths of both parents within a fairly short time. They might marry. Francis Drexel had known of the marriage proposal to Katharine, which she rejected. Any one of them might remain single. One or more might enter a convent. Their father had written to a friend: "My daughters are all good practical Catholics — whether any of them will have the vocation to become a religious I cannot say — If they should, I will not oppose it."[69] Emma Drexel preferred that her daughters marry; she believed that they would do more good in the world as pious women of wealth and status than as cloistered nuns. Emma, who had considered the religious life for herself and whose sister had entered a convent, told her daughters, "I do hope God will not give you, my children, a reli-

68. This provision was due to what was called a "Spendthrift" clause in the will. Will of Francis Drexel, SBS Archives.

69. Francis Drexel Correspondence, SBS Archives.

gious vocation. If He does, I must submit; but I shall never permit you to enter a convent until you are at least 25 years of age."[70] Their father's will would accommodate any of these possible vocations. His daughters' decisions concerning marriage, the single life, or the convent were still in the future when Francis Drexel wrote his will.

The loss to the community of the example of and daily commerce with Francis Drexel was nothing compared to his loss to his daughters. Elizabeth, Katharine, and Louise were now quite literally the "All Three." They no longer had the guiding hand of either parent. The estate trustees, Uncles Anthony Drexel and John Lankenau, along with George Childs, a close family friend and the owner and editor of the *Philadelphia Ledger,* were solicitous of the Drexel sisters, looking after and advising them, but all the many kindnesses of relatives and friends could not make up for the loss of their father and mother. For a short period of time they lived with Uncle Anthony and his wife, just as more than twenty-five years before Elizabeth and baby Katharine had stayed with them after the death of Hannah Drexel. Anthony Drexel, by then the single head of the Drexel family banking firm, took his nieces in hand. He no doubt talked with them about their future and security. He found Katharine particularly interested and adept in financial matters. His biographer, Dan Rottenberg, called Katharine the "shrewdest business head among her generation of Drexels," including Anthony's three sons. "Kate seemed eager to learn from her Uncle Anthony about the relative value of investments and the creditworthiness of specific bonds. Tony for his part was grateful to find someone of the next generation who responded enthusiastically to his mentoring instincts. But of course Victorian society offered no place in banking for a woman. Some suitable activity would have to be found for her."[71] Eventually, the Drexel sisters moved back into the family home on Walnut Street to plan the rest of their lives. While her uncle Anthony might not have considered the convent a "suitable activity" for Katharine, she would and did.

During the illness of Emma Drexel, both Katharine and Elizabeth seriously considered entering the convent. The religious life had had its attractions for Katharine from young girlhood. She was at home as much in a church or a convent as she was at St. Michel. As a small child she had enjoyed playing in the chapel at Eden Hall while she and Emma waited to pick up Elizabeth at the end of the school day. She had enjoyed the convent

---

70. Repeated in a letter from MKD to O'Connor, January 27, 1884.
71. Rottenberg, *The Man Who Made Wall Street,* p. 50.

parlor when her mother visited with her aunt, Madame Louise. Additionally, the Carthusian monastery in France had provided her with an image of a peaceful life. Becoming a religious was an idea that Elizabeth rejected almost immediately after the death of her mother. Elizabeth confided to her journal: "Sweet it is to weep at the foot of the Cross and there, Thank God! I have found refuge and consolation. But now the finger of the Lord clearly points me the way of the active life. There I will find my cross if I pick it up and follow Jesus. There will the footsteps of my mother mark out for me a well-beaten path."[72] Elizabeth resolved to carry on for her mother and to follow in her footsteps. It was an idea that had come to her at least a year before Emma's death, when she wrote the following in her journal:

> Our meditations on the life of Christ would seem to teach us that to suffer patiently the will of God is even more pleasing to Him than even to accomplish great things for the glory of His name. When I resume in my own mind the edifying life of my darling mother, so full of activity and usefulness, so pure in its intention of pleasing God, all her charities which the world at large dwells on so much — all her devotion to duty — her turning resolutely aside from the influence of the world — all, all beautiful as they are, seem to me less than her final sufferings endured (and so hard to endure) at the hand of God and her surrendering herself to Him at His call in the vigor of her age, and in the very middle of her work.[73]

While Elizabeth had chosen the active life and Katharine was beginning to long for the peace of the cloister, neither of the sisters was willing to take the decisive steps that would break their circle. Both of the older sisters felt responsible for Louise, who at twenty-one was still quite young. So they stayed together and planned various ways to carry on the charities of their parents and means to promote and honor their memories. They met regularly, as had their mother, with the Dorcas charity, something the sisters would do until duty called them elsewhere or they were no longer able.

Bereft of her own father, Katharine turned more and more to her spiritual adviser and father, Bishop James O'Connor of Omaha. They had written to one another regularly after his departure for the West. Their correspondence flourished as she grew older. Concerning Katharine's convent thoughts, Bishop O'Connor advised her, "Think, pray, and wait, and all will

---

72. ELD Journal, Good Friday 1883.
73. Baldwin, *St. Katharine Drexel*, p. 35.

turn out for your peace and happiness."[74] He was initially adamantly opposed to her joining a convent, believing that she would do more good with her example as a pious woman living in the married state in the world. It took many years of thinking, praying, and waiting by both Katharine and Bishop O'Connor until he would consent to her entering a convent, and then he had very specific ideas about the type of convent she should enter. The development of Katharine's spirituality and the process of her search for a vocation are the next story to be unfolded through her interactions with her spiritual adviser, her confessor, and her sisters.

In the meantime, the portrait that emerges of Katharine Drexel from her childhood and young adulthood is one of a bright, likeable young woman with a religious seriousness that was a little beyond the norm. She and her family exhibited all the hallmarks of what is termed Catholic devotionalism that became popular in the latter half of the nineteenth century. Their piety centered on the sacraments of the Church, aided by individual and family prayers, including the rosary; devotional readings, including prayer books and guides, as well as lives of the saints; the practice of fasting and abstinence according to the rules of the Church; and the practice of charity.[75] She demonstrated remarkable love and loyalty to her family, especially to her parents and sisters. She never seems to have questioned her family's financial or social standing. Her attachment to her mother was particularly strong, yet she was also extremely close to her father. Indeed, when he died, Katharine suffered a physical and nervous collapse. She lost a considerable amount of weight, became lethargic, and retreated even further into the exclusive company of her sisters. Her condition would have been recognized today as clinical depression and treated accordingly.

The precarious state of her health was one of the reasons Bishop O'Connor would give for withholding his consent for her to enter the convent. Katharine also exhibited a great willingness to adhere to authority. She was the dutiful daughter to her parents and the dutiful spiritual daughter to her religious advisers. Her desire was always to please and never to offend; obedience came naturally to her. Interestingly, in the years ahead, the exercise of authority and leadership would also come naturally to her. The external events of her early years do not begin to tell the entire story of those years or of the years to come. That she learned the lessons her parents sought to

---

74. O'Connor to MKD, August 5, 1883.

75. Jay P. Dolan, *The American Catholic Experience: A History from Colonial Times to the Present* (Garden City, N.Y.: Doubleday, 1985), pp. 221-40.

teach her about what it means to be Catholic is evident. What those lessons in virtue, spirituality, and philanthropy would lead to will be the subject of the following chapter; the events will tell the story of a remarkable young woman and budding saint as she argued with a bishop of the Church about her vocation; eventually, she argued herself into a convent and the founding of a new religious order.

CHAPTER 2

"Make Haste Slowly":
The Discernment of a Vocation

There was a long epistolary argument between Bishop James O'Connor and Katharine Drexel over whether or not her desire to enter the convent constituted a true vocation. She, quite naturally, insisted that she was called by God to become a nun in a contemplative order. He, on the other hand, did not believe that her vocation was indeed a gift from God, but a distraction from what he thought was her true place in society. In the course of their fifteen-year relationship, Bishop O'Connor counseled her in her growing spiritual quest. For the last six of those years, the question concerned her vocation. It was difficult for Katharine to persist in her desire for a vocation in the face of his opposition, and, eventually, it was nearly impossible for her to accept her specific vocation to found an order of nuns to serve Native Americans and African Americans. Her ultimate moment of defiance of the bishop over her decision to enter the convent could not have been predicted by her previous actions and attitudes, but it followed a time when she developed a more deeply spiritual life and more strength of character. It was a period of turmoil not readily evident to those about her.

Watching a swan glide across a pond, one sees a majestic bird move effortlessly. It is a serene scene, peaceful and calm. However, beneath the water, the feet of the swan are actively working away, sometimes through the muck and mire of the pond. Similarly, what one saw of Katharine Drexel as a young woman in her twenties reflected the serenity of the swan gliding across the pond; her life was unruffled, charmed by wealth and love. It is true that both of her parents had died, but it is the natural order of things for parents to predecease their children. Katharine still had her youth, beauty, wealth, social position, and a long life before her. She and her sisters enjoyed an intense intimacy that needed no outsiders while, at the same time, they extended their relationships to their large family and close family friends.

On the other hand, there was a depth to Katharine that was not apparent to her family and friends. They saw the swan gliding on the pond. Could they have seen beneath the surface of her charmed exterior, they would have seen a battle raging. Not even to her sisters would she confide her torments. This was not a case for the "All Three" to solve together, even though it would eventually have a profound effect on every one of them. Katharine was wrestling with the existential question of how to give the most meaning to her life so as to give the greatest glory to God and to secure for herself the highest place in heaven. In short, she was a serious Christian searching for her vocation. She wanted to know what God wanted her to do with the rest of her life. Was she called to the married state to serve God as a wife and mother, as Emma Drexel had done before her? Was she to spend her life as a single woman dedicating herself to charity and friendship? Or was she called to the life of a religious to spend her years in cloistered prayer and meditation? She felt herself pulled one way and then another.

Keeping Spiritual Accounts and Early Religious Impulses

One of the earliest manifestations of her relationship with O'Connor was the commencement of a spiritual journal, which began in 1873 when Katharine was still only a young teenager. Under his guidance, Katharine's budding spirituality was given direction and shape. Her spiritual journals helped her to focus her religious intentions and mark her progress, as well as her failures. Her journals are at times wise, amusing, and heartbreaking. Here is an excerpt of an entry written when she was just fourteen:

July 8, 1873

Vacations have now commenced and I now take resolution to say prayers, etc. for ¾ of an hour every day. First I will say the beads for Grandma Langstroth, then my Scapular prayers, Sacred Heart and cord of St. Joseph for a happy death and that I will make a good confession. Then a meditation and Fr. Faber, [read] five pages [of Fr. Faber's *Spiritual Conferences*]. I will try to be patient and kind, overcome v[anity] and p[ride], etc., etc. My meditation today is on death. Every single thing we do is making death easier or harder. There are 3 kinds of preparation for death — 1. the entire series of life; 2. a conscious and intentional fashioning of our lives generally with a view to death; 3. the special preparation for death, viz. spiritual exercises, retreats, and penances which have death for their object.

REMEDIES OF SELF-DECEIT
Finding out one's self-deceit.

1. Offering our actions to God.
2. Self-distrust.
3. Docility to our Director.
4. Meditation on the perfections of God, and reverence for God.
5. Simplicity.
6. Love of the Blessed Sacrament and our Guardian Angel.
7. Confidence in God.[1]

First, there is the determination to pray for three-quarters of an hour every day, though one wonders to what the "etc." refers. It most likely takes the form of reading from the lives of saints, various religious tracts, or the Bible. Again there are those et ceteras following "I will try to be patient and kind, overcome v[anity] and p[ride]." It is clear that she wants to become a more virtuous person, but to what other vices might she be alluding? Later journal entries mention purity and sensuality, neither of which is surprising in an adolescent.

What is more striking in this particular entry is the subject of her meditation: death. This demonstrates a tremendous depth and maturity in a fourteen-year-old. She had already taken seriously the teaching that life is but a prelude to death, a liminal event to the eternal hereafter. Further, Katharine recognized that one of the greatest stumbling blocks to a good life, and thus a good death, is self-deceit. According to Catholic belief, the fallen nature of man makes it easy, in fact inevitable, for the individual to fall into sin, with self-deceit masking evil, clouding the intellect, and disordering the will. Additionally, she knew, even at fourteen, that she could not trust in herself alone. She needed to rely on someone with a wiser head than hers — her spiritual adviser; moreover, she needed to cleave to the Church and the sacraments. Fundamental were her faith and hope in God to bring her to himself. To this theme of faith and hope in God, she returned throughout life, both in her personal life and in her more public life as the founder of an order of sisters sent out to labor under very trying circumstances.

1. ASBS, vol. 1, July 8, 1873.

A few months after the previous entry into her spiritual journal, Katharine wrote the following:

Another year has again come 'round and I will renew my resolutions again for I am but little better than then in purity. I was much better in May than I am now because I suppose I have relied too much on myself. P[ride] and V[anity] is just the same, or a _very_ little better or worse. In impatience, with God's help I am a little better although I have not had the same occasion for sinning against it. During the year 1874, I am resolved:

1. To overcome pride and vanity
2. To speak French
3. Attention to Prayers
4. Attention to Studies

If God will help me, however, I intend and must do what Fr. O'Connor has told me to do . . .

1. Never to omit my morning prayers, but to devote 5-8 minutes in the Morning devotions in the prayer-book.
2. During the day and if prefer when clock strikes offer up all your
    a. actions to God.
3. Make a meditation in "Following of Christ" or other book for about
    a. 10-15 minutes, or perhaps less time. Read a life of a saint or some
    b. good book such as "Monks in the West" every three months.
    c. Novels of day, etc., every once in a while.
4. Examine conscience thoroughly every day to see if the duties proposed have been fulfilled.
5. Take the advice of your Confessor for he has more responsibility than you, and believe what he tells you. Try to go to confession less as if you were going to execution. Try to go as a repentant child who is sorry for having offended a good Father, and joyful at receiving his pardon.[2]

Obviously, Katharine was honest in examining her conscience; whether she was overly scrupulous is another question. She realized, however, that her pride and vanity were getting in the way of her ability to rely on the constancy

---

2. ASBS, vol. 1, p. 31, January 1, 1874, emphasis in original. Hereafter, only emphasis added by the author will be noted.

of God and the good advice of her elders. Bishop O'Connor's advice struck a good balance for her. He wanted her to focus not so exclusively on religion, but to read a novel now and then. Because of her tendency to view herself in such a sinful light, she had come to dread the confessional. "Try to go to confession less as if you were going to execution. Try to go as a repentant child who is sorry for having offended a good Father, and [be] joyful at receiving his pardon." O'Connor wanted her to be a good daughter of the Church, but here he is actually limiting her prayer time and discouraging the kind of scrupulosity that made her fear the confessional. "She often prayed to be delivered from the scruples and she begged grace 'to confide in God, to conquer scruples and to be humble and kind.'"[3] Yet, she failed time and again. Her one consolation seemed to be the Eucharist. "I wish very much at present to receive dear Jesus, for it has been so long since I have been to Holy Communion. But I am so awfully unworthy of this greatest of favors, sinning every second [*sic*] intend from today to try — please help me! Therefore [I shall] endeavor to be less selfish and to be kind."[4] Katharine, like most conscientious Christians, was constantly making resolutions. The liturgical calendar of the church year helps to create a rhythm of the occasions for making resolutions, calling the faithful to the examination of conscience, along with prayers and the creation of plans for personal improvement. This liturgical rhythm surrounds the sacraments of the Church. Thus for Lent of 1874, Katharine made the following resolutions:

> Next Wednesday will be Lent and so to please God and mortify my flesh, I resolve:
>
> 1. Not to eat between meals
> 2. Not to take water between meals
> 3. Dinner, everything but once
> 4. No butter, no fruit
> 5. To speak French
> 6. To give money to the poor[5]

She notes in September of 1876 that her spiritual adviser, not surprisingly, "has told me that my predominant passion is scrupulosity and a certain fear."[6] It is

---

3. Sr. Patricia Lynch, SBS, *Sharing the Bread in Service: Sisters of the Blessed Sacrament, 1891-1991*, 2 vols. (Bensalem, Pa.: Sisters of the Blessed Sacrament, 1998), 1:14.

4. ASBS, vol. 2, October 1873.

5. MKD, Collected Journals, March 1874.

6. ASBS, vol. 2, September 1876.

obviously a fine line for a spiritual adviser to walk in trying to foster nascent spirituality in a young person yet quashing an unhealthy scrupulosity. Katharine was an intelligent and strong-willed young woman. She relied on her confessor and spiritual adviser for the advice she found difficult to carry out.

Four years later she was still struggling with the same issues, though she was more precise in keeping track of her successes, which appear to be few, and her failures, which appear to be many.

> Resolve that during this year to try to overcome:
> Impatience
> Attention to lessons

> I, Katie, put these resolutions at the feet of Jesus, Mary and Joseph, hoping they will find acceptance. May Jesus, Mary and Joseph help me to bear much fruit in the ensuing year, 1878.

Pride	Vanity
Jan. — about same	Jan. — Worse
April — little better	April — same — not try again
May — Little Better by God's Help	May — bad — not try — overcome
June — slight relx from last	June — I never try — overcome
July, Aug. Sept. — I think a relax	July, Aug. Sept. — Bad
November — <u>relaxed</u>	November . . .

Impatience	Attention to Study
Jan. — worse	Jan. — little, little better
April — little better	April — bad
May — about the same as April	May — bad
June — better	June — no better
July, Aug. Sept. — better perhaps	July, Aug. Sept. a little, Little Better
November "	November . . .[7]

Here is a young woman in her nineteenth year who is keeping her own accounts, as she calls them, of her efforts to master her vices. But by her own estimation, she is in most cases "bad," "no better," and on occasion com-

---

7. ASBS, vol. 1, p. 3, January 1878.

pletely "overcome" in her attempt to improve herself. At her best she is only a "little better." Pride and vanity are, as always, her main stumbling blocks. For Lent of that same year she made the following observation about herself: "Lent has commenced and still I am as bad as ever and perhaps worse. How is it ever possible that I could treat Him so badly after all He has done for me. I hope I will make a good Confession next Saturday and the Bread of Life will strengthen me against all evil. Is it not wonderful to think of that infinite love shown by Him to us miserable sinners."[8]

In her struggle with her sins and in her failed resolutions, Katharine was the "Everyman" of Christendom. She was sincerely sorry for her sins and knew she must rely on God both to forgive her sins and to give her the grace to avoid further sin. Even when she found improvement, she rebuked herself for her pleasure and vanity in assessing her progress. Following Lent of 1878, she noted, "I am a little better but like a vain wretch I am proud of it. Should I not thank Jesus for helping me? . . . I hope I shall not relapse. May J[esus] M[ary] J[oseph] help me not to."[9] In the fashion of a saint, Katharine was willing to continue fighting the continuous battle with sin, even the sin of scrupulosity. She demonstrated in her spiritual notes a growing trust in God's love and an understanding and appreciation for the Eucharist. As she matured chronologically, she also matured spiritually. Her schooling officially ended in 1878, and to her it seemed as if her future were "vague and uncertain." Her classroom work was over, but her education continued, especially in the area of her spirituality.

In 1881, Katharine wrote of the importance of self-emptying: "Always try to approach the Holy Table with more and more love. Divest your heart of all love of the world and of yourself and then you will leave room for Jesus."[10] After this entry into her spiritual journal, she wrote, "Thank Our Lord for having redeemed your soul with His Most Precious Blood." In self-emptying, in *kenosis,* one makes room for God to act, acknowledging one's dependence on God rather than on oneself.[11] Later that year, she acknowledged her dependence on God and her personal insignificance as she wrote her resolutions for 1882.

8. ASBS, vol. 1, p. 3, February 2, 1878.

9. MKD, Collected Journals, May 1878.

10. MKD, Collected Journals, 4, 1881. Date according to Anthony Costa, "The Spirituality of Saint Katharine Drexel: Eucharistic Devotion Nourishing Apostolic Works" (diss. for licentiate in theology, Pontificiam Universitatem S. Thomae, 2001), p. 12.

11. *Kenosis,* though a common term today in discussions of spirituality, was not a term used in the context of nineteenth-century spirituality. The use of the term is fully developed in chapter 4.

Oh Dear Little Infant Jesus, by your humble crib, I will make my reso-
lutions for the coming year. In the presence of the Blessed Virgin, St.
Joseph, my Guardian Angel, and St. Catherine, and in your presence,
Infant Jesus, I here protest that of myself I can do nothing.

Do not think of self but of God in all things. To renounce self. By frequent
offerings, by hastily stopping the least vain thought or thought of self.
No cake for 1882.
No preserves until June, 1882.
No grapes, No Honey until July 1st.[12]

Part of Katharine's self-emptying was carried on throughout her life by denying herself the physical pleasures of filling herself up with the sweets and
good foods that she had always enjoyed. This was a great sacrifice, because
she loved good food. According to St. Francis de Sales, moderate fasting or
abstinence is useful for "elevating our spirits, keeping the body in subjection,
practicing virtue, and in gaining a greater reward in heaven, it is valuable for
restraining gluttony and keeping our sensual appetites and body subject to
the law of the spirit. Although we may not fast very much, yet the enemy has
greater fear of us when he sees that we can fast."[13] Katharine, in her spiritual
enthusiasm, would fall occasionally to immoderate fasting and abstinence,
alarming her family, possibly harming her health, and causing Bishop O'Connor to limit her fasts and her self-proscribed foods. Later, when she was
actively contemplating her vocation, she would ask for permission to "come
down to convent rations," but he would not, at first, consent, and when he
did allow her so-called convent rations, it was within limits that he set.

The Beginning of Discernment

During Emma Bouvier Drexel's illness and death Katharine turned more
inward, relying on her spiritual strength. Her mother's death in January 1883
rudely awakened within her a need to contemplate her own future. Her meditation on death as a fourteen-year-old, almost ten years before, was but
an abstract exercise compared to the reality of it. During Emma's illness,

12. Costa, "Spirituality of Saint Katharine Drexel," p. 12.
13. St. Francis de Sales, *Introduction to the Devout Life,* trans. and ed. John K. Ryan
(New York: Image Books, 1989), p. 185.

Katharine had teased her mother by telling her that if anything happened to Emma, she would enter a convent. Knowing that Emma's preference was for her daughters to marry, this was but a gentle tease on Katharine's part. Yet, there was truth concealed in the tease. She was beginning to consider seriously a religious vocation. With her mother's passing, the charmed circle of the Drexel household was broken for the first time, and an uncertain future stretched before the bereaved daughters. Within a few months, Katharine sent her spiritual adviser the following letter.

Right Rev'd. & dear Father;

As you can readily see by the bulk of this letter I have availed myself of your extremely kind permission. In presenting "my papers" for your perusal I feel that I am imposing upon time that can ill be spared from important business. And yet, I would not confide these papers to any one else. I confess, I have come to no conclusion about my vocation in writing them; but I know that I cannot do better than submit everything to you whom God in His mercy has given me to lead me to Him & Heaven. — I hope the matter of my "papers" may prove intelligible; I fear it may not. I have made a novena to the Holy Ghost & have received the prayers of several very holy souls. After that I have tried to lay open my heart to you. But it is a difficult matter to know ourselves, & I trust I have not been self-deceived. — If my papers are all wrong, please tell me & in what way & I shall make as many attempts as you may require of me. If you were to tell me you thought that God called me to the married state, I should feel that a great weight were off of my mind & yet I should not in the least feel satisfied with the consequence of such a decision, namely, — a low place in Heaven. Does it not appear that my own corrupt nature leads me to the married state, & the Holy Ghost prompts me to choose the better part? — Again the religious life seems to me like a great, risky, speculation. If it succeeds I gain immense treasures, but if I fail I am ruined.

Please do not feel obliged, dear father, to answer me for months, if it is not convenient for you to do so soon. I am in no hurry for the response. I think it is clearly my vocation at present to remain an old maid. My reasons for desiring a speedy decision as to my vocation have now been removed. — The gentleman who was paying me attention had proposed, & I have refused the offered heart. I have every reason to believe that it was not a very ardent one. No one (not even my sisters) knows of this little affair except Papa, who gave me my free choice, saying he desired but my happiness.

If Lise & Louise knew that I am writing to you, they would certainly ask me to send their warmest remembrances. I hope we shall never forget what you were and are to us in our first great sorrow.

With a big apology for boring you with such a mass of egotistical matter, believe me entirely

Your unworthy child in Christ,
K. M. Drexel[14]

With this letter, Katharine is following the advice of her confessor in Philadelphia, Fr. Daniel McGoldrick, SJ, to apply the plan of St. Ignatius in trying to decide a course of action by making a list of reasons in favor of entering the religious life paralleled by a list of reasons opposed to the religious life. Katharine, never one to do things by halves, did the exercise twice, first with personal reasons for and against the religious life and then with personal reasons for and against the married life. She did not appear ever seriously to consider a calling to the single life, or she would have done the exercise a third time.

MY REASONS FOR ENTERING RELIGION	MY OBJECTIONS TO ENTERING RELIGION
1st. As Jesus Christ has given His life for me, it is but just that I should give Him mine. — Now in religion we offer ourselves to God in a direct manner, whereas in the married state natural motives prompt us to sacrifice self.	1st. How could I bear separation from my family? I who have <u>never</u> been away from home for more than two weeks. At the end of one week have invariably felt home-sick.
2nd. We were created to love God. In the religious life we return Our Lord's love for love by a constant voluntary sacrifice of our feelings, our inclinations, our appetites. Against all of which nature powerfully rebels; but it is by conquering the flesh that the <u>soul</u> lives.	2nd. I hate community life. I should think it maddening to come in constant contact with many <u>old-maidish</u> dispositions. I hate <u>never</u> to be alone.
3rd. I know in truth that the love of the most perfect creature is vain in comparison with Divine love.	3rd. I fear I should murmur at the commands of my Superior and return a proud spirit to her reproofs.

14. MKD to O'Connor, May 21, 1883.

4th. When all shadows shall have passed away I shall rejoice if I have given in life an <u>entire</u> life to God.	4th. Superiors are frequently selected on account of their holiness, <u>not</u> for ability. I should hate to owe submission to a woman whom I felt to be stupid and whose orders showed her thorough want of judgement.
5th. In religious life our Last End is kept continually before the mind.	5th. In the religious life how can spiritual dryness be endured?
6th. A higher place in Heaven is secured for all eternity.	6th. When with <u>very slight variety</u> the same things are expected of me day in and day out, year in and year out, I fear weariness, disgust, and a want of perseverance which might lead me to leave the Convent. And what then!!
7th. The attainment of perfection should be our chief employment in life. Our Lord laid a price upon its acquirement when He says, "<u>If</u> thou <u>wilt</u> be perfect go, sell what thou hast and give it to the poor and thou shalt have treasure in heaven; and come follow Me. . . . He that followeth Me <u>walkest</u> not in darkness." How can I doubt that these words are true wisdom. And if true wisdom, why not act upon them?	7th. I do not know how I could bear the privations and poverty of the religious life. I have never been deprived of luxuries.
8th. [Lost]	
9th. If I should leave all I possess, I am sure that my wealth would be employed by my father and sisters to far greater advantage or at least to as great an advantage as I myself could employ it.	

To this list there are appended two additional reasons, both numbered four: "4th. I question whether I would not when stimulated by earthly love perform greater things in life than when moved by duty or the pure love of God." This reason appears to belong in the column opposing religious life. However, the last number four could easily go in either column. "4th. Does God estimate the greatness of human actions according to the work accomplished or according to the motives which induced the actions?"

FOR THE MARRIED STATE	OPPOSED TO THE MARRIED STATE
1st. I am drawn to love those that love me and in proportion to the love given.	1st. Why then should I not love God? In Heaven I shall surely see that His love is infinitely superior to that of any creatures.
2nd. I should like to be loved with that devoted and special affection (I imagine) a true husband feels for and shows to his wife.	2nd. Is this not vanity and pride?
3rd. I consider it desirable to be assisted by the judgement of a husband in whom I have every reason to suppose I can rely on with entire confidence.	3rd. On whom can we more truly rely with entire confidence than upon God? His judgement is manifest by means of a superior and a spiritual director.
4th. Marriage appears to me to open a new field for many good and desirable actions.	4th. Does not religious life also open a large field for performing acts of virtue and benefiting our fellow beings?
5th. Certainly temptations to spiritual disgust would be considerably lessened when even natural motives conduct — as they do in marriage — to the practice of virtue. Witness the self-sacrifice of the mother for her child, the wife for her husband.	5th. Should I not have that confidence in God which would lead me to know that His grace is sufficient to save me from despair and disgust in His service. And do natural motives profit for eternal life?
6th. I like the independence and individuality of being at the head of my own affairs.	6th. [None]
7th. I think it a glorious destiny to bring forth souls.	7th. Could I with my temperament do this without sin? I very much fear that I should find it extremely difficult — impossible — unless God surely calls me to the married life. In that case I have this lesson of experience to rely upon. His grace had aided me to perform without sin actions which I could not even think of before. . . . As far as my nature is concerned I feel no obstacles to the married life except those mentioned. Unless indeed I

	should find my husband tyrannical and unreasonable. Then I should be a wretched woman and should bitterly mourn having sacrificed my life to a man and blame myself for the vanity.
8th. I should like the joys of motherhood.	
9. The wealth with which God has blessed me would naturally seem to be given me for employment in the world.[a]	
a. Contained in letter from MKD to O'Connor, May 21, 1883.	

In making these lists, Katharine was clearly trying to be as honest as possible as she laid before her spiritual adviser her thoughts and concerns about the religious life versus the married life. It is also clear that the topic of the religious life had been brought up in previous correspondence between her and the bishop. Those letters are now lost. Katharine thought she leaned decidedly to the religious life, though her spiritual adviser did not believe he detected a true vocation for another six years, and she herself had at this point come to "no conclusion about my vocation in writing them [her lists]." He observed that her lists supporting the religious life contained no real personal reasons in its favor, only rather abstract ones. On the other hand, her reasons for opposing the religious life, as well as those in favor of married life, were very specific and personal. It is hard to imagine a woman going into a convent when she "hates community life," or would find it irksome "to owe submission to a woman [she] felt to be stupid," or does not think she can bear "the privations and poverty of the religious life." These are the very basics of religious life. In the married state, she would look forward to "independence and individuality," "motherhood," and the enjoyment of a love that is a "devoted and special affection" from her husband. Again, these are the very basics of married life and personal and specific reasons for desiring that state. Yet there is a decided fear of marriage expressed should she marry a "tyrannical and unreasonable" man. Everything else in her lists appears to be so dispassionate and reasonable that this sudden explosion of emotion and fear is shocking. Her spiritual adviser, for his part, was compassionate about her desires but unimpressed with her reasoning. Nineteenth-century letter-writing style and rhetoric aside, his is a rather condescending response softly couched.

Dear Child,

Yours of the 21st., with accompanying paper, is received.

Will you be persuaded once for all, that your letters always give me great pleasure, and that I shall always be most happy to help you *in via domini* [in the way of the Lord].

Most of the reasons you give, in your paper, for and against entering the states considered, are impersonal, that is abstract and general. These are very well as far as they go, in setting one's vocation, but additional and personal reasons are necessary to decide it. The relative merits of the two states cannot be in question. It is of faith that the religious state is, beyond measure, the more perfect. It must be admitted, too, that, in both, dangers and difficulties are to be encountered and overcome. One of these states is for the few, the other for the many.

In the religious state, a young lady becomes the mystic *"sponsa Christi"* [bride of Christ]. She gives her heart to Him, and to Him alone. If she loves others it is in Him, for Him she does so. And loving Him with this undivided, and exceptional love, she seeks to liken herself to Him as perfectly as possible, the practice of the three virtues that were peculiarly manifested by Him, during His mortal life, — poverty, chastity, and obedience. If she desires this union with our Lord, and is not daunted by the difficulties to be overcome in acquiring the perfection it implies, and calls for, there is nothing in her natural dispositions, and no such want of virtuous habits, as would make it imprudent in her to aspire to it, she has what is called a religious vocation.

Now, my dear child, coming to your case, you give general, but no personal reasons for becoming a nun, unless your reasons for entering the married state, should be considered as such. But these reasons, too, are general, and point to dangers that exist for all who get married. If they would justify you, they would justify all women in entering religion.

On the other hand, you give positive personal reasons for not embracing the religious state. The first — the difficulty you would find in separation from family, does not merit consideration, as that would have to be overcome, in any case. The second — your dislike for Community life, is a very serious one, and if it continues to weigh with you, you should give up all thoughts of religion. You would meet many souls there, but some, even among superiors, who would be far from perfect. To be in constant communion with these, to be obliged to obey them, is the greatest cross of the religious life. Yet to this, all who "would be perfect," must be prepared to submit. Indeed, toleration of their faults and shortcomings, is in the

Divine economy, one of the indispensable means of acquiring perfection. The same must be said of "the privations and poverty," and the monotony of the religious life, to which you allude. If you do not feel within you the courage, with God's help, to bear them, for sake of Him to whom they lead, go not further in your examination. Thousands have [borne] such things, and have been sanctified by them, but only such as had foreseen them, and resolved, not rashly, to endure them for our Lord.

Think over what I have here said, at your leisure, and let me know what further conclusions you may come to.

> Truly yrs. *In Dno,*
> +J. O'Connor[15]

This exchange of letters began a struggle between Katharine and the bishop over her life's true vocation that would take six years and the intervention of the pope to resolve. The letters are key to understanding the inner workings of Katharine's mind and the growth of her self-confidence. She makes clear her moments of doubt considering her calling and her abilities. But her letters also demonstrate her growing strength of character and her burgeoning spirituality. For his part, Bishop O'Connor holds up a mirror for her to look into, all the while pushing, prodding, or holding back as he saw fit. Later in the summer, he wrote to her:

Dear Child,

God, I trust, will reward the simplicity with which you have opened your heart to me, His unworthy minister, by enabling me to help you to a choice of the state of life He would have you enter. I know He must love you with a special love, and I am full of confidence that He will not allow me to mislead you. . . .

You write, "I find it difficult to think of the married state, I can find peace in thinking of the religious life." This is a strong "personal" indication of a vocation to religion, especially when accompanied by your little desire for society, and your hesitation to put your happiness in the hands of a husband.

What most makes me hesitate to say that you have a vocation to religion, is the fear that you might not have the strength to endure the sacrifices it calls for. From your home, from your table, to the cell and the

15. O'Connor to MKD, May 26, 1883. *In Dno* means "in the Lord."

refectory of a nun, would be a very great change, indeed. And what makes me hesitate, in this matter, should cause you to do the same. How then, may the doubt be removed? By continuing in the course you have already begun. One or two days a week come down to convent rations, and, on other days, for a time, abstain from the one dish you most relish. Dress occasionally, and especially when you see company, in the colors that least become you. These acts of self-denial, in addition to what you already do, will, I think, soon enable you to measure your strength.

That you may get a clearer insight than you have into the daily life, privations, and consolations of a religious, I send you *An Apostolic Woman,* a book I read with deep interest a year ago. . . .

You are in doubt in regard to a matter of the gravest importance to yourself individually. It is a doubt that, usually, takes time to solve. Don't be in a hurry. Think, pray, wait, and all will turn out for your peace and happiness.[16]

How difficult it must have been for a twenty-five-year-old woman to be told that she must wait — that these things "take time." O'Connor suggested that Katharine's biggest problem would actually stem from the privations of a nun's life, but he did allow her the opportunity to "try out" a few of its privations. Any parent, even a spiritual one, would be wise to advise his or her child not to be too quick to enter into such a serious, demanding, and permanent commitment as the religious life. At the same time, the bishop challenged her to test her strength. By expressing the difficulties to be overcome, he pricked her pride so she could prove that she was up to the challenge. It was the perfect psychological tactic to use on the strong-willed Katharine.

Not content with having to wait while doing the minimum suggested by Bishop O'Connor, and mindful that ultimately the call to a religious, or any, vocation was directly from God to her at the prompting of the Holy Spirit, Katharine begged to do more:

God is to lead my soul in the road He wills & I wish to follow Him & obey His call. It seems to me that He calls me "to come down to convent rations" not only on "one or two days in the week" but everyday unless my doing so should attract attention. Now whether this is really the desire of the Holy Spirit, or whether it proceeds from my very scrupulosity, or a

16. O'Connor to MKD, August 5, 1883.

wish to show you that I have courage, I am at a loss to determine. . . . Your great kindness makes me confide that you will direct me on this occasion, & also tell me what course God wishes me to adopt when I am again uncertain as to His will in such trifling matters. I fear undertaking anything, no matter how small it may be unless it is in conformity with the Divine Will, because [He] gives me the strength necessary to perform what He prompts; but if I follow the inspiration of pride He will not support me & I shall fail. I have not yet told you that I have been receiving Holy Communion three times a week since the first of July.

If you should approve of my coming down to convent rations everyday would you think it *en règle* [within the rule] five times a week to take soup for supper in place of tea or coffee [nun's rations] which is not procurable in anything but a wee cup after dinner at our late dinners [nun's supper time]? This soup, in addition to bread (2 rolls), fruit, & cheese.[17]

Throughout the process of discernment for her vocation, Katharine continually asked for advice and counsel from Bishop O'Connor, then chafed under it and pushed him to remove or extend whatever limits he might have set upon her. In this letter, she even began to doubt her own motivation for her desire to deprive herself of the pleasures of the Drexel family table. She questioned whether it was the prompting of the Holy Spirit or her own pride and desire to show the bishop that she was up to the deprivations required at the refectory table of the convent. She tried to wheedle and cajole her own way. She sought openings in the bishop's logic and thought processes to win his approval for her plans.

The frequency of the bishop's letters to Katharine and their great detail are remarkable. His motivation for being involved with her and the discernment of her vocation was never made explicit in any of his writings. He was the bishop of an enormous diocese that covered 367,265 square miles, including all or part of what are today seven states. During his tenure, its population grew by 400 percent, even while the square miles were reduced.

The Union Pacific Railroad was completed in 1867 and opened up the upper Midwest to migration from the East. The Burlington Railroad moved into Nebraska in the 1870s and 1880s, making it more accessible to migrants. The Oregon and California trails crossed Nebraska, and many settlers took advantage of the offer of free, 160-acre homesteads and stayed there, instead of continuing the difficult journey on to California or Oregon. Later Nebraska,

17. MKD to O'Connor, September 8, 1883.

by means of the Kinkaid Act, would increase the acreage of homesteads to 640 acres to help settle the less hospitable western plains of the state. White settlers were served in various Catholic schools by the Sisters of Mercy and the Benedictines, who became a stable presence in the diocese, but orders of nuns could not be found to serve the needs of the Indians. With such an influx of white settlers, part of O'Connor's job was to keep peace between the settlers and the Indian tribes of his diocese. When he was first appointed bishop, his diocese contained all or parts of the Pawnee, Ponca, Omaha, Oto, Sioux, Shoshone, Crow, Cheyenne, Winnebago, and Arapaho tribes. The last battles of the Indian wars were fought there while he was bishop. He feared for the literal survival of the Indians, for some of the tribes were down to only a handful of clans. Most of the Indians in Nebraska were forcibly resettled in wretched conditions in Indian Territory, now the state of Oklahoma. Today, only four tribes remain within the state: Sioux, Poncas, Winnebagos, and Omahas.

That O'Connor would arrange not one trip, but eventually two trips, to his Indian missions for the daughters of Francis Drexel indicates his deep concern for the welfare of the Indians and his firm belief that the Drexel women would be important to their spiritual and temporal salvation. Of the three Drexel women, Katharine showed the most interest in the plight of the Indians. After Francis Drexel, Katharine was the Drexel to whom Bishop O'Connor was closest. Their close relationship provided an opportunity for the bishop to formulate a plan for Catholic evangelization of the Indians, but it took years to finally come into shape. In the meantime, Bishop O'Connor encouraged her philanthropy to the Indians and was a careful spiritual adviser to her. He tested her one way and then another, and he took an interest in everything about her.

He was concerned with her eating and sleeping habits, her toilette, even her amusements. He never seemed to restrict his concern to her spiritual life; rather, he realized the essential unity of her person in body and soul. A few days after he received her letter about convent rations, he wrote back:

> Do not undertake anything in the line of penance without consulting me or your confessor. With such as you, the devil usually changes himself into an angel of light, tempts them to undertake too much, so as to weary, and ultimately disgust them with self-denial. Let your motto, then, in such matter be: *Festina lente* [Make haste slowly]. Do nothing that would make you seem to disregard family usages. Two days on convent rations, is as much as you can bear at present. These rations in your case, should include soup at your evening meal. . . .

Continue to receive Holy Communion three times a week, if you can do so without inconvenience to the family. Never refuse to go out with your sisters, when they are anxious that you should do so. Lead, as far as possible, an interior life. Think often of the presence of God, and of your angel guardian. Reflect on the <u>relative</u> emptiness of worldly things. Compared to the love and service of God, and the salvation of the soul, they are, indeed, "vanity of vanities."

Then, be utterly indifferent as to the state of life to which you may be called. Seek only to know God's Will in this matter, wait, pray, and before long that Will, in one way or another, will be made known to you.[18]

Exactly what penances she was planning is unknown, as her previous letter is missing from the collection. However, given her propensity toward scrupulosity and her view of herself as especially sinful, one can imagine what a sensitive and creative mind might develop. Here the bishop served as a reasonable counterbalance to her occasional extremes. In reminding her to make haste slowly, he wanted her to get outside of herself a little, to partake of the joys of family life, and above all, not to call attention to herself by exterior demonstrations of religiosity. He urged her to perfect her interior dispositions, rather than making more obvious, external privations and devotions that might call attention to herself; yet, she rebelled at such restrictions.

She and her sisters made an enormous effort to comfort their father after the death of their mother and to run the household in the style and manner she had taught them. While Katharine might have been eager for outright approval from Bishop O'Connor for her choice of vocation, she was also not especially keen to break the remaining family circle as long as her father lived. Katharine was content to be an "old maid" for the time being. She was supported by the comfort of Bishop O'Connor, who wrote her later in August, "Every day since the receipt of your last letter, I have made a special commemoration for you at Mass. I shall continue to do so, till God's Will in your regard is made clear to you, that is, as clear as can be expected in such matters. Whatever may be the issues of your investigations, it will be no slight consolation to you in the future, to have taken so much pains to learn the Will of your Divine Master in regard to the state of life you should embrace."[19]

---

18. O'Connor to MKD, September 14, 1883.
19. O'Connor to MKD, August 28, 1883.

While the daughters were concerned about their father's well-being, he was concerned about them. Francis Drexel removed himself from active participation in the family business to devote himself more fully to Lise, Katharine, and Louise. He appears to have been unaware of Katharine's great anxiety over her future vocation, and that, even in Europe, she relied on Bishop O'Connor for advice and fretted about her devotions and her vocation.

And now your troublesome child has a few questions to ask. Would you consider it in accordance with the *"festina lente"* to devote one & a half hour each day or two hours, to prayers, rosary and a quarter [to] meditation? Or if I should wish to pray for a longer time would you consider it prudent to do so when I have the opportunity? . . . Also whilst traveling when I am forced to ask advice on any little point of direction to a confessor who does not know my soul can I afterwards submit the advice to you although given in the secrecy of the confessional?

. . . I believe I am partially afraid of becoming again interested in what I have learned from experience to be transitory. I ardently hope I shall never all through life forget the truths which struck me so forcefully by Mamma's death-bed. There, I could clearly solve the problems of life. Teach me, dear Father, to make it a way to heaven. Any one but you would think that I were morbid or sad in indulging such thoughts, and I should not tell them to any one else.[20]

O'Connor responded: "You ask me if I consider an hour and a half or two hours sufficient time for you to devote to prayer each day. I think one and a half hours quite enough, whilst you are traveling. When you return, send me a list of your daily devotions, and I will <u>overhaul</u> it. In your case, somebody <u>should</u> do this." Clearly, left to her own devices, Katharine would know no bounds to her spiritual exercises. He did not recommend any books of devotional reading until she returned from Europe. He recommended instead that she read novels or travel books and keep a journal of her impressions from her travels. "To read a good novel occasionally will not hurt you, and may help you, so you must not consider any indulgence of this kind opposed to the higher purposes you formed on the occasion referred to above [the grace and direction she gained from being with her mother through her illness and death]."

Then begins a long passage on her vocation:

20. MKD to O'Connor, October 8, 1883.

And now, let me acquaint you with the conclusion I have reached in regard to your vocation. It is this, that you remain in the world, but make a vow of virginity for one year, to be renewed every year, with the permission of your director, till you or he think it well for you to omit it or make it perpetual. This, I think, is what is best for you to do now, and as far as I can see, in the immediate future. Your vocation to <u>religion</u> is not pronounced, and without a very decided vocation, one in your position should not enter it. On the other hand, your vocation to celibacy, and perhaps to a life of celibacy, is sufficiently evident to warrant or even require you to give it a trial. Should the future make known to you that God asks of you the practice of this virtue only for a time, nothing will prevent you from entering another state of life. Should you, on the other hand, feel obliged to remain the *Sponsa Christi,* to the end, you can do so, and make use of the liberty you will enjoy in the world to be of immense service to others, by deed, and example. Give this matter a few days' consideration, and fervent prayer, and if you conclude to adopt the course I have recommended, you would do well to make your first vow at the next sanctuary of the Blessed Virgin you visit after the receipt of this note. At all events, let me know what you think of my view of the matter. Should you conclude to make the vow, all that is necessary for you to do is, to promise our Lord, in any form of words, or even mentally, to practice for love of Him, till that day and year, the holy virtue of chastity. You <u>need</u> not mention the matter even to your confessor.[21]

It is curious that the bishop, while not forbidding her to mention his recommendation of a vow of virginity to her confessor, expressly discouraged her from talking about it with another cleric in a position to advise her. Bishop O'Connor's letter caught up with her in Venice on November 16, 1883. She immediately followed his recommendation to make a vow of celibacy. Katharine made her first vow before the Madonna of St. Mark's, a painting of the Virgin piously attributed to St. Luke. Even though she submitted to her director's advice, she was not very happy about her circumstances. She wrote back a strongly worded response:

The outlook in the future to a life of perpetual celibacy is contrary to my <u>present inclinations to the religious life</u>. If, however, God calls me to remain in the world, to be exposed to its temptations, to be obliged to serve

21. O'Connor to MKD, October 25, 1883.

it, to remain in the world and yet not be of the world, to know how great is the beauty of God's House, and yet to have duties which constantly withdraw from it, to feel that God has given graces, which to quote your own words "<u>must</u> be used under direction lest they lead from the path of prudence" and yet to be deprived of daily direction such as those in religion receive, to be looked down upon as an old maid — If all this is for God's greater glory — I must drown inclination and say <u>Fiat</u> [Let it be done. Echoes the Virgin Mary's response at the Annunciation]. Most likely I can, <u>with God's grace</u>, do more for Him in the world.

I shall reduce myself to an hour and a half prayers each day since you think it "quite sufficient whilst traveling." But at the same time I am going to ask you whether there is to be <u>no exception</u> to the rule. . . .[22]

She had mentioned to the bishop more than once her vain distaste of being thought of as an "old maid," so it is easy to surmise that one of the things he detected in her desire for the religious life was a desire not to be pitied as an old maid, a single woman, for the rest of her life. It is true that she had had at least one suitor, but it is also clear that she did not seek the acquaintance and affection of young men. She was not averse to society, but it never had tremendous appeal for her either. Yet, in the discussions her mother used to carry on with her sister, Madame Bouvier, in the convent, about the relative merits of marriage versus the religious life, the merits of the unmarried state did not seem to be an issue, perhaps giving young Katharine the impression that it was a state to be avoided as not entirely desirable. Bishop O'Connor saw clearly that the desire to avoid one state was not reason enough to choose another, especially one as difficult as that of the religious woman. He wanted her to develop specific, positive, and personal reasons for desiring to enter the convent. The way she wrote of her "*present* inclinations to the religious life" (emphasis added) suggests that she might have other inclinations at some time in the future, making her present inclination appear somewhat tentative. On the other hand, she pushed her director to find exceptions to the rules she had asked for and which he had laid out for her benefit.

In his next letter, he relented on the rules for one hour and a half of daily devotion, but raised more specific questions concerning her vocation.

An occasional spiritual "spree" is as admissable [*sic*] in one who follows a cautious "rule of life," as is an occasional big dinner in one of abstemious

22. MKD to O'Connor, November 20, 1883.

habit. But let the spree be only <u>occasional</u>. The examination for confession, or the preparation for communion need not count in the hour and a half, but neither of these exercises should exceed a quarter of an hour. Better the examination were even less. When at some sanctuary, then, of course, you can go on a spree, but it should be a moderate one and not give scandal. [He does not want her to worry or alarm her sisters and her father.]

You say: "The outlook in the future to a life of perpetual celibacy is contrary to my <u>present inclinations to the religious life</u>." You must not look at your obligation in this matter as perpetual. It is only temporary, lasting from year to year, and ending entirely, and before God, whenever the year closes. I have recommended this course as a tentative measure, since, as I told you, I do not consider your vocation to the religious state sufficiently pronounced. It may become so in no long time. In this, as in most other matters, development is the order of God's works.

And what has made me hesitate about your vocation is that in your own examination on this subject, you told me you felt it would be hard for you to pass your days, and every hour of each day, with women, and, if I do not forget, under the rule of a woman — in a word, to endure the kind of society to which religious vows would consign you. A natural repugnance of this kind, if really felt and lasting, would be an insuperable objection to your becoming a nun. All the other requisites of a vocation you have, at present, as far as I can see, but this dislike for the human or natural side of the religious life, whilst it lasts, would make it highly imprudent for you to enter it. Your yearly vow, may obtain for you the grace to overcome it. But even if it do not, it will enable you to measure your strength in regard to a virtue to which you are so much inclined, and which can be practiced in the world, no less than in religion. And, then, should you find that in this matter you have overestimated your resolution and your power, you will be free to adopt the course that reason will suggest. It is no new thing for the voluntary *Sponsa Christi* to be found in the world, though not of it, benefiting, encouraging, and edifying those who are exposed to its dangers and its hardships. And I really think, dear Child, that you are one of those to whom God gives this hard, but glorious, and most meritorious vocation. Thus far, you have had everything to tempt you to take a very different course, but you have not taken it. God has given you almost every earthly good, but you have counted them as loss compared with the love of Christ. And this has not been the result of surrounding controlling circumstances, but of your own free choice, made and sustained by the grace that has been given you. In this view of your case, however, I may be mistaken. When I see you, which I hope will be soon, we can discuss the matter more nearly, and in detail. In the meantime, have God <u>alone</u> in view in this whole affair. Do not trouble yourself about what the world may think of any course you may feel called on to take. God's holy will should overrule all considerations of this kind.[23]

Perhaps he was trying to appeal to her vanity and to challenge her when he wrote of the vocation to the single state: "It is no new thing for the voluntary *Sponsa Christi* to be found in the world, though not of it, benefiting, encouraging, and edifying those who are exposed to its dangers and its hardships. And I really think, dear Child, that you are one of those to whom God gives this *hard, but glorious, and most meritorious vocation*" (emphasis added). At the same time, he tried to alleviate her fears about the nature of her vow to celibacy by pointing out that it was but an annual vow; it would not be perpetual unless by her own free will she chose it to be so.

Crisis in Discernment

The next letter recalls in a heartbreaking manner the lesson learned from her mother that all not pertaining to God is vanity and will be swept away. It tells of the lessons learned by anyone who travels to ancient lands. It brings to mind the bitter, hard lessons of childhood about the nature of reality:

> Dear Father, I shall try to correspond with the graces you obtain for me. I deeply appreciate all your goodness to me and by reason of the confidence with which it inspires me I am going to take the liberty of occupying this evening a little of your time. Do please be patient with all the egos it will be necessary to use in opening my whole heart to you. It is a very sorrowful heart because like the little girl who wept when she found that her doll was stuffed with sawdust and her drum was hollow, I too have made a horrifying discovery and my discovery like hers is true. I have ripped both the doll and the drum open and the fact lies <u>plainly</u> and <u>in all its</u> glaring reality before me: <u>All, all, all</u> (there is no exception) is passing away and <u>will</u> pass away. European travel brings vividly before the mind how cities have risen and fallen, and risen and fallen; and the same of em-

---

23. O'Connor to MKD, December 16, 1883.

pires and kingdoms and nations. And the billions and billions who lived their common everyday life in these nations and kingdoms and empires and cities where are they? The ashes of the kings and mighty of this earth are mingled with the dust of the meanest slave. The handsome sculptured sepulchres, the exquisitely finished Etruscan vases, the tombs of Egyptian mummies are <u>exposed in museums</u>, the dust of the great which these sepulchres and vases were intended to preserve are scattered to the winds unless perhaps with the exception of the mummy whose face grins from without his winding-sheet upon every idle eye who chooses to gaze within the gilded case once so reverently respected. Day succeeds day and when, as Byron so beautifully expressed it, when the heavens grow red in the western sky "the day joins <u>the past eternity</u>." How long before the sun and moon, and stars continue to give forth light? Who can tell? Of one thing we are <u>sure</u>. In God's own time — then shall come the Son of Man in great power and majesty to render to each <u>according</u> to his works. The reward and punishment for these will <u>not</u> pass away, nor does <u>the</u> day — Eternity — then open before us. An <u>eternity</u> of happiness infinite, or an eternity of misery infinite. <u>The</u> question alone important to me and the solution of which depends upon how I have spent my life and <u>the state of my soul at the moment of death</u>. Infinite misery or infinite happiness! There is no half and half, either one or the other. And this question for me is to be decided <u>at most</u> in seventy years, seventy short years compared to eternity, seventy long years of time. God grant that the time or trial and probation and exile may not last for seventy years longer! — And 93 years after my death my body will be a bony, grinning skeleton like that of the deceased who lay on the bones and skulls of the Capuchin convent in Rome. On this bony arm was tied a tag with "died 1774." — This is ripping open the doll and discovering it to be made of saw-dust! A melancholy grin, frightening grin, disillusionizer! — All is stuffed with saw-dust. . . .

And now to return to the little girl, what was the consequence of her finding out that her doll was stuffed with saw-dust? She says, "she does not want to play with dolls anymore." Once being fully convinced that dolls are not flesh and blood she asks herself seriously what is the good of fondling that which in reality is a bag of ugly sawdust. Now dear Father, <u>that</u> is my case. I am disgusted with the world. God in His mercy has opened my eyes to the fact of the *vanitas vanitatis,* and as He has made me see the vile stark emptiness of this earth I look to Him — the God of Love — in hope. He will not leave me to despair because of the dreariness of all the joys which cannot satisfy my heart. . . . I hope that God may place me in a state of life where I can best know Him, love Him, serve Him for whom alone I am created. I am ambitious. I desire to become the disciple of Our Lord Jesus Christ. What am I to do <u>now</u> — what am I to do in the future? — In today's meditation my text chanced to be "Why asketh thou Me," concerning the doctrine of Jesus and His disciples. "Ask them who have heard what I have spoken unto them: behold they know what things I have said." And therefore, what course should I <u>now</u> adopt to become a disciple, please instruct me, dear Father? Do you wish me to try any line of mortification in order to see for what God gives me strength. If so, tell me and I shall endeavor. Or if I fail it will be either through self-confidence and want of confidence in God, or because God wishes me to fail. I have no longer any dislike of spending my life in the society of religious women or under the rule of a woman, <u>if</u> God gives me the grace to see His Will in her commands. With me it is, I think, impossible to like men except with my inferior nature mingled with passions which <u>must</u> be kept under. Of course, I do not include in my fear of men, those who are consecrated to God and who are His representatives on earth. The following, however, is where I <u>do</u> find difficulty; but with the aid of God cannot this be overcome? I <u>have a vigorous</u>, remarkable <u>appetite</u> and <u>if</u> you should decide that I have a religious vocation, or even if I were to remain in the world as a disciple of Christ, this would, it appears to me, be an impediment unless conquered. I am not a <u>gourmet</u> because I am a gourmande [*sic*]. Nature does not like to be hungry which it must if cut down to convent rations. Now twice every week, according to your directions, I do try and with the help of God's Grace I have always succeeded in bringing myself down to, or near to the portion of a religious. Also on the other days I follow your advice and abstain from the one dish I most like. At least I do this at lunch and dinner; at breakfast as we only serve bread and butter and eggs, I dock off butter, although that is what I least care for. Sometimes <u>too</u> I doubt whether I abstain from the dish I most desire, and once or twice forgot myself and partook of the favorite viand, and was obliged to substitute another. — So far, for my confession! And now for a difficulty. . . . Three times my loving sisters have observed and commented on the smallness of appetite <u>on some</u> occasions. They are quiet now; tell me. . . . Also whilst I am in the world shall I dress tidily, neatly and carefully, having an idea to the becoming, or shall I do the reverse?

One thing more in answer to your letter. I have not had "everything to tempt me to take a very different course from what I have taken." It has been altogether the result of surrounding, controlling circumstances, viz:

— the mother whom God gave us. <u>She</u> plainly saw the *vanitas vanitatis,* and did not hide the fact from us. . . . We plainly saw and now how we can rejoice that she spent every moment of her life in the service of God! — Please do not think, however, that Mamma directly influenced me to think of becoming a nun. . . . I remember her saying ever since I was a mere child, "I do hope God will not give you . . . a religious vocation. If He does I must submit, but I shall never permit you to enter a convent until you are 25 years of age." And in her last illness when she spoke of leaving us, I used to playfully <u>threaten</u> her with "You had better not go away from us, darling, or else I shall run off to a convent." . . .

. . . I have overdone the case at the end of page 3 in saying that I have no longer "<u>any dislike</u>" to being under the rule of a woman. Under the rule of some women I should love to be. . . . Suppose I were to be under the rule of a cranky superioress. I should not <u>like</u> it; but don't you think Our Lord would give me the grace to bear all things . . . ? — And now, good bye to self. I am sorry for occupying so much of my good Father's time.[24]

This is an uncharacteristically emotional letter. Katharine was not pleading and begging to get her way or laying out rational reasons in favor of her desired course of action. She was opening a wound to Bishop O'Connor, pouring out her heart. These are not new discoveries she had made. She had known from childhood that drums were hollow and dolls were stuffed with ugly things. Nonetheless, the analogies of the discoveries of childhood are cleverly linked to the realities of the rise and fall of cities, states, and empires, the leavings of which are now found only in museums for the curious to gawk at. The lessons of *vanitas vanitatis* learned at her mother's knee were reinforced by her trip through Europe. For a young woman who had witnessed the centennial of her own young nation, the antiquity and history of Europe had greater import than the fact of its age. Europe represented for her an object lesson in the teaching of Christ: "Heaven and earth will pass away, but my words will not pass away" (Mark 13:31). She reacted with horror to this reality and naturally desired to become part of that which was permanent, that which would tie her, while she was in this world, to the permanence of a life in Christ in the next world. This letter is linked to the journal entry of the fourteen-year-old whose meditation for the day was on death and her realization that all she would do in life would be preparation for death. Desiring a "good death," with the secure hope for a heavenly reward, the now

24. MKD to O'Connor, January 27, 1884.

more mature Katharine Drexel sought the permanent things through the life of a professed religious. She discounted her previous comments about not wanting to serve under the rule of women, even that of a "cranky superioress," and she was willing to submit even to such a woman because it would be God's will and God could be depended upon to grant her the necessary grace to endure whatever hardships would come her way.

That she should be worried about the transitory nature of the created world and the things that men and women value is perfectly understandable given her background and inclinations. What is surprising about this letter is the degree to which she is concerned about her concupiscence. She continues to fret about her eating habits as a gourmand, but her references to her fear of men and of her "inferior nature" and its passions, which "must be kept under control," are truly surprising. Aside from her repeated vows to increase within herself the virtue of purity, her letters and journals provide no specific accounting for her fear of men and her obvious fear of her own sexuality. It was easier to deal with the problem of food, which is an external temptation, than to deal with passions that arise from within, unbidden and unwanted. One suspects that in her scrupulosity and the relative innocence of her time, Katharine did not recognize her attraction to men as a normal phenomenon. She does not appear to have had any experience with the opposite sex, other than of the most benign sort. In her social position, she was always chaperoned. She had the one proposal of marriage, but the young man's name rated nary a mention in her journal. Whatever desires she experienced, she most likely never spoke of them to anyone, including her sisters. What was hidden became something shameful and something to fear. The convent may have represented safety, and this may have colored her decision to enter the religious life.

In his response to Katharine's impassioned letter, Bishop O'Connor made no reference to her fear of men, except to point out that while there may be cranky superiors, there are also cranky wives and cranky husbands. He did say he was glad she made her vow in Venice and that the Lord "has already begun to enrich [her] with His gifts." He wrote, "You appreciate [the gifts], for now, more clearly than ever before, you see and feel that *'Quod aeterna non est nihil est'* [That which is not eternal is nothing at all]. Ragbabies, or dolls filled with sawdust, are all things earthly compared with those of eternity! Happy are they who are convinced of this in youth . . . and regulate their lives accordingly!" He urged her to continue with the rules he had given her and to add no additional mortifications. As to her toilette, he advised her to dress according to her station, with "due limitations." In reference to her comments about a cranky superior, he reminded her that "only great saints can do this."[25] With present-day hindsight, O'Connor's remarks carry considerable irony, but in truth, Katharine never had to serve under women who were cranky or inept. For most of her religious life, she was the superior who demonstrated competence and holiness, not crankiness.

Clearly Bishop O'Connor saw Katharine as a very religiously serious young woman, but he worried about her excesses. He reminded her of the devil, who "knows he cannot induce such as you to do what is evidently evil. Hence he changes himself into an angel of light and tries to get [people] to do good inordinately. He urges them to do more than they will be able to perform, in hope that they will grow weary of well doing. Though it is an old device of his, beginners in God's service are constantly deceived by it. Indeed, very few are able to detect it for themselves. This is why in your acts of self-denial I have called your attention to the well known rule, *'Festina Lente.'"*[26] Katharine, for her part, did not tire of her attempts to do good. She often failed in her own eyes, as is witnessed by her annual lists of voluntary table deprivations and daily devotions, but she never showed any inclination to give up or even scale back in order to take an easier route to heaven. She always asked to be able to deprive herself more and to devote more time to her devotions. Hers was a spiritual pride and vanity that would not admit the possibility of any interference from the deceiving "angel of light."

After their father's death in 1885, Elizabeth and Louise worried about Katharine's complete lack of appetite and her general lack of interest in life, even life within the family among the "All Three." Naturally Louise and Elizabeth were distraught over the sudden and therefore unexpected loss of their father, but it must have seemed to them that Katharine was slipping away as well.

The one thing that held Katharine's attention was the plight of the Native Americans and blacks, or in the lexicon of her day, the Indians and the colored people. Though as a teenager she had taught Sunday school for black children in Philadelphia, her initial philanthropic thought after receiving control of her share of the interest from her father's estate was to help the missions for the Native Americans. Her first personal philanthropy had been the purchase of the statue of the Immaculate Conception for Fr. Hylebos's Indian mission. No doubt Bishop O'Connor's letters describing the needs of the Indian missions in his diocese also spurred her interest in Native

---

25. O'Connor to MKD, February 15, 1884.
26. O'Connor to MKD, August 1, 1884.

Americans. Her sisters concentrated their philanthropy for the benefit of black Americans, yet the efforts and interests of each of the Drexel women complemented and overlapped with the interests of the "All Three." They worked together to honor their father's memory by donating $50,000 to endow the Francis A. Drexel Chair of Moral Theology at the new Catholic University in Washington, D.C. They also cooperated on Elizabeth Drexel's initial project, the development of the St. Francis de Sales Industrial School for Boys to teach young orphaned boys technical skills that would enable them to earn a living. It remains today as a monument to Francis Drexel and his patron saint. Louise's largest project would be St. Emma's Industrial and Agricultural Institute in Virginia, a military-style school where young black men could learn employable skills. It was called St. Emma's Military Academy, in honor of Emma Bouvier Drexel.[27] Katharine built a school for the Sisters of Notre Dame de Namur in Philadelphia for the education of poor black children. Katharine would eventually turn more of her efforts to the very pressing needs of black people, but her initial philanthropic sympathy and endeavors were primarily for the Native Americans.

As a young girl under the tutelage of Mary Cassidy, Katharine had written a story based on the heroic work of the Ursuline nuns with seventeenth-century Native Americans in Quebec. "These ladies born to the mild climate of France, brought up amid all the luxury that wealth with rank could procure, had come to the wilderness to spend a life of unimaginable hardship among poor Indian children in order that these darkened souls should receive that gift of faith which these generous women burned to impart."[28] It is fascinating to conjecture that the fifteen-year-old Katharine had somehow foreseen her own future. She could not have, but her comments about the Ursulines leaving luxury and wealth to impart the gift of faith under great hardships in a western wilderness did in fact foreshadow her future.

After her father's death, Katharine's thoughts turned even more to that future, one more inclined toward the convent. Her desire was for a contemplative order. "To tell the truth, it appears to me that God calls me to the religious life. But when is it prudent for me to obey the call? Next week? This Fall? This Winter? In what religious order? Please tell me, dear Father, what I shall do to save my own soul, to save as many souls as possible, to devote myself and all that I have to God and to His Church. You know that I have a leaning to the contemplative life, but you and Father Ardia [her confessor]

---

27. St. Emma's closed in 1972.
28. ASBS, vol. 1, p. 48, 1874.

both say no to that; you know that I yearn to bring the Indian into Mother Church."[29]

Bishop O'Connor was not swayed by Katharine's repeated attempts to get him to change his mind, nor would Katharine be put off indefinitely. In this letter, she asserted that entering the religious life was not for her a question of "if" but of "when." Her mind was made up. Bishop O'Connor used everything in his arsenal of logic to dissuade her from the convent, including her health.

> The conclusion I have come to in your case is, that your vocation is not to enter a religious order. The only order to which I could have thought of recommending to you, is the Sacred Heart; but you do not have the health necessary to enable you to discharge the duties that would devolve on you as a member of that society. God cannot be presumed to wish us to do what he has not given us the means to perform. You cannot count on health, and a long life, in the world, as your late restoration proves, but the nature of the disease from which you suffered, is such that the restraints and duties of religious life would be almost sure to bring about a relapse, and perhaps, permanent disability. Then, your inclination to that sort of life is not strong enough to justify me in recommending you to give it a trial, especially in view of your physical disqualifications for it.[30]

He added that God's mission for her was to remain in the world and live her life as she had been doing: giving aid to the poor, the blacks, and the Native Americans; being an example to the rich, whom he called "the poorest of the poor"; and helping her sisters and influencing them for their temporal and spiritual good. It appears that Katharine had expressed a fear of being alone after her sisters married, but he assured her that God and his angels and saints would be with her as well as himself and other spiritual guides who would come her way throughout her life.

Not only did she fear being alone, but she also feared that she might give in to the temptations of the world and somehow turn from God and the happy death she so desired. O'Connor responded in the same letter to her concern. "The very fear you have of the world, and your inclination to fly from it, are an earnest of your safety in the midst of its dangers. . . . If you did not fear

---

29. MKD to O'Connor, August 1885, quoted in Sr. Consuela Duffy, SBS, *Katharine Drexel: A Biography* (Philadelphia: Reilly Co., 1966), p. 126.

30. O'Connor to MKD, August 29, 1885.

the world, and yourself, then, indeed, I should greatly fear for you."[31] His last recommendation to her in this same letter was to renew annually her vow of virginity, not only for the merit it would bring her, but also for its strength and consolation. It was one way to keep the flesh constantly under the control of the spirit. Every temptation overcome made the next temptation easier to overcome, and to do so because one had dedicated herself to God would further strengthen her conviction. In his next letter to Katharine, Bishop O'Connor recommended a few books for spiritual reading, but admonished her to stay away from reading "mystic or ascetic fare without letting me know what it is. And, under all circumstances, try to possess your soul in peace. Excitement and unrest do not come from God. Pause and reflect, and pray whenever you are inclined to be impetuous and disturbed by any matter."[32]

Apparently Katharine was not taking seriously the motto *Festina Lente*, for the bishop had to tell her that in "practicing your present devotions, you are far from standing still. You are advancing, and as rapidly as prudence will allow. Growth in holiness, is, like all other growth, gradual and orderly. When forced it is not healthful. You are going after Our Lord, and traveling under direction, you are going as He would have you go."[33] Of course, nothing, if desired, comes quickly enough for a young person. She had written that she wanted to go on regular retreats, but the bishop held her to one annually. She wanted to try out a convent, which he would not permit. She wanted to practice a more ascetic form of living, including more fasting, and this at a time when she was still ill following her father's death. She did not want to make haste slowly; she wanted to make haste, period.

Katharine's listlessness and loss of appetite, combined with her fasting, far beyond what her spiritual adviser allowed, brought on jaundice and internal complications from severe weight loss. Today she would be diagnosed as suffering from the eating disorder called anorexia combined with clinical depression. How very different she was at this time from the young woman who worried about entering a convent because the refectory fare did not live up to her standards as a "gourmand." Her sisters were alarmed at her failing physical condition and took her to Europe seeking a cure at famous spas. The trip was also undertaken so the three sisters could view various European schools upon which to model their St. Francis de Sales Industrial School. The "All Three" sailed for Europe on July 31, 1886, with the first order of business

---

31. O'Connor to MKD, August 29, 1885.

32. O'Connor to MKD, October 1, 1885.

33. O'Connor to MKD, December 3, 1885.

being the restoration of Katharine's health. They took her to the doctors at Schwalbach, a German spa town. Katharine took the five-week cure: "daily [mud] baths, one half glass of the Weinbrunner Spring waters twice daily, quantity to be gradually increased."[34] Katharine wrote to Miss Cassidy, "I have gained eight pounds, honest weight. All my clothes are beginning to be too small. Dyspepsia much better."[35] She was perhaps a little premature in her assessment of her physical progress. Elizabeth wrote to Miss Cassidy, "Our stay [in Schwalbach] certainly benefited Kate; her face has fattened, her color is better — but the main trouble still remains, along with a delicate digestion. We had hoped for a more decided cure. The doctor says she will feel the good of the waters after leaving them and sends us onward our way."[36]

Somewhat physically restored, Katharine joined her sisters in touring a half dozen or so industrial schools in France, taking time out to visit the *couturiers* in Paris to replenish their wardrobes with the latest styles. However, as always, a Drexel family trip was an occasion for a religious pilgrimage. Katharine, all the while, was seeking confirmation of her call to religion by prayer and fasting, so much so that Bishop O'Connor wrote to her,

> I come again to caution you against fasting. I want you to bear with my insistence in this matter. In all candor I tell you I have the highest opinion of your judgement in other matters, but in your spiritual direction of yourself, you are not to be trusted. Very few are; and we all, at times, make serious mistakes in the management of our own spiritual affairs. . . . Let me then, as your spiritual advisor, recommend, and as far as I can, command you not to fast or abstain. . . . You will have other opportunities enough of denying yourself in other ways besides food. You can mortify the will, the eyes, and the tongue in ways it is needless for me to enumerate.[37]

Katharine tried to keep her fasting within bounds, but this was a topic that would have to be visited periodically. In the meantime, Katharine and her sisters toured the many pilgrimage sites in Spain, eventually making their way to Rome.

In Rome, the sisters naturally wanted an audience with Pope Leo XIII. He undoubtedly knew in advance of the rich philanthropy of the Drexel

---

34. ELD to Cassidy, August 12, 1886.
35. MKD to Cassidy, August 27, 1886.
36. ELD to Cassidy, September 5, 1885.
37. O'Connor to MKD, October 30, 1886.

family. The sisters had two audiences with the pope and attended one of his personal masses. In an oral interview during the Catholic Students Mission Crusade Convention held in Dayton, Ohio, August 18-21, 1921, Mother Katharine described what led up to her boldness to speak before the pope:

> When I was still in my youth, God's Providence brought me into touch with three magnificent missionaries, Bishop Marty, Monsignor Stephan, and Bishop O'Connor. Bishop Marty and Monsignor Stephan told me of their personal experience with the [Sioux] Indians of Dakota, and with joy I gave them the means to erect a boarding school for the Indians. Bishop O'Connor tried in vain to obtain priests to open a mission for his Arapaho and Shoshone Indians in Wyoming. He could find sisters, but no order of men. What could sisters do without a priest? I was willing to give the means to put up the mission buildings, but without priests to minister to the sisters and the heathens — what use?
>
> At this time my then unmarried sisters and I were going on a trip to Europe. Bishop O'Connor asked me whether I would not try to find in Europe an order of priests willing to work for this Indian mission of his. I remember summoning up my courage and asking in several European monasteries, but always in vain.
>
> Then we went to Rome and had a private audience with Pope Leo XIII. Kneeling at his feet, my girlish fancy thought that surely God's Vicar would not refuse me. So I pleaded missionary priests for Bishop O'Connor's Indians. To my astonishment His Holiness responded, "Why not, my child, become yourself a missionary?" In reply I said, "Because, Holy Father, sisters can be had for the missions, but no priests."[38]

This was certainly not the answer that Katharine was expecting to her question. In her private conversation with Pope Leo, she confided that she was seriously considering a vocation to a contemplative order of sisters, but that she was also very interested in the plight of the Native Americans and that she had been helping the Indian Bureau to build and staff missions. "It has seemed to me more than once, Your Holiness, that I ought to aid [the Indians] by my personal work among them as well [as giving money], and if I enter an enclosed congregation I might be abandoning those whom

---

38. Duffy, *Katharine Drexel*, p. 100. The dates of the two audiences the Drexel sisters had with Pope Leo XIII appear to have been January 27 and January 30, 1887. It is not known at which of these audiences Katharine had her private talk with Leo XIII.

God wants me to serve."[39] It is no wonder that Pope Leo suggested that she become a missionary. Her private interview with the pope ended with his blessing for her "and all [her] future works."[40] The audience left Katharine in tears, weeping in confusion and perplexity. As she tried to make sense of the pope's words to her, she still heard regularly in Europe from Fr. Stephan and Bishop O'Connor, who were keeping her up to date on events at the Indian missions she was helping to fund. When Katharine gave money, she always wanted an accounting of how it was being used and to what results.

She did not tell anyone about her private conversation with the pope, but she continued to insist that she was called to the religious life. Bishop O'Connor wrote her:

> You are certainly doing immense good where you are [in the world]. It were [*sic*] not wise to abandon the certain for the uncertain. You are making bountiful provision for the most abandoned and forlorn of God's creatures on this continent. You have the means, you have the brains, you have the freedom to do this work well. [The work referred to here is her philanthropic endeavors in the Indian mission field.] In religion you could direct your income to this or some other good purpose, but your talents and energies would be directed by others. You would therefore not have the freedom necessary to do this work well and to interest others in it, which you have in the world. You are doing more for the Indians now, than any religious, or even community of religious has ever done, or perhaps could ever do for them in this country.[41]

It is clear that Bishop O'Connor was interested in directing both her money and her personal assistance to the Native Americans.

It seems not to have occurred to either Katharine or Bishop O'Connor that she might become the founder of a missionary order of sisters, even though he believed no order of sisters in the United States was fit or willing to undertake Indian missionary work. For his part, he simply did not believe that she had a religious vocation and felt that she could do more good being in the world. For her part, she felt called to the religious life as a contemplative sister within the cloistered walls. In the letter quoted above,

---

39. Quoted in Katherine Burton, *The Golden Door: The Life of Katharine Drexel* (New York: P. J. Kenedy and Sons, 1957), p. 88.

40. Burton, *The Golden Door,* p. 88.

41. O'Connor to MKD, March 5, 1887.

the bishop suggested to the heiress that to solve the problems of finding missionary sisters for the Indian missions he would get the permission of Archbishop Ryan of Philadelphia to invite the Sisters of Providence from Montreal, Canada, to establish a branch novitiate in Philadelphia. There, the French-speaking sisters with extensive experience with Native Americans could learn English before heading west. Katharine Drexel's role would be to fund the enterprise. This was only one of many counterproposals that Bishop O'Connor would make to her over the period of her discernment. Katharine was willing to fund a novitiate for the Sisters of Providence, but the Sisters were not able to spare any of their novices to take up more missionary work than the order already had under way. As Bishop O'Connor had foretold, "Nuns are generally unwilling — and it is well that they should, as a general thing, be unwilling to leave the beaten track on which they have been accustomed to travel."[42] Even on her European recovery and fact-finding trip, her vocation was constantly on her mind, and the letters between Katharine and her spiritual adviser were plentiful. She also had repeated letters of invitation from Bishop Marty, Fr. Stephan, and Bishop O'Connor to visit their Indian missions after her return home from Europe.

The Drexel sisters sailed for the United States on April 19, 1887, on the SS *Etruria*. By late September, the "All Three" were on a train headed west in the company of Bishop O'Connor. They stopped over a day in Omaha, where the Drexels bought gifts for the Indians they would meet at the missions. After another day of train travel, Fr. Stephan met them at the top of the railhead. Setting off over the roadless prairie, Kate rode in a carriage or buckboard with Fr. Stephan and Bishop O'Connor, while Elizabeth and Louise rode horseback. This was not the luxurious travel that the Drexel sisters were accustomed to — there were no hotels and no room service. They were roughing it in the true western fashion with tents, campfires, and even the occasional springless buckboard.

The first mission the party came to was at the Rosebud Agency in South Dakota. Katharine had funded a school there and subsidized its staffing by Jesuit priests and the Sisters of Saint Francis from Stella Niagara, New York. It was named the St. Francis Mission in honor of her father, Francis Drexel. The party arrived at the mission unannounced. The eastern women were given a first-floor room with makeshift beds in the as-yet-unfinished convent. They awoke in the morning to Indian faces against their curtainless window and the sound of giggles. Louise described some of her impressions of the day:

42. O'Connor to MKD, March 5, 1887.

Indian children at 7:00 a.m. Mass. At nine o'clock Mass congregation of Indians. Large crowd. Squaws in bright colored shawls and dresses, some with faces painted red, some yellow, some with paint down the hair part, some with papooses held to their backs with shawls. Men wrapped in unbleached sheets, some in fancy costumes, some in European clothes. All with long hair. Size of squaws. After Mass general "howing." Ox killed for feast. Eaten raw by Indians. Distribution of gifts. . . . A collection of Tepees and log huts, ox tails, hoofs, rag strewn on village green. Picturesque sight to see Indians flocking to the Mission, some on foot, some on horseback, some in wagons. Bracelets on arms. Some of the squaws have their ears pierced in two places. Children at Mission well-cared for. Forced march to Valentine, covering a distance of 34 miles in 4½ hours. 64 miles ridden in two days.[43]

The next mission the Drexels visited was the Holy Rosary Mission at the Pine Bluff Agency, so named because of Emma Bouvier Drexel's special devotion to praying the rosary. There they met the famous Oglala Lakota Sioux warrior and chief, Red Cloud. They presented him with a gift of a handsome bridle and saddle and gave his wife a lovely fringed shawl. They paid him a special honor by visiting him in his own home, leaving behind a store of sugar. They were introduced to Red Cloud as the ones who had built and would maintain the mission school for the education of his people. Red Cloud's friendship with the Drexel sisters and ultimately the Sisters of the Blessed Sacrament turned out to be extremely important when, in the 1891-1892 Sioux uprising, he intervened with his warring braves to save the Holy Rosary Mission from a certain massacre.

The Drexel sisters visited many missions, but, in addition to their introduction to the Sioux at the St. Francis Mission, an experience that must have impressed them was with the Crow Indians at the Immaculate Conception Mission in Stephan, South Dakota. The Immaculate Conception had been Emma Bouvier Drexel's favorite title for the Virgin Mary. There, after a feast, the Indians put on a dance for Katharine and her sisters, "clothed for the most part in paint, with sleigh bells at their knees and feathers in their hair."[44] It must have been a thrilling but unsettling sight for the prim

---

43. LBD Travel Journal, September 25, 1887.

44. From Journal of LBD, quoted in Sr. M. Dolores Letterhouse, SBS, *The Francis A. Drexel Family* (Cornwells Heights, Pa.: Sisters of the Blessed Sacrament, 1939), p. 322.

Miss Drexels of Philadelphia to be presented with the spectacle of mostly naked men dancing to the beat of the drums. Katharine wrote to Bishop O'Connor, who had left their party after the stay at Holy Rosary Mission: "It seems to me that these Immaculate Conception Crow Indians take a palm for intelligent faces, and noble form." She added:

> On Rosary Sunday, I took a vow of obedience for three months to you as my Spiritual Director. I enclose a copy of the rules as I understand them. May I trouble you to correct them where they are wrong; to add to them as you think fit and then to mail them back to me.
>
> Candidly I must own that I am very much tempted to gluttony, more than *gourmandise.* I have no submission nor humility nor spirit of mortification with regard to eating. — And yet, indifference must be acquired, and my will brought into agreement with the Divine Will, if I would say with St. Paul, "I know how to abound and to be brought low, to be hungry, etc." — Teach me, Reverend Father, the way to do always the Will of God. — Sometimes I think it would be best to eat just what others eat so as not to be singular. All this I submit to you, and also antidotes to pride and vanity.[45]

She constantly came back to food as a special weakness of hers, along with pride and vanity. It would appear that her exaggeration of her gluttony might be an attempt to get her spiritual adviser to approve her desire to fast. At this point in her discernment, her pride and vanity were actual, spiritual sins. She took pride in and was vain about her religious inclinations. Additionally, she probably wanted to demonstrate to the bishop that she had the stamina for the rigors of religious life, which he maintained were too strenuous for her, both physically and mentally. In a letter to her adviser dated May 31, 1888, Katharine explicitly stated, "I wish to pass as being mortified in eating, as one who frequently even fasts!!!"

The following, marked by her own hand as "STRICTLY PRIVATE," may be "the rules" she referred to in the October 13, 1887, letter.

Not to eat between meals.
Not to eat dessert (fruit excepted).
Not to take sugar in tea.
Pray one hour and a half each day, viz.:

45. MKD to O'Connor, October 13, 1887.

20 Minutes	Mass
15 "	Thanksgiving
15 "	Rosary
15 "	Visits to the Blessed Sacrament. If I belong to the Third Order of St. Francis, then the prayers of the Order will take up a great part of the 15 minutes. Also once a week five minutes preparation for Confession will have to come out of this.

¼ hour visit to the Blessed Sacrament if I do not pray more than 1½ hour.

5 minutes	preparation for Holy Communion.
10 "	Night Prayers.

What shall I take for Particular Examen Practice? I have been advised to take the following : — "To do everything with the view of pleasing God." Simplicity of Intention.

In making my preparations for Holy Communion is it not best to use a prayer-book and read some "Preparation" as I am very dry when left to prayers of my own composition, perhaps; however, they may be more acceptable to God on that account. The same question I must ask with regard to ¼ hour visit to the Blessed Sacrament, — shall I use prayer-book?

Shall I read over from time to time your letter deciding why I should not enter a convent?

Shall I, when I am able (even neglecting temporal affairs for same) read one quarter of hour spiritual reading say Ullathorne's "Ground work of Christian Virtues." Or Life of the Blessed Virgin as she is in the Gospels by Canon Nicholas, or Rodriguez's "Xian Perfection," or "Spiritual Combat." Are there other books you would prefer my reading?[46]

O'Connor responded that she should not read many religious books; "indeed, the fewer the better. . . . You must bear in mind that the works in which you are engaged are a constant prayer, and an exercise of sublime charity. Don't unfit yourself to discharge them, by undermining your health

---

46. Undated, but contained with various other 1887 writings by MKD. It appears to belong to her letter dated October 13, 1887, because in his letter of October 22, 1887, the bishop refers to her letter of the thirteenth and "the rule" as answers to her questions and makes suggestions for her reading.

or wasting much time in desultory pious reading. . . . You must think and pray enough to give your thoughts and actions the right direction, but no more. . . . You have opportunities to <u>act</u> for God and your neighbor, vouchsafed to few. But, as I said above, this very action is, in itself, the most meritorious sort of prayer."[47] At this point in her discernment process, he continued to express concern for her physical state, which was indeed quite fragile, and her religious cast of mind that was ascetic and contemplative. She believed that she could be happy and serve God the most by continuous prayer and mortification. He tried time and again to get her to see her philanthropic actions and personal example as the way of life most pleasing to God. It was a constant battle between them.

What was a tremendous success on Bishop O'Connor's part was his invitation, along with those of Bishop Marty and Fr. Stephan, to visit the Indian missions in the West. They prevailed on the Drexel sisters to make another trip west in the autumn of 1888. The sisters stood as godmothers to three Indian children who took the names Katharine, Elizabeth, and Louise for their baptismal names. Katharine came home to Philadelphia with a great enthusiasm for aiding the Native Americans by building schools, churches, and convents at Indian missions and by establishing new missions where there were none.

> [She engaged] a firm of architects to draw up plans for the construction of boarding schools which she determined to erect for the Indians whose poverty she had witnessed and whose needs she realized. Within five years, as a result of her zeal for souls and her love of God and her neighbor, her benefactions stretched in a long line of mission schools from the great Northwest to the Mexican border. They were built among the Puyallups in Washington, the Cheyennes and Arapahos in Wyoming, the Sioux in North Dakota, the Coeur d'Alene, Nez Perce in Idaho, the Mission Indians in California, the Chippewas in Wisconsin, the Crows and Blackfeet in Montana, the Cherokees, Comanches, and the Osages in Indian Territory and Oklahoma, and the Pueblo Indians in New Mexico. Kate with her keen, orderly business instinct followed a definite procedure in all this. She paid for the land and the erection of plain, serviceable buildings. Then the grounds and the buildings were deeded to the Catholic Indian Bureau.[48]

47. O'Connor to MKD, October 22, 1887.
48. Burton, *The Golden Door,* pp. 106-7.

Not only did Katharine build up the missions, she also found nuns to staff them. She and her two sisters donated $30,000 to the Sisters of Saint Francis of Philadelphia to work in the missions.

She and her sisters were not separated by their charitable works, as they feared they might be; rather they were united, even if Kate gave, in her early years, more attention to the Native Americans than to the blacks. She had learned from Fr. Stephan that the Native Americans and the African Americans were "color relations."[49] Still, Katharine was teased by Louise, "You have only some hundred thousand souls in your Indian field, but I have ten or more millions in my Negro harvest."[50]

In the meantime, Katharine was worried about Louise, who had received a proposal of marriage from a Protestant young man. Louise refused the gentleman, to the relief of her sisters, but Katharine believed it was her duty to introduce Louise to eligible Catholic suitors. However, the plan was perhaps backfiring on her. She wrote to Bishop O'Connor, "Naturally, I love to flirt. . . . When I am with men I find it difficult not to flirt."[51] Might she be caught in the snare set for her younger sister? This was not the first time her attraction to men had come up. In the late spring, he reassured her, after telling her that "[You are] . . . doing more for God, yourself, and others than you could do in religion," that "You must not forget that dangers encompass you, you have the passions of other people, you have a woman's heart, and a woman's affections, you must be on your guard, if you desire to persevere in the path you have led for the last couple of years. Should you tire of it, you can take another less difficult to travel [marriage] — or one that is thought to be such — but whilst in it, look deliberately at nothing that would turn your thoughts from the object you have in view."[52] His very next letter continued the same theme. "Have we not all been warned to prepare our hearts for temptation, when we come to the service of God? . . . So don't be at all surprised when your turn comes. . . . Don't be surprised at coming now and then, on that soft spot you mention. No woman's heart is without it. The only question is, whose image shall it receive? Shall it be that of a mortal, or of Him 'at whose beauty the sun and the moon stand in wonder'?"[53]

Despite his admonishments to her, Bishop O'Connor recognized his

49. Fr. Stephan to MKD, February 23, 1886.
50. Letterhouse, *Francis A. Drexel Family*, p. 337.
51. MKD to O'Connor, June 24, 1888.
52. O'Connor to MKD, March 14, 1888.
53. O'Connor to MKD, March 30, 1888.

position as her spiritual adviser: "I take full responsibility for having 'kept you out of the convent' till now. The more I reflect on the matter, the more I am persuaded that you are where God wishes you to be at present. Should I see any certain indications of his will that you should enter religion, I shall not fail to direct your attention to them."[54] The bishop strongly believed Katharine Drexel's philanthropic work on behalf of the Indian tribes to be of the utmost importance in God's divine providence. " 'A little help,' now, may keep the Indians on [the reservations] from total extinction."[55] Extinction was a real possibility for many of the tribes that had been severely reduced in number by disease, war, and famine. The once-mighty Huron tribe and the Oto Indians each had fewer than 400 members at the end of the nineteenth century.

Vocation Acknowledged

Because the bishop explicitly took responsibility for her place in the world, she was able, however briefly, to give herself over to his guidance: "Here is your child, spare her no point. Make her, according to the strength which God gives her, and instrument for the *ad majorem Dei Gloriam* [to the greater glory of God]. It seems to me that I can never be made such an instrument unless you discipline me."[56] However, by late autumn, Louise was engaged to be married to Edward Morrell, and Katharine was in rebellion against herself and against her spiritual director.

> Rt. Rev'd and dear Father: —
>
> I am reduced to reading over all the letters you ever wrote me on the subject of my having no vocation for the religious life. I entreat you, <u>for God's sake re</u>-consider the matter and see if our Lord will not give me the grace to enter the more perfect state — the religious state. . . .
>
> As it now is, I am perpetually in trouble of soul, warring as it were with my better nature. The peace which I felt last year in obeying you, gives me an assurance that the same peace and security would overshadow me in obeying a superior. <u>I did not renew my vow of obedience to you</u> . . . (emphasis added).

54. O'Connor to MKD, May 16, 1888.
55. O'Connor to MKD, May 16, 1888.
56. MKD to O'Connor, August 1888.

Please, Rt. Rev'd Father, read over this accompanying letter of your own written more than five years ago, — five years in the world has caused me to drop the "positive personal reasons for not embracing the religious life." 1st — separation from family costs little. 2nd. I have not at present, 1888, as much dislike for community life as I have a dislike for social intercourse with those in the world with whose aspirations I do not feel in sympathy. To be thrown into company with those whose interests are in the world, and whose daily strivings are for the world. . . . This I dislike. I love and revere the society of those whose business in life is simple, — viz.: that of knowing God and loving God, and of serving Him. If Our Lord permits me to choose in this vocation of mine, I choose the religious state, firmly resolved, <u>with God's help</u>, to bear privations and poverty, "monotony of religious life," and obedience to even an unreasonable superior (when such is the case) — to bear these for the sake of Him to Whom they lead. Vanity of vanity, all is vanity, except knowing, loving, and serving God. This alone can bring peace to my soul. . . .

. . . I am so afraid Our Lord will reject me on account of my unworthiness. Up to this point I have not dared to ask Our Lord to give me a religious vocation. I have said "May the most just, high, and adorable Will of God be done." If I have not this religious vocation can I pray and have prayers said for it? In your charity please pray for

Your child *in Dno.*, K. M. Drexel[57]

This was such an anguished letter that Katharine could not bring herself to mail it to the bishop, her friend and adviser for so many years. She had not previously acknowledged to Bishop O'Connor that she had not renewed her vow of obedience to him. Perhaps it was an action she at first simply put off but later found she could not in good conscience continue. Two weeks later, she was in an even greater state of angst concerning her vocation; she was willing to risk open rebellion against Bishop O'Connor should he continue to maintain that she did not have a true vocation to the religious life. She felt so certain of her direction in life that she was willing to follow it on her own, in spite of what he might caution to the contrary.

57. MKD to O'Connor, written November 11, 1888, but not mailed until November 26, bundled with another letter written on the later date. Across the earlier letter she requested that he return his letter to her written on May 26, 1883. See pages 64-65 for the referenced correspondence. *In Dno* is Latin for "in the Lord."

May I trouble you to read the enclosed. It was written more than two weeks ago and I had stamped it ready for sending to you, then concluded to wait. The sentiments in it remain the same, and have remained the same, only I am suffering greater anxiety lest Our Lord should deprive me of a life near Him, in union with Him. My God! What can I desire better than this. "If thou wilt be perfect. . . ." I will it. Our Lord's words ring in my ears. How I wish to spend the rest of my life entirely given to Him, devoted to Him by the three vows which would happily consecrate me to Jesus Christ. This night I feel a sadness out of which it is difficult to rally. Several times during our trip out West, I remember you said to me with an amused expression, "What makes you look so sad?" My heart indeed was sad, is sad, because in your judgement I am condemned to living in a world whose ways I detest. I cannot say "Deus meus, et Omnia" [my God and my all] as long as I am not consecrated to Our Lord. As He is, or as I desire Him truly to be "my All," I wish to love Him in poverty, chastity, and obedience. I wish to give Him "all," relying that He Who loves me will become "all" to me. It appears to me Our Lord gives me a right to choose the better part, and I shall try to draw as near His Heart as possible, that He may so fill me with His love, that all the pains I may endure in the religious life may be cheerfully endured for the sake of Jesus, the Lord of Love. — Do not, Rev'd Father, I beseech you say "What is to become of your work?" What is to become of it when I shall give it all to Our Lord? — Will Our Lord at the Day of Judgement condemn me for approaching as near Him as possible by following Him, and then leaving my yearly income to be distributed among the Missions, or for the Missions in some way that I am sure could be devised if only Our Lord will free me from all responsibility save that of giving myself to Him. . . . Joyfully I shall run to Him. I am afraid to receive your answer to this note. It appears to me, Rev'd Father, that I am not obliged (emphasis added) to submit my judgement to yours, as I have been doing for two years, for I feel so sad in doing it, because the world cannot give me peace, so restless because my heart is not rested in God. Will you, Rev'd Father, please pardon the rudeness of this last remark, in view of this, — that I am trying to tell you the truth. . . .

P.S. I intend to try and grow in love of Our Lord, so that all sacrifices in the religious life will be cheerfully endured. . . . In your charity, Rt. Rev'd Father, pray that I may do God's holy Will now and always.[58]

58. MKD to O'Connor, November 26, 1888.

The date on this letter is Katharine's thirtieth birthday. At thirty, she must have felt that it was time to stop her vocational drifting and settle on her life's work. It was unity with God, her "All," and not the unity of the "All Three" that was her chief concern. Her youngest sister, Louise, whose social life Katharine had fretted over and manipulated, was undertaking her own vocation as wife and mother. Louise's marriage to Edward Morrell was set for January 17, 1889, just a few weeks hence. Surely, most people thought that Katharine would soon follow suit and be happily married. The closely knit circle of the "All Three" would be unalterably broken. In her letter, Katharine maintained that it was her right to choose the calling she felt best for herself and reminded the bishop that she was no longer under an obligation to follow his direction in the matter of her vocation. It was settled in her mind that she would join an order of nuns and become a complete *sponsa Christi,* and all she truly asked of him were his approbation and his prayers. His response was immediate:

> I had come to regard it as <u>certain</u> that Our Lord had chosen you for Himself, but, for reasons with which you are familiar, I inclined to think He wished you to love and serve Him as His spouse, but in society. This letter of yours, and your bearing under the long and severe tests to which I subjected you, as well as your entire restoration to health, and the many spiritual dangers that surround you, make me withdraw all opposition to your entering religion. In all that has passed between us in regard to your vocation, my only aim and anxiety have been to help you discover God's will in the matter, and that, I think, is sufficiently manifest. Something, too, which I heard, when in the east, a couple of weeks ago, of well-meant <u>plans</u> made by your own flesh and blood to <u>entangle</u> you and Lizzie in mere worldly alliances, confirms me in this view of the case. A vocation like any other grace, <u>may be lost</u>, and those who have it should not be too much exposed, or expose themselves needlessly.
>
> The only matter that now remains to be determined is, which order you should choose? Have you a decided preference for some of them? . . .
>
> There are three orders the rules of which it would be worth your while to examine: The Sacred Heart, the Sisters of Mercy, and the Ursulines of Brown County, Ohio. . . . Don't be impatient. The matter to be considered is a serious one for you, so let your motto be: *Festina Lente.*[59]

---

59. O'Connor to MKD, November 30, 1888.

How quickly Bishop O'Connor capitulated to Katharine's calling to a religious vocation when finally she was willing to go against his command to remain in the world serving God as a single woman. Lynch suggests that the main reason for the bishop's turn of mind was that Katharine's uncle Anthony Drexel "was planning a financially advantageous marriage for her with a non-Catholic."[60] Because of Francis Drexel's will, his daughters' husbands could not inherit their trust funds, but the husbands could certainly influence their wives on how to spend their yearly income. A non-Catholic husband could adversely affect how the Drexel money was spent, diverting Drexel money away from Catholic causes and charities. This would obviously be a tremendous loss for the Church missions for blacks and Native Americans. "Bishop O'Connor . . . knew this one woman [Katharine Drexel] endowed the western missions more generously than the entire American Catholic community."[61] As late as 1902, Katharine Drexel, then Mother M. Katharine, SBS, funded almost 60 percent of the activities of the Bureau of Catholic Indian Missions, not to mention the monies she gave the missions run by the Sisters of the Blessed Sacrament.[62] Had Katharine married, the fate of the Indians might have been very different. Both President Grant and Bishop O'Connor believed that the Native Americans faced extinction without missionary help. Katharine was almost single-handedly supporting the Catholic missions. Therefore, her marriage to anyone, but especially to a non-Catholic, might have had disastrous effects on the people she had been helping. On the other hand, her entry into certain congregations of sisters or orders of nuns could also have a profound effect on her ability to control her trust funds.[63]

The usual procedure for one entering a cloistered convent of nuns was to endow the convent with all one's wealth. Katharine, who had at one time

60. Lynch, *Sharing the Bread,* 1:31.

61. Anne M. Butler, "Mother Katharine Drexel: Spiritual Visionary for the West," in *By Grit and by Grace: Eleven Women Who Shaped the American West,* ed. Glenda Riley and Richard Etulain (Golden, Colo.: Fulcrum, 1997), p. 204.

62. William H. Ketchum, *Report of the Director of the Bureau of Catholic Indian Missions,* in SBS Archives.

63. In a congregation, or community, sisters renew annually what are called "simple vows" of poverty, chastity, and obedience and undertake an active ministry outside of the cloister. In orders, nuns make "solemn vows" of poverty, chastity, and obedience for life and live within the cloister leading a life of prayer and meditation. The terms "congregation" and "order," as well as the terms "sister" and "nun," tend to be used interchangeably. Today's orders of nuns are no longer sequestered unless they choose to be so. Indeed, many sisters and nuns no longer live within convent walls.

yearned for the nun's cloistered life of prayer and meditation, no longer wanted the life of silence. She rejected Bishop O'Connor's proffered orders. She wrote him, "I want a missionary order for Indians and for Colored People."[64] She and her Philadelphia confessor were looking into the Franciscans and the Benedictines, whom she admired. Her main criteria for a community were that it allowed daily Communion, that it served the needs of blacks and Indians, and that it was not too strict for her. Once she decided which community of sisters to join, she would make provisions for the disposal of her annual trust income. Bishop O'Connor continued to counsel her on her options.

> There remains [*sic*] the Benedictines and the Franciscans. For reasons some of which I will give you when I see you next month, I beg you not to bestow a thought on the former. All religious institutes, or rules are good, as they have the approbation of the Church, but <u>all orders</u> are not, for not all live up, even fairly well, to their rule. To enter an inobservant order is not only to fail to find the helps to perfection which such organizations should afford, but almost to insure the loss of even ordinary piety. The Franciscans of Philadelphia, and in most places, are, I have every reason to believe, laborious, devoted women. But, then, they are not ladies. . . . But you should bear in mind that for a lady of your antecedents, position, and habits, to be able to pass her whole life in the most intimate, daily and hourly intercourse with women of the peasant class, would require a fortitude that is vouchsafed to very few indeed. . . . The order of grace, should, as far as possible harmonize with the order of nature. Unless where God clearly and unmistakenly demand [*sic*] the sacrifice, no one should do life-long violence to her natural instincts and habits.

He recommended the Order of Mercy. "There is no better community in the Church than the Mercy Community of Pittsburgh . . . there is no place I should be as well pleased to see you enter as there. I know that community thoroughly, and I can recommend it without the <u>slightest</u> hesitation."[65]

The Sisters of Mercy, who also had a convent in Philadelphia, had served in some of the Indian missions of the bishop's diocese. Furthermore, his brother, Michael O'Connor, the first bishop of Pittsburgh, had brought the first Sisters of Mercy from Ireland to America to establish their convent

---

64. MKD to O'Connor, December 15, 1888.
65. O'Connor to MKD, December 21, 1888.

in his diocese. His cautions about the Benedictines, if true, were certainly sound. His concerns about the Franciscans did not cause Katharine to count them out. However, she was again beginning to feel the pull of her original attraction to the cloistered life. She first wanted to rid herself of her temporal affairs.

Katharine's plan for divesting herself of the responsibility of her income from her father's estate was for the Church to organize a Bureau for Colored and Indian Missions in Washington, D.C. This new bureau would be funded not only by her personal income, but also by an annual, nationwide, special collection on the second Sunday of Lent.[66] The day-to-day functions of the bureau would be handled by a professional staff, but its oversight would be the responsibility of a board made up of five bishops. The problems of the Native Americans were so severe that Katharine dreaded leaving their fate to the mercy of a large or general assembly of bishops: "I fear such an assembly of Bishops would not think of the importance of the Indian. — There are 7 million colored people in the U.S. and only 600,000 Indians. I would have to devise some method to save these 600,000 souls so that the interests of the colored 7 million would not prevent the speedy help which these 600,000 Indians require in order to fit them for the opening of their reservations in 25 short years. — The Colored question may press, but does it press to the same extent as the Indian Question? May God enlighten!"[67]

Founding a New Order

Katharine wanted to dispose of her income and to enter a convent imme-diately, there to discern further the direction her life in religion must take. Bishop O'Connor told her to allow her sisters to administer her income until she took her vows. Little did she suspect that O'Connor would have another and greater demand yet to make of her. He had become convinced that she should found a new order exclusively for Indians and colored people. His first letter to mention this plan is missing, so we are not privy to his reasoning. When he second mentioned it, he wrote, "Why then, should you hesitate [to found a new order], unless you mean to be your own guide in the matter?"[68]

---

66. The first Sunday of Lent collection for Catholic Home Missions in the United States is a practice that continues to this day.

67. MKD to O'Connor, February 12, 1889.

68. O'Connor to MKD, February 12, 1889.

He knew it would be a tremendous challenge to her, but he was fully convinced of its importance for both Katharine and the races she desired to help. Then he laid before her the greatest challenge of her life.

> The more I have thought of your case the more convinced I become that God has called you to establish an order for [the Indian and colored people]. The need for it is patent to everybody. All the help the established orders can give in the work will be needed, but a strong order devoted to it exclusively is also needed. You have the means to make such an establishment. Your social position will draw to it subjects and friends without number. God has put in your heart a great love for the Indian and the Negroes. He has given you the taste and the capacity for the sort of business which such a foundation would bring with it. All these things point more clearly, than an inspiration or a revelation could, to your duty in the premises. . . .
>
> Reflect carefully on what I have told you, and let me know your objections to my decision in your case.[69]

The bishop was most emphatic with Katharine because he feared that her headstrong, willful nature would take precedence over her spiritual side. Even though her friend the director of the Bureau of Catholic Indian Missions, Philadelphia Archbishop Patrick John Ryan, along with Father Joseph Stephan and her spiritual adviser, agreed that Katharine should found a new order, Katharine herself had, as O'Connor knew she would, grave misgivings about such an important step.

She responded with great distress to the thought of founding a new order.

> 1st. I have never decided whether a life devoted to prayer and contemplation would not be more acceptable to God. . . . Then in the Contemplative Orders daily Communion is permitted and this is not the case in active Orders, and as one single Holy Communion gives Our Lord more pleasure, and God more glory than all the work and toil and labor for God, of all the men in the world, — then I feel that a Contemplative Life where daily Communion is usual, would give Our Lord more pleasure than if I were to devote myself to active life. . . .
>
> My second reason for not wishing to found an Order for Indians and

69. O'Connor to MKD, February 16, 1889.

Colored is that I appreciate that a founder of an order should be animated with every virtue capable of fitting her to carry out the object of her order. If she has not the right spirit, <u>who</u> should have it? I know of the self-sacrifice necessary in the missionary life! I know the privations, the trials, the temptations, and I could go through all these in a manner suitable for edifying the religious in my order?

3rdly. Is not an old and tried order more efficient in this Indian and Colored harvest? . . .

4th. Could the Indian and Colored work not be better done by employing <u>all</u> the orders? The orders to be employed by the . . . Bureau [to which] I would leave <u>all</u> my income. . . .

Rt. Rev'd and dear Father, I hope Our Lord will teach me to do His will. I see Him thirsty at the Well and tired. I wish to slake His thirst, according to His Will and in the manner He wills. I wish to be a docile instrument, etc., if it be His Will for me to found an Order I shall do it. I know Our Lord wished for souls, — but does He wish me to <u>ask</u> Him for them in prayer and contemplation, or does He wish me to found an order. The responsibility of such a call almost crushes me, because I am so infinitely poor in the virtues necessary.[70]

Bishop O'Connor brushed aside her concerns as "simply scruples."

I was never so quietly sure of any vocation, not even my own, as I am about yours. If you do not establish the order in question, you will allow to pass an opportunity of doing immense service to the Church, which may not occur again. . . . I regard it as <u>settled</u> that you are to establish a new order, and I shall go to Philadelphia merely to arrange details. The Church has spoken to you through me, her unworthy organ, and you must hear her or take the consequences. Do you wish for a decree of a general council in this matter, or for a decision ex cathedra of the Pope?[71]

The bishop here took a stronger stand than ever before with Katharine. He was more emphatic about her founding an order than he ever was about her not having a vocation. Moving from not believing that she had a vocation at all to deciding that she must found a new order or take the consequences was a tremendous turnaround by the bishop. It must have taken

70. MKD to O'Connor, February 24, 1889.
71. O'Connor to MKD, February 28, 1889.

Katharine by surprise, yet she yielded to the idea of becoming a founder almost meekly and remarkably quickly. In a letter dated March 19, she wrote to Bishop O'Connor: "The Feast of St. Joseph brought me the grace to give the remainder of my life to the Indians and Colored, — to enter fully into your views [to found a new order] and those of Rev'd Stephan as to what is best for the salvation of the souls of these people. . . . As long as I look on myself, I cannot. Our Lord gives and will give me the grace always to look at Him." Perhaps her immediate acceptance was because she had indeed had a personal *ex cathedra* decision from Pope Leo XIII when he had told her in 1887, "Why not, my child, yourself become a missionary?" At the time, she did not know what the pope meant. With the fullness of time, making haste slowly and prayerfully, and with the intercession of her spiritual adviser, Bishop O'Connor, the pope's meaning became clear to her. She was called to found a new community of sisters dedicated to the welfare of Native Americans and blacks. It was as the leader of her community, the Sisters of the Blessed Sacrament for Indians and Colored People, that Katharine would work out her salvation on earth. She became a saint of the Catholic Church for her spirituality and temporal works. When Bishop O'Connor wrote that he had destroyed some of her letters because of their personal nature, she presciently teased him back, "I nearly forgot to tell you that I was rather disappointed that you destroyed my letters. They might be needed for my canonization."[72]

On May 6, 1889, almost six years after she wrote Bishop James O'Connor her lists of reasons for and against a religious vocation, Catherine Mary Drexel entered the novitiate of the Sisters of Mercy of Saint Mary's Convent in Pittsburgh, Pennsylvania, where she was to learn how to be a religious, how to live in community, and how to lead a community of women before starting out with her own sisters. She would be a postulant and a novice sister under obedience to the mistress of novices and the superior of the convent before taking her own vows as the founder of the Sisters of the Blessed Sacrament for Indians and Colored People and moving back to her family home, St. Michel, until a new motherhouse could be built. Taking the name of Sister Mary Katharine Drexel, she became the first professed sister of her order on February 12, 1891. Except for the 1890 tragic death of her sister Elizabeth, newly married to George Walter Smith, and the death of Bishop O'Connor the same year, Katharine did not leave the Mercy Convent for twenty months. She spent her time with the Sisters of Mercy still seeking

72. MKD to O'Connor, June 24, 1888.

God's will, praying, and waiting. It was a fairly quiet interlude before the great effort of launching a new order.

This chapter has charted the development of Katharine Drexel's youthful spirituality and the difficulty she had discerning her life's vocation. Had she followed Bishop O'Connor's initial and long-standing advice to remain a single woman, holy and philanthropic, there would have been no story about her at all. Had O'Connor simply agreed with her desire to become a nun after the death of her mother, the outcome for Katharine and those she eventually came to serve would have been quite different. A young woman in her middle twenties most probably would have been incapable of founding a congregation of sisters dedicated solely to the temporal and spiritual benefit of Native Americans and blacks. Had she gone into one of the contemplative orders, there to pray and meditate for the remainder of her days, would she have been recognized by the Catholic Church as a saint? No doubt she would have been just as holy as a contemplative sister; but would she have accomplished the profound good that she did through the Sisters of the Blessed Sacrament? It took a woman who could defy a bishop to found and sustain a new order of women missionaries. Her firm strength of character in the face of hierarchical opposition was the result of her belief in the reality of her call from Christ. She could hold to such a conviction with tenacity because her deepened spirituality allowed her to hear and heed the word of her Lord. The fruit of her vocation is the subject of the next chapter. It will outline the trajectory of the order she founded, from its inception to its peak and decline.

CHAPTER 3

Growth of the Order

When Katharine Drexel founded the Sisters of the Blessed Sacrament for Indians and Colored People in 1891, it was one of 134 orders of Catholic women religious founded in the United States since its founding. It was one of 5 orders founded in the same year.[1] When Mother Katharine died, there had been 343 orders of Catholic women religious established in the United States. Most orders were transplanted from Europe and never truly took root in American soil, and were disbanded after a few years; more failed than succeeded.[2]

That Katharine's order has endured to the present day is a mark of its founder's vision and charism, despite the general apathy and occasional hostility of her fellow Americans and coreligionists to the Sisters of the Blessed Sacrament and those they served, and despite the inherent harsh conditions in which the sisters found themselves, whether in the North, the South, the East, or the West.

This chapter focuses on the growth of the order of the Sisters of the Blessed Sacrament, and mainly on the first forty-three years when the founder was still the mother general and active in its development, before summarizing its continued growth into the 1960s and eventual post–Vatican II decline to the present day. The establishment of the missions of St. Catherine's (Santa Fe, New Mexico), St. Francis de Sales (Powhatan, Vir-

1. Of the orders established in 1891, the Sisters of the Perpetual Rosary and the Little Sisters of the Assumption were from France, the Sisters of the Assumption were from France by way of Canada, and the Sisters of the Immaculate Conception were a new American order.

2. George C. Stewart Jr., *Marvels of Charity: History of American Sisters and Nuns* (Huntington, Ind.: Our Sunday Visitor, 1994).

ginia), St. Michael's (St. Michael's, Arizona), Immaculate Mother (Nashville, Tennessee), Blessed Sacrament (Beaumont, Texas), and Xavier University (New Orleans, Louisiana) and the outlying southern Louisiana schools is discussed in some detail, as they illustrate the challenges and difficulties Katharine encountered in carrying out her mission to be a mother to the Native American and African American peoples. But first we must establish the internal context for the order, because it was an order that easily could have been stillborn.

Katharine Drexel had reluctantly embraced Bishop O'Connor's vision of an order founded for the benefit of "Indians and Colored People." Newly ensconced in the Mercy Convent, she wrote to the bishop:

> This convent life is full of joy for me and I take a most unmortified satisfaction in this respite from responsibility, which brings me peace. There is one thought, however, which causes me unease — it is the thought of why I am here *viz:* — to prepare me for a future life of responsibility, and what is more, a life which is most apt to be one of opposition, trial, subject to even criticism of the Church. Then as it were to have the very salvation of so many hang as it were upon my instrumentality! The undertaking you proposed, Reverend Father, seems enormous and I shall freely acknowledge that my heart goes down in sorrow when I think of it. To be the head of a new order! New orders always, I think, have to pass through the baptism of the cross.
>
> All of these dismal thoughts are not generous to Our Lord, and in the chapel and meditation I am striving to overcome this selfishness and self-seeking, and to look upon the future life you propose for me with cheerfulness since you say it is the will of the Lord.[3]

This must have been a very difficult time for her as she tried to focus on the present and to ignore the daunting future: "I try to think just as little as I can about the new order, endeavoring to attend solely to my own progress in perfection."[4] She counted on Bishop O'Connor's continuing support and comfort to sustain her.

However, before she had even had her reception into the Mercy novitiate, O'Connor became ill. Archbishop Patrick John Ryan had to preside at her veiling on November 7, 1889. O'Connor had written to her that "nearly

3. MKD to O'Connor, May 12, 1889.
4. MKD to O'Connor, May 31, 1889.

all the works destined to be of special service to the Church, began in trial," but he did not realize how prescient he was in writing those words.[5] He died on May 27, 1890. His death left Sister Katharine bereft of his support and consolation. She did not think that she could go on with the foundation of a new order without him. Archbishop Ryan offered her his support: "If I share the burden with you, if I help you, can you go on?"[6] She could and did, but it was never easy, and the earliest days were the most difficult.

Not all the women who came to the Sisters of the Blessed Sacrament persevered in their vocations. Of the forty-one women who entered either at the Mercy Convent in Pittsburgh or at the temporary novitiate at the Drexel family estate, St. Michel, nineteen left. This was an unusually high dropout rate. More established orders saw 17 to 25 percent leave.[7] There were many frustrations caused by the newness of the SBS order. They could not move directly into the motherhouse, St. Elizabeth's, because it was still being built. The day before the celebration to lay the cornerstone for the new motherhouse, a stick of dynamite was found, presumably placed by a neighbor distraught at the thought of a school for black children so near his home. There were rumors that "all the Catholics who were on the platform would be blown to Hell."[8] When they finally moved in, the facility was still under construction, with no heat and no lights. The water froze in the pitchers during especially cold winter nights, and the sisters burned candles for lighting. They could not go immediately to the missions in the West because the community was still in its infant stages and needed to grow more spiritual and sororal bonds before it spread out across the country. It was not until 1894 that the first mission was established, as the sisters took over the mission school of St. Catherine's in Santa Fe, New Mexico.

Surely a few sisters were frightened away by frustrations and intimidating activity, but this was only one reason that sisters left the order. Some departed due to poor health; others joined congregations that would send them immediately to the West. One wanted a more contemplative order. Only one left after having made her final vows and without being released from the vows. Seven were asked to leave, usually for reasons that, had they been more obedient to their superior, would not have warranted their re-

5. December 27, 1888.

6. ASBS, vol. 3, p. 110.

7. Sr. Patricia Lynch, SBS, *Sharing the Bread in Service: Sisters of the Blessed Sacrament, 1891-1991*, 2 vols. (Bensalem, Pa.: Sisters of the Blessed Sacrament, 1998), 1:401 n. 24.

8. Sr. Consuela Duffy, SBS, *Katharine Drexel: A Biography* (Philadelphia: Reilly Co., 1966), p. 179.

moval. These reasons included lack of "prudence, discretion, or charity"; being "pettish," "temperamental," or a hypochondriac; or, worst of all, for producing "friction" in the community.[9] These were infractions of immaturity and lack of obedience on the part of the young sisters. *Perfectae Caritatis* put the principle of obedience this way: "Religious engaged in the active apostolate . . . must always be imbued with the spirit of their religious community, and remain faithful to the observation of their rule and a spirit of submission due to their superiors."[10] *Optatam Totius,* in speaking of seminarians, carries the principle of obedience to an even higher level whereby the religious is expected to "accept the authority of superiors from a personal conviction, that is to say from a motive of conscience (cf. Rom. 13:5), and for supernatural reasons."[11] Those asked to leave were lacking in that love that is the surrender of the will. Those who stayed — and after the earliest years most did stay — were bound together by their vows and their individual convictions that each one had been called personally by Christ to become a missionary in the order of the Sisters of the Blessed Sacrament.

The order consisted of Choir sisters and House sisters. The House sisters performed most of the more menial jobs of the convents and missions and taught the domestic arts to students, while the Choir sisters were more educated and performed the academic teaching duties. Choir sisters had priority over House sisters. This division of the sisterhood was common to European orders, but uncommon in the United States. However, it was practiced by the Sisters of Mercy, where Katharine had done her novitiate, and by the Sacred Heart Sisters of Eden Hall, where her aunt had been the superior. All the SBS sisters wore the same habit, and all performed many of the same chores about the convent. No one was exempt from physical labor, except those who were ill or aged. This division of House and Choir sisters was eventually dropped in 1958.

All the earliest sisters were Caucasian. It was not because Katharine believed that African American women were inferior or not capable of being good nuns that they were not originally welcomed into the order. "Why, should they [African American women] not be religious [nuns]? . . . They are sent to do the work of the religious, without the graces or protection of the religious. It is too much work and too exposing a work without spiritual

9. Lynch, *Sharing the Bread,* 1:60-67.

10. *Perfectae Caritatis,* 35.2, in *The Sixteen Documents of Vatican II,* introduced by Douglas Bushman; gen. ed., Marianne Lorraine Trouvé (Boston: Pauline Books and Media, 1999).

11. *Optatam Totius,* 11, in *The Sixteen Documents of Vatican II.*

merit and protection the religious life affords. If it be possible — as seems the case — that the Colored girl may live in religion, why should she not do so, and enjoy its advantages?"[12] She alluded to a heated discussion on the possibility of a racially mixed congregation in a letter to her brother-in-law, Edward Morrell, and presumably her sister Louise, who "strongly favored" a mixed congregation. Her other sister, Elizabeth Smith, had the opposite opinion. She thought that a mixed congregation would be "sheer madness."[13] Katharine's decision to maintain a Caucasian-only order was political, not a product of prejudice. Her main fear was that her order, dedicated as it was to the service of "Indian and Colored People," would be seen as being in competition with the African American orders of nuns for members. The only two orders of black women in the United States at the time of the founding of the SBS were struggling for members and financial support. Both the Oblate Sisters of Providence in Baltimore and the Sisters of the Holy Family in New Orleans, the African American orders, received financial support from Katharine, who also promised not to raid their supply of possible candidates. In the early 1890s, Mother Mathilda Beasley of the newly forming Sisters of the Second Order of St. Francis approached Katharine about the possibility of her fledgling African American order of nuns being trained under SBS auspices. Katharine turned her away because her own SBS order was still very young and not yet well formed, and she felt the established black order in Baltimore or New Orleans would better serve Mother Mathilda. However, in 1927, the newly forming African American community of the Handmaids of Mary placed their Sr. Dorothy, who would become their mistress of novices, in Cornwells Heights to be trained under the guidance of the SBS mistress of novices, much the way that Katharine and her first SBS sisters were trained by the Sisters of Mercy in Pittsburgh. The first African American to become a Sister of the Blessed Sacrament would not join for several more decades.

However, about the same time that Katharine was turning down Mother Beasley, Georgianna Burton, a young woman of Seneca Indian background, converted to Catholicism in New York against the opposition of her Native American family. Needing a place to stay, she sought refuge at the SBS mission of St. Michael's in Arizona. She had hoped to join what would have been the first order of Native American nuns that was being organized by Fr. Francis Michael Craft. When Fr. Craft's efforts to found the Indian order fell through, Burton turned to the SBS for admission. By a vote of the congre-

12. Lynch, *Sharing the Bread,* 1:42.
13. ASBS, vol. 3, p. 22.

gation, she was accepted, and she entered the novitiate at the motherhouse on January 15, 1893. Native American women freely joined the order, while black women could not. The SBS would one day became color-blind in their admission policies, but that day was far distant from the time of Georgianna Burton.

Even before the founding of the SBS, Katharine was besieged by bishops and priests seeking her funds for their schools and missions. She filled those requests as fully as she could, dispensing more than $100,000 while she was still in the Mercy Convent. Her first supplicant visitor after she left Pittsburgh for St. Michel was Archbishop Francis Janssens of New Orleans, and though she gave him funds for the meantime, it would not be until the preparation for the founding of Xavier University in 1915 that her sisters would establish a mission in his city.

One of the Indian missions Katharine had supported before entering the convent was St. Stephen's in Wyoming, a mission for the Shoshone and Arapaho Indians she had funded since 1885. It was a mission plagued with staffing difficulties from its beginning. Bishop Maurice Burke of Cheyenne wrote to her in 1889:

> You certainly cannot be expected to do any more. . . . Our position, how-ever, in Wyoming is not understood, and this fact is to our real disadvan-tage and embarrassment. . . . I am bishop in name only. . . . I am here in a vast desert without inhabitants and without any means under heaven to accomplish any work in the interest of the Church or of religion. . . . If I had the zeal and the ability of St. Paul, I could accomplish nothing here. I am without people, without priests, without any means whatever of living or staying here.
>
> . . . Your work among the Indians has been and is indeed a charity so great that words cannot express it. If a little of what you have done for the poor Red Man of this desert, were done by others who had the means and the power to do it, for the poor whites who are scattered here and there throughout this vast territory like sheep without a shepherd, many souls would be saved that are now lost to the faith.[14]

Bishop Burke kept in touch with her over the years. He could not secure priests or nuns for his mission, which had been built with Drexel money. The Sisters of Charity were to staff the mission in June of 1890, but were recalled

14. ASBS, vol. 3, p. 146.

to Fort Leavenworth before they could start a school. Then four Protestant women were secured to undertake the school, but they, too, were unable to open it. Katharine sent out letters to other orders of sisters looking for staff for the mission. No sisters were willing or available to undertake the mission. Katharine learned of this last failure at the profession of her vows, where Bishop Burke was present. She secured permission from Archbishop Ryan to make an investigatory tour of the Wyoming mission. In her mind, it would be the first mission of her new order. On her trip, she inspected the buildings and made supply lists of what would be needed to open the school. When she left to return to Philadelphia, both she and the bishop of Cheyenne expected that she would return in the spring with SBS sisters to staff the mission. She was in for a major disappointment, because Archbishop Ryan, perhaps at the suggestion of Mother Sebastian, the superior of the Mercy Convent in Pittsburgh, denied her request to open St. Stephen's Mission.[15] He deemed her community too young and inchoate to undergo such a difficult assignment. At that time, Mother Katharine was the only professed member of the SBS community. This was, however, the only setback that she experienced. If it made her angry or upset, she did not express or record it. Instead, she looked upon the experience as an opportunity to teach her infant order a lesson in humility.

> We should, then, Sisters, endeavor to sanctify ourselves during this period of grace which He has given to us. If we desire to build the house of holiness, we must begin by laying a good firm foundation and the firmer the foundation the higher we can build. . . . Humility will carry the superstructure and be sure that your house will not stand unless it is built on the virtue of humility. If we are not humble, tell me — of what use are we in God's service? It is on condition that we are humble that He will bestow His grace upon us. In bestowing upon us the name of Sisters of the Blessed Sacrament He seems to desire us in a special manner to be humble; for in no act of His life or even in His passion and death, did He show His humility as He did in the Sacrament of His love, not even in the Incarnation. . . . He hides all of His glory even that of His Humanity — under the form of ordinary bread. If we have this virtue we shall also have fraternal charity which is the bond of union, for if we listen to the voice of humility which is truth, we shall see so much imperfection in ourselves that we will not notice the faults of our Sisters much less speak of them. During this time

15. Duffy, *Katharine Drexel,* p. 176.

of preparation [before going out to the missions] we will not lack material to practice our future work with the little ones of Christ.[16]

Years later, she would write about her thwarted plans to open St. Stephen's with her own sisters: "Oh how audacious I was in those days. Almighty God was certainly good to save us from such a mistake. I see now what a wild scheme it was. It would have been the ruination of our little Congregation."[17]

St. Catherine's, Santa Fe, New Mexico

The first mission the Sisters of the Blessed Sacrament founded was to serve Native Americans in the pueblos surrounding Santa Fe, New Mexico, in 1894. St. Catherine's School was built in 1886-1887 with funds supplied by Katharine Drexel. It suffered the same staffing problems as did St. Stephen's. The Sisters of Loretto opened the school and taught there for two and a half years; the Benedictine fathers served there but withdrew after a year; and then three laywomen were contracted to run the school but were unable to do so. The school closed in June 1893 for lack of teachers. Archbishop Placide L. Chapelle of Santa Fe made the trek to Cornwells Heights, the new name of the area around the SBS motherhouse, to induce Mother Katharine to send SBS teachers to his school. Again, Archbishop Ryan said, "No. Let Archbishop Chapelle try to secure another community for the present." Mother Katharine again looked upon the delay as an opportunity to teach humility: "Sisters, we can make an act of humility, we are not fit instruments for apostolic labor among the Indians of New Mexico. Do not let this, however, deter us in the work of our sanctification. If we persevere courageously in the uphill work, dying to ourselves and letting God reign in our hearts, He will in His own time choose us to go and work in His vineyard and bring forth fruit that will remain. Let us strive to grow in all the virtues, especially the virtue of humility."[18]

When she learned in the spring of 1894 that Chapelle had been unsuccessful in finding teachers for St. Catherine's, Mother Katharine again approached Ryan for permission to make a trip to Santa Fe to assess the needs of the school. This time Ryan agreed, and Mother Katharine and another

16. OASBS, p. 73, 1892.
17. ASBS, vol. 3, p. 188, no date.
18. ASBS, vol. 4, p. 20, 1893.

sister traveled to Santa Fe. While there, she engaged workmen to repair and alter the buildings of the school. Upon her return to the motherhouse, and with Ryan's permission, she selected nine sisters to be the order's pioneer missionaries. The first group of four sisters departed the motherhouse on June 13, 1894. The second group started out a few weeks later, only to be caught up in a national railway strike that more than once threatened mob action and endangered the sisters. The sisters telegraphed Mother Katharine to ask whether they should try to continue their journey. She responded that "if continuing journey seems dangerous REMAIN in La Junta." There was no consensus as to exactly what Mother's instructions meant or whether or not there was the possibility of danger ahead, so the group went on anyway. Mother Katharine was upset that her sisters misunderstood her instructions. She wrote to them afterward, "I feared your going despite the danger. . . . I explain this, not to pain you, but that you may know your Mother better on another occasion. I have offered the judgment you formed of me in atonement for the many times I have doubted Our Lord's love. Indeed a little penance was well merited and made me understand the Sacred Heart better and how want of confidence must grieve Him."[19] The five sisters joined the original four in Santa Fe just as a funeral was under way for an Indian child with the band playing "Nearer, My God, to Thee."[20] The sisters must have wondered what they had gotten themselves into.

Mother Katharine gave the sisters a few weeks to settle in before leaving to visit her first mission. She wrote frequent letters back to the sisters in the motherhouse when she traveled. Even though she was away, she was still mistress of novices, in addition to being the mother general of the order, and their spiritual formation was always on her mind. She wrote the following en route from Kansas:

> If we have died to self in life and lived in God's presence, and near Him and with Him, in union with Him in life, surely on that day when eternity shall commence to us, God's own beautiful life will glorify all our thoughts, words and actions because His Will and Light will appear in them and thus they will glorify Him for ever and ever. The splendor will not fade as do the golden tints of these clouds that pass when I am writing to you. Oh even now they have assumed a leaden hue and they appear but fleeting clouds! So will self will, self seeking, self-judgment be on our day

19. ASBS, vol. 1, p. 127.
20. Duffy, *Katharine Drexel,* p. 191.

of eternity. Let us do God's will and see God and God's judgment whilst traveling to eternity. Then we need not fear that only the fleeting clouds will remain in our thoughts, words and actions. All these will be laid up in Heaven as a treasure that will not fade.[21]

When she arrived at St. Catherine's, only nine students were enrolled in the school. She asked Bishop Chapelle and his priests to visit with the Indian elders to convince them to send their children. When that was done and the school and convent were in good order, she took leave of her sisters, whom she called "My Nine." She wrote to them not to be discouraged in their slow start: "I loved you before my visit, more since my visit and during it. . . . As I think of His paternal love, it does not seem improbable to me that He has plucked some of the fruit from you by not permitting the children to come all at once, because He wisely saw that would be too heavy for the slender branches. That is at least now, if they come all at once. Growth must be gradual to be enduring."[22] The first planting was successfully under way. By the end of the first year of SBS direction, St. Catherine's had enrolled eighty-four children of both sexes. It would grow gradually and endure for more than one hundred years, until 1999.

St. Francis de Sales, Powhatan, Virginia

Because her vocation was to serve both the African American and the Native American peoples, Katharine Drexel, once St. Catherine's School was secure, looked for ways to introduce her order directly into the service of African Americans. Her sister Louise and her husband had been most interested in the plight of African Americans. Their Virginia school for young men of color was opened in 1895 under the direction of the Christian Brothers. Katharine approached Bishop Augustine Van De Vyver of Richmond about opening a sister school for young black women on an adjacent piece of property. He was more than happy with her proposal and immediately gave his consent. She purchased 600 acres along the James River to construct her new academy, which she called St. Francis de Sales, in honor of her father. It was more informally referred to as Rock Castle, the name of the area. It was the first of many schools for African Americans she would finance.

21. ASBS, vol. 4, p. 146, September 1894.
22. ASBS, vol. 4, p. 154, September 1894.

Eventually the bulk of her funds and the efforts of her community would be directed to serving the black community. Her prediction that the needs of the large number of African Americans would overwhelm the needs of Native Americans came true, even within her own order.

Rock Castle took four years to build, from July 1895 until the fall of 1899. In July 1899, Mother Katharine and a companion went out to the school site to ready it for the arrival of its first teachers. She had chosen nine sisters to be its first faculty. When she arrived at the nearby train station, the farmer she had hired to manage the property, a former slave, greeted her with bad news. The new barn at St. Francis de Sales had been vandalized and burned to the ground. Once again, the Sisters of the Blessed Sacrament were not wholeheartedly welcomed by their new neighbors. Mother Katharine was undaunted, even though the fire cost the order another $4,000. The school opened on time, in the fall. The sister assigned to be the first superior at Rock Castle had been in a carriage accident the previous spring, so another had to be appointed in her place. Even though St. Francis de Sales was intended as a boarding school for African American girls, its first student was an Indian from St. Stephen's School in Wyoming. Indians and blacks were all brothers and sisters of color to the Sisters of the Blessed Sacrament. One could occasionally find an Indian among the black orphans in Holy Providence School at the motherhouse in Cornwells Heights. In the first semester of St. Francis de Sales School, thirty-one students enrolled. A small tuition was charged to those who could afford it; otherwise the girls' room, board, clothing, and medical care were provided by the order.

The new buildings were not without their problems. Because they had been empty for so long, the rats had moved in. It took more than a year to get the rat problem under control. More importantly, the heating system did not work, and in a winter that turned out to be unseasonably cold, this was a disaster. The sisters' efforts to get the contractor to repair the system failed, so they replaced it with another system. The order then had to sue the initial contractor. The suit failed in the lower courts, but the congregation won on appeal, so the company eventually paid for the new system as well as punitive damages to the order.

From the beginning, Mother Katharine had envisioned her missions making visits and performing social services in the areas surrounding them. In the Rock Castle area were many poor black families; many included former slaves. Their poverty brought with it a great deal of sickness. The sisters shared food and medicine with the poor in their neighborhood. They even went into homes where typhoid had struck down the inhabitants. A nearby prison also benefited from the services of the sisters. Their first prison visitation must have been very difficult, as the prisoner was condemned to die for his crimes. The sisters prepared him for baptism, which he received on December 29, 1902, two days before his execution.[23] Mother Katharine felt very keenly for her daughters at Rock Castle. For their first Christmas in Virginia, she wrote to them:

> My very dear children in the Blessed Sacrament
> At St. Francis de Sales:
> You will not be with my flock at St. Elizabeth's at Christmastide. I shall miss each dear child of mine with whom it has been my privilege to be in such close relations in those sweet Christmases of the past. And, you too, will miss us, just a little, I hope. This is natural. Our Lord gave us our nature and He will not be displeased with us because we miss each other. . . . You have left us to bring in imitation of Our Lord the blessings of redemption to the souls for whom He is born in such poverty, abandonment, and suffering.
> See His little arms; they are opened wide to receive the souls you will bring to Him in Virginia. Last year the house of St. Francis de Sales stood as it does now on the rolling hilltop overlooking the James; but to the eyes of Faith, how different now from then. It encloses within the walls, as the case in Bethlehem, its God. And you, His spouses, are there as St. Joseph and Mary to adore and worship and love Him in His first Christmas at St. Francis de Sales. Really, I see little difference in one way, between His birth at Bethlehem and His birth in this land where He has never been before on this Christmas day — the spot where my dear daughters will be at the Midnight Mass of 1899.[24]

It is clear that she, who remained a consecrated virgin, nonetheless expressed deeply held emotional maternal ties with her spiritual daughters. The point of missing one's separated family members is expressed in terms similar to those employed within the Drexel family when they were separated on their various trips abroad or to the country or seaside. She was so attached to her sisters and in awe of the work they did that she actually tried to kiss their feet during a 1913 visit. They were horrified at her attempt. She explained herself this way: "It was no real joke, my trying to kiss your feet — privileged feet

23. Duffy, *Katharine Drexel*, p. 207.
24. MKD to SBS at St. Francis de Sales, December 1899.

indeed of the Sisters of the Blessed Sacrament who walk in distant parts from the dear motherhouse and away from parents and friends to bring the glad tidings of the redemption. You who have left all things to follow Jesus, Jesus Himself is and will be your reward in the eternal motherhouse where each Sister of the Blessed Sacrament has her throne awaiting her."[25]

St. Michael's, St. Michael's, Arizona

In 1896, while St. Francis de Sales was being built, Mother Katharine bought land in Arizona to establish a mission for Navajo Indians. She called the mission St. Michael's; it is still actively staffed today by the Sisters of the Blessed Sacrament, but its beginnings were inauspicious. As early as 1744, two Franciscan priests ventured into Navajo country and reported that the Indians there were receptive to learning more about Christianity. However, the Navajos were a pastoral people living in a harsh climate in a remote country that was less than inviting to missionaries. Unlike the Pueblo peoples of New Mexico, they knew little of Christianity at the end of the nineteenth century. Under Grant's Peace Policy, the Presbyterians had been given the Navajos around Fort Defiance, Arizona, to proselytize, but their efforts were unsuccessful. In the early 1890s, the Methodists and the Episcopalians had attempted missions among them, which also failed. Mr. Frank Walker, who was one-half Navajo and who was later hired as the handyman, caretaker, and interpreter for St. Michael's Mission, wrote to Archbishop Jean Baptiste Salpointe about the Navajos in Arizona: "The Navajos speak more Spanish than English. Medicine men have no influence on the younger element of their race; their religion is dying out. The Navajos are well disposed to receive the teachings of the Catholic priests. Strange to say, although the reservation has had for many years a great number of Protestant preachers of all denominations there is not, I think, a single Protestant Navajo."[26]

Father Stephan, of the Catholic Indian Bureau, sat down with Mother Katharine in 1895 to plan a Catholic mission there. With funding from Mother Katharine, he bought a parcel of land six miles outside of Fort Defiance and a mile from the 3.5-million-acre reservation. He asked various men's reli-

---

25. MKD to St. Catherine's, August 1913. Quoted in Lou Baldwin, *St. Katharine Drexel: Apostle to the Oppressed,* ed. Rev. Paul S. Quinter, Elena Bucciarelli, and Frank Coyne (Philadelphia: Catholic Standard and Times, 2000), p. 148.

26. December 14, 1896. Mr. Walker had also served Mother Katharine in the same capacity at St. Catherine's.

gious orders to staff the mission with priests, but none would promise to do so permanently. St. Michael's seemed to be heading toward the same predicament as St. Stephen's in Wyoming. Fr. Stephan was so keen to open a Catholic mission for the Navajos that he offered to leave the Bureau and staff the mission himself, but Mother Katharine thought he had best stay at the Bureau. He contacted the Cincinnati Province of Franciscans about staffing the mission. He reported back to Mother Katharine: "I spoke to a Franciscan Father of the Province of Cincinnati who are good, pious, and hard working priests, like the Sanguinists. I got real encouragement and hope we may get them for the Navajo Indians. They are mostly Americans and adapted for the work; there is a 'go ahead' in them."[27] He may have been encouraged, but the answer of the Franciscans was still vague. Mother Katharine visited them personally in the fall of 1897 and secured their commitment to St. Michael's. So strong was their commitment to the Navajo that they have been at St. Michael's ever since.

It took some doing to untangle the title to the property that Fr. Stephan had bought for the mission, because some of it belonged to the federal government and could only be granted as a homestead to an individual, and not to an institution or congregation of priests or nuns. The Franciscans, who take a vow of complete poverty that does not allow them to own property, could not take legal possession of the title. Also, there were problems with white claim-jumpers, who tried to get bits of the site in complicated legal maneuverings. Eventually the property considerations were ironed out, and three Franciscan priests arrived at St. Michael's on October 5, 1898. They oversaw the construction of the buildings and made the necessary improvements to the land to support the mission. Everything was underwritten by the Sisters of the Blessed Sacrament.

The next major hurdle was the very difficult Navajo language, which, of course, none of the priests spoke. It was an unwritten language. The priests "originated a new code to record it. With the help of two boys, Charley Day, aged nineteen, and Sammy Day, sixteen, they went through Webster's [dictionary] from A to Z."[28] The priests also used the Montgomery Ward mail-order catalogue with the children to identify Navajo terms for various items. Eventually they would write the first books ever published in Navajo, a Catholic catechism and an ethnographic dictionary of the Navajo language, which were printed on a St. Michael's printing press.

27. Fr. Stephan to MKD, August 12, 1997.
28. Duffy, *Katharine Drexel*, p. 219.

The mission of St. Michael's was in the desert, so finding a good source of water was important. The only water on the property, a stream, was not drinkable and not even clean enough to wash clothes in. Mother Katharine wrote to her sisters in Cornwells Heights about the water situation in Arizona:

> Shall we find limpid waters? That depends on your prayers. Today we visited the little church at Newton, and I told our Lord the truth when I said to Him it was easy for Him to give you all to drink. . . . I told Our Lord that better would it be for us to drink muddy temporal waters always in this short span of life, provided that He gave us His own pure living waters. With that great gift we shall never thirst, and the Navajos will never thirst, but will become God's own most dear children in the Blessed Sacrament to them as *the* gift of God dwelling in their hearts, as in a sanctuary. Yet Our Lord can give us, if He wish, both the spiritual and temporal waters.[29]

To make matters worse, the muddy stream occasionally flooded over its banks, so one of the buildings had to be moved to higher ground to save it from damage in flash floods. Finally clean water was found after several dry wells were dug.

The next challenge was to secure students for the school. The Navajo elders believed that schooling in the government boarding schools had rendered their children unfit for life on the reservation.[30] They were leery of the white man's education. Mother Katharine met with them to discuss the curriculum for St. Michael's. They stressed to her a need for vocational training, so she planned a curriculum that included harness making, carpentry, wagon construction, shoemaking, and the native arts of weaving and silver smelting, along with basic courses in English, mathematics, geography, U.S. history, and, of course, religion. She held a feast to entice the Indians. She also attended their feasts and ceremonies. She even once partook of a "wee bit" of a peyote button during one such ceremony. She reported that the ceremony was not unlike the Catholic celebration of the Eucharist, except that it went on for five or six hours. The peyote, she said, was "very bitter."[31] As a gesture of good will and to allay the elders' fears, she invited them to send five Navajo children, accompanied by three Na-

29. ASBS, vol. 7, p. 13, no date.
30. Lynch, *Sharing the Bread,* 1:111.
31. ASBS, vol. 7, p. 29, no date.

vajo elders, to St. Catherine's in Santa Fe to see the SBS Indian mission and education at first hand. The parents also feared they would be cut off from their children once they were ensconced in boarding school. Mother Katherine assured them that parents and other family members would always be welcome and that she would provide accommodations for them, as well as hay for their horses. The Navajo headmen were impressed, especially after they witnessed her playing a friendly game with their children of throwing stones at a tin can. They promised to send their children to the school once it opened.

Mother Katharine was interested in every aspect of the development of the new mission. After the rat infestation at Rock Castle, she was perhaps overly concerned about the rats and mice in Arizona. The Day family, who lived on the property, had complained of rats, so she wrote to the priests: "In one of my private letters I intended asking you if you will be kind enough to procure some 'Rough on Rats' and put it around the Day's house in the various rooms and [in the other buildings]. . . . It would be well to distribute some 'Rough on Rats.' I know from experience how destructive mice are; in an empty building they usually hold sway."[32]

She visited St. Michael's in October of 1902 to see if it was ready for her sisters. She found that the five rooms set aside for the twelve sisters did not have roofs. By the time they arrived at the end of the month, four of the rooms were roofed. It was typical for the sisters to move into an uncompleted mission, school, and convent. In fact, St. Michael's was bereft of heat and indoor plumbing for the sisters until the 1940s. The children and their needs always came first.

Missionary work, even that sustained by the supernatural, entails physical and emotional hardships. Mother Katharine had put it this way in trying to cheer her sisters at St. Catherine's mission: "But remember this always: it is the supernatural which has called you here and it is only the supernatural which will sustain you and keep you here."[33] Yet those missionary sisters who left their homes and families for places far from home and lacking in the amenities of home found themselves exhausted from their labors. Physical comforts, or discomforts, were nothing compared to the actual work of the missions.

The actual workday of the Sisters of the Blessed Sacrament began at

---

32. MKD to St. Michael's, April 9, 1902.
33. Katherine Burton, *The Golden Door: The Life of Katharine Drexel* (New York: P. J. Kenedy and Sons, 1957), p. 153.

4:30 in the morning, when the sister in charge of cooking arose to start the fire and to milk the cows and bring in the eggs, and the "caller" sister began to awaken the other sisters. Before breakfast, the sisters spent one-half hour in meditation in the chapel followed by reading the daily office and Mass. Breakfast was accompanied by a lecture on the rule of the order and followed by the making of beds and other light "charges," or chores. The sisters began their regular assigned work after their morning chores. Some sisters taught students, while others made home visitations, another important aspect of their missionary work. Others did heavier housecleaning in the chapel, convent, or school, or looked after the convent's gardens and livestock. The heavy chores were shared by all the sisters on a rotating basis. Sometime during the day, they were required to spend one-half hour visiting the Blessed Sacrament and fifteen minutes each in spiritual reading and in the examination of conscience. The main meal of the day was the noon dinner. Throughout the day, silence reigned, except in relation to assigned duties. Even during meals, except on Wednesdays, the sisters practiced silence. Dinner was accompanied four times a week by readings from a spiritual book. After dinner, the sisters enjoyed a short recreation time before returning to the duties, which would carry on until late afternoon. Another recreation, usually a walk, carried the sisters through until supper. After supper, the sisters could take another walk, visit the Blessed Sacrament, complete their grading of the children's work, or finish other work of the day. They also spent their evening hours in a sewing circle, making and mending clothes for the children and themselves. Their day done, they were allowed to share its highlights with one another. After night prayers in the chapel, the convent lights were turned off at 10:00 in the evening. On major feast days and holidays, talking could begin at breakfast, and extra food was allowed at all meals; on those days there would be no school or other assigned charges to take them away from their sororal pleasures.[34]

It can be seen from this list of daily activities that Katharine Drexel was as concerned for her sisters' spiritual health as she was for their physical and emotional well-being. It was a strict regimen, but one with a purpose. Her sisters spent a minimum of two hours a day fostering their spiritual health. She had them flexing their souls as well as their muscles. Their food might have been nourishing but spare, but their superior ensured that their daily nourishment by the Eucharist was extended by the adoration of the Blessed Sacrament and that the supernatural would sustain them in their efforts. It

34. ASBS, vol. 7, pp. 54-55.

was a regimen that appeared to be successful. After one of her annual visits to St. Michael's, she wrote to her sisters there, "See Jesus and Mary in your Sisters when you speak to each of them or serve them. Love one another as Jesus has loved you. It pleased me much to see your cheerfulness at the recreation. Continue this holy cheerfulness. Let there be no 'Sister Vinegars' at St. Michael's."[35]

Immaculate Mother, Nashville, Tennessee

Thomas Byrne, the bishop of Nashville, had been in touch with Mother Katharine since 1900, when he asked her to open a mission and school for African Americans in his diocese. She was unable to meet his request at first, but wrote him a check for $2,667 to cover one-third the cost of building a church in Nashville for black Catholics. The bishop was persistent. He managed to see Mother Katharine in 1904 while she was visiting her missions in the West. His doctor had sent him to the desert for his health, and there he met Katharine and finally convinced her to open a school for African Americans in Nashville. He had observed that her sisters in Santa Fe were doing well in what he called "uphill Work," and was convinced they would succeed in his diocese.[36] It would be quite challenging to establish the school because of the objections of the politically powerful. Santa Fe had been an anthill compared to the mountain of objections and difficulties in Nashville.

In 1904, Katharine Drexel oversaw an order of 104 sisters eager to serve in the mission fields. She was no starry-eyed reformer but a realist, who nonetheless felt called to a very difficult apostolate. On the retreat she made before entering the convent in Pittsburgh, she made the following resolution:

Ask the Eternal Father what He wants of you. Vocation — all right. New Order — all right. Does God wish me to do anything better, or leave undone what I do?

Resolve: Generously with no half-hearted, timorous dread of the opinions of Church and men to *manifest my mission*. To speak only and when it pleases God; but to lose no opportunity of speaking before priests

---

35. Quoted in Baldwin, *St. Katharine Drexel*, p. 121, no date.
36. Quoted in Lynch, *Sharing the Bread*, 1:144.

and bearded men. Manifest yourself. You have no time to occupy your thoughts with that complacency or consideration of what others think. Your business is simply, "What will my Father in Heaven think?"[37]

The strength of her resolve would be tested in Nashville. Race relations there were such that the white population was adamantly opposed to a black school near them. Mother Katharine proposed to buy a large house in a white neighborhood and convert it into a school for black girls. She could survey the property only from an enclosed carriage, lest the identity of the prospective buyer and her intentions be made known. The property was bought for $25,000 through a lawyer, Thomas Tyne, who turned the deed over to the Sisters of the Blessed Sacrament. Two days after the purchase, on February 13, 1905, the local newspaper printed the name of the purchaser and the intended use of the property. The white citizens read that a grammar school and several years of high school were about to open in their neighborhood. There was an uproar when the facts became known, and a battle was played out in the press and in the courts.

The original owner tried to rescind the sale. Mother Katharine wrote to the banker who had owned the house, Samuel J. Keith, to try to mollify him. It is interesting that he had addressed his letter to her in care of Drexel & Company, rather than writing to her convent.

My dear Sir:

I am just in receipt of your letter of February 17, transmitted to me from Drexel & Company. I hasten to answer it, and to express my regret that you and your neighbors should feel as you do concerning the purchase of the property. I think there is some misapprehension on the part of you and your neighbors which I would like to remove. The Sisters of the Blessed Sacrament, who have purchased the property, are religious, of the same race as yourself. We will always endeavor in every way to be neighborly to any white neighbors in the vicinity; we have every reason to hope we may receive from our white neighbors the cordial courtesy for which the Southern people are so justly noted.

It is true we intend to open an industrial school and academy for Colored girls, but the girls who come there will only be day scholars. In coming to the academy and returning to their homes, I am confident they will be orderly and cause no annoyance.

37. May 1889.

I observed very carefully when in Nashville, that the property which we purchased was within very few blocks of numerous houses occupied by Colored families, and therefore, even were the property to be the residence of Colored teachers, which it is not, I think no just exception could be taken to the locality selected.

I can fully realize, I think, how you feel about your old revered home, around which so many attachments of the past — the sweet relations of home life — hover. I acknowledge I feel the same with regard to mine, and confess that some time ago, when passing it in the trolley cars, when I saw a bill of sale on it, a whole crowd of fond recollections of father, mother, sisters, etc., came vividly to my imagination. Then I more than ever realized how all things temporal pass away, and that there is but one home, strictly speaking, that eternal home where we all hope to meet our own, and where there will be no separation any more. And so temporal things, after all, are only to be valued, inasmuch as they bring us and many others — as many as possible — to the same eternal joy for which we were created.

With warmest trust that all misapprehensions be removed, believe me,

Very sincerely yours,
M. M. Katharine
(Drexel)[38]

Keith's apprehensions were not removed by her letter. He offered the bishop $2,500, to be given to any Catholic charity the bishop might choose, if he would prohibit the establishment of a school for African American children on his former property. The bishop demurred in support of Mother Katharine. Keith then published her personal letter to him as a paid advertisement in the *Banner of Nashville.* Mother Katharine was unhappy to see her private correspondence in a public newspaper.

When the men failed to dissuade Mother Katharine from her objective, the women in the neighborhood took up their collective pen. They wrote the following to her in a joint letter: "In conclusion, we beg to say that we highly appreciate and cordially commend your worthy enterprise among the Colored People. There are a number of localities in and around the city where Colored People live, and where no objection would be made to the location of your school. On the contrary, it would be welcomed as a distinct

38. Duffy, *Katharine Drexel*, pp. 257-58.

good and a social blessing."[39] For those women, any place but in their own neighborhood would have been acceptable. Having once been burned by having her personal letter published, Mother Katharine did not respond to the women and went on quietly establishing her school. She wrote, however, to her sisters:

> I cannot tell you how I regret that any letter of mine on the subject should appear in print. The very best is to let the whole affair die out — at least in the press if it won't die out before the Mayor and the City Council. If the Apostles were sent as sheep amongst the wolves, they were told, *therefore,* be as wise as serpents harmless as doves. To have this matter stirred up in the press is only to fan the flame. I have resolved not to answer another letter sent me by these parties, since they come out in the press. It seems but prudent to protect our cause by being very quiet, since there seems to be a certain prejudice which I hope will blow over by quietly minding our preservation of the good we have undertaken without aggressiveness. . . .
>
> It is encouraging to meet some opposition in *your* work. . . . It is appropriate for a Convent of the Blessed Sacrament — Christ dwelling within us — and the School of the Immaculate Mother, to have people of the city have no room for our precious Charge. They say, "There is another place on the City's outskirts," for our educational work. How truly was the Cave of Bethlehem *the* great educator of the World! This was indeed the School of the Immaculate Mother.[40]

Despite the opposition from some white citizens of Nashville, Immaculate Mother opened on September 5, 1905, with a mass celebrated in the school chapel by Bishop Byrne and attended by the sisters, their 54 pupils, and a few well-wishers. The newly opened school attracted attention from another group of protestors. Byrne had originally planned a school for Catholic students only. However, Katharine Drexel stressed to him that her mission was to Indians and colored people, regardless of their religion, and that if he wanted her to open a school for black children in his diocese, it would have to be a school open to those of all religions. Her stance was confirmed by a vote of the SBS Council. The invitation to black parents to enroll their children in Immaculate Mother looked like an attempt at sheep stealing to Protestant black ministers. Their anti-Catholic sentiment surfaced because

39. ASBS, vol. 8, p. 177, July 1905.
40. July 14, 1905, quoted in Duffy, *Katharine Drexel,* p. 259.

they did not want their members' children attending a Catholic school. Parents seemed undaunted by the opposition to the school and signed up their daughters in great numbers. The original building was outgrown by the end of the first year, and by the spring of 1907, a new building served 195 students. Active opposition to Immaculate Mother School disappeared.

Its only other serious trial was an outbreak of typhoid in 1908 that killed one of the sisters. What it could not survive — and none can lament it — was the integration of public schools in 1954, when Immaculate Mother closed and the students were transferred to the Cathedral School and Fr. Ryan High School.

The opposition to the establishment of Immaculate Mother was a very civilized affair compared to that encountered in other places. Perhaps the most frightening demonstration of resistance occurred in Beaumont, Texas, for the Ku Klux Klan was very active in that part of Texas. In 1917, the Sisters of the Blessed Sacrament, at the invitation of the bishop, established a mission school for African American children and built a small parish church in Beaumont. In the early 1920s, race relations in large northern cities, throughout the South, and especially in southern Texas deteriorated greatly. There was money to be made in the new Texas oil fields, but white laborers predominated and would not allow African Americans any jobs, except the lowest-paying ones. Blacks who had served in racially segregated units in the armed forces during World War I had experienced social freedom and equality in Britain and Europe. They were beginning to demand the same at home. In Beaumont, the Ku Klux Klan openly suppressed African Americans. Many of the city's prominent judges and politicians belonged to the Klan. The sisters complained to their mother general, "No civic protection can be hoped for, because all the officials here belong to the infamous party."[41] In March 1922, the Klan posted a sign outside the church that served the mission school and convent that read, "We want an end of services here. We will not stand by while white priests consort with nigger wenches in the faces of our families. Suppress it in one week or flogging and tar and feathers will follow." The next sign read, "If people continue to come to this church, we will dynamite it." The Klan had already tarred and feathered one of the parishioners and run his family out of town. The Klan also tarred and feathered a "sympathizing" judge and held a Klan march through town. The situation looked desperate for the church. Katharine Drexel offered body-guards for the priests (the sisters had not been threatened with harm) and

41. Mother Mary of the Visitation to MKD, March 21, 1922.

also guards for the property. The sisters' protection was unceasing prayer. On March 25, a severe rainstorm with thunder and lightning spawned a tornado that picked up and destroyed two buildings that were known Klan headquarters. The Beaumont Klan never threatened the church or mission again, but its original intent had been far more dangerous than what had happened earlier in Nashville.

The same subterfuge of having to buy property through third parties due to racism and anti-Catholic bigotry, as in Nashville, would be carried out time and again by the Sisters of the Blessed Sacrament, most notably in the establishment of Xavier University in New Orleans.

In the intervening ten years between Immaculate Mother and the expansion of the sisters into southern Louisiana, the order grew by about fifty new sisters. It was a slow but steady increase that allowed the sisters to open twelve new missions, only one of which was in the West. While, in general, the sisters were occupied in their schools and missions, their founder had to take care of practical matters pertaining to the establishment of a new order. For instance, in their early years, the SBS operated under the Mercy Rule. The SBS Rule received its initial approval from the Vatican in 1907. Mother Katharine followed the advice she received from Mother St. Frances Xavier Cabrini: "If you want to get your Rule approved, you go yourself to Rome and take it with you." She went to Rome and helped the rule through its translation into Latin and acceptance, first, by the Sacred Congregation for the Propaganda of the Faith and, then, by Pope Pius X. In 1911, Archbishop Ryan, who had been Katharine's firm supporter for twenty years, died. While she continued to have friends and supporters in the hierarchy, none was ever again as important to her. Her rule reached the end of its five-year testing period in 1912.

That year the order ventured into Harlem in New York City, where Mother Katharine contracted typhoid fever after she cleaned and helped renovate two old buildings for a school and convent. When she developed the full symptoms of the disease, she was in the West, making her annual visits to the missions there. She did not want to alarm her sisters, so merely wrote that they should pray hard for a special intention for her. She finally became so ill with the typhoid and pneumonia that her brother-in-law, Colonel Morrell, went west to bring her back to Philadelphia. At Christmas she wrote to her sisters, "Of all the Christmasses in the past, this is the Christmas in which it behooves me to thank you for the efficacy of your prayers *through Our Lord in the Blessed Sacrament.* Your prayers have made me well, thank God. . . ."[42]

42. MKD to SBS, December 25, 1912.

By the next spring, she was fully recovered and able to travel to Rome to make final adjustments in the rule and to get it approved. On her ship was a bishop, Joseph Schrembs of Cleveland, eighteen of his priests, and seventy laypeople, all making a pilgrimage to Rome. The non-Catholics on the ship, *Invernia,* must have felt like they had gotten on the wrong boat. There were several masses daily, benedictions, and processions of the Blessed Sacrament twice a day, and the Sacrament was exposed for adoration all day long. Mother Katharine was delighted. Mother Mercedes, her traveling companion, noticed that her superior spent two hours each day kneeling in adoration before the Blessed Sacrament. While in Rome, it turned out that her cousin, Lucy Drexel Dahlgren, and her daughter, resided in a suite at the Barberini Palace, where they offered rooms to the two sisters. Dahlgren tempted Mother Katharine with the money she would save by staying with her. However, the spirit of poverty overtook Mother Katharine, who worried, "What about precedence? Will any of my Sisters feel they should partake of the hospitality of their friends because my example in Rome would lead them to infer that I approved such a step?"[43] Another offer of hospitality, which she accepted, came from some American Franciscan sisters who had a convent in Rome. A convent was much more to her liking than a Renaissance palace. The rule achieved its final approval on May 15, 1913.

Their business concluded, the sisters returned home by way of Germany and Ireland, where they sought vocations for the order. This sweep through Germany and Ireland garnered them four vocations. Eventually over one hundred young women would find their way to the Sisters of the Blessed Sacrament from Ireland. Many who came had not sufficient education to enter directly into the order, so a junior novitiate high school was opened at the motherhouse to accommodate their needs and those of other girls who thought they might have a vocation. Blessed Sacrament High School operated from 1931 to 1952 and was an important element in providing sisters for the Native American and African American missions and schools. Nearly one hundred sisters of the order began their vocations at Blessed Sacrament High School.

Xavier University, New Orleans, Louisiana

The founding of Xavier University in New Orleans provides a good opportunity to study the order's growing influence on Catholic education for Native

43. ASBS, vol. 9, p. 114, May 1913.

American and African American children and youth. Mother Katharine had purposely stayed away from forming schools and missions in or around New Orleans because the city was the home of an African American order, the Sisters of the Holy Family, even though the bishop of New Orleans had approached her time and again about the great need of his black Catholics. She responded with funds to support the building and maintenance of schools and teaching salaries for the Sisters of the Holy Family and other sisters and priests who taught African Americans in New Orleans and across southern Louisiana. The following is a typical letter from Archbishop Francis Janssens: "There is nothing in my administration of the diocese that worries me more than our Colored People. I cannot find the means to counteract those who try to capture them. In other dioceses they may look out for conversions of Colored People and I have to look out for perversions. I often feel discouraged. With your kindness to our diocese in the way of pecuniary help, please add the prayers of the community for me."[44] When a hurricane drowned two thousand of his people and damaged or destroyed six churches and a convent, he turned quite naturally to Mother Katharine for aid: "I am downcast and feel sick at heart. But the name of the Lord is blessed. You and the Sisters must pray a little more for me."[45] Later in the same year, he was pressured by both whites and blacks over the issue of creating separate churches for black Catholics to attend.

> Our white Catholics are unwilling to help the Negro for Church and school purposes; and many influential Negroes, especially Mulattos, are opposed to special Colored churches, not because they go to church themselves, but because they imagine the different churches will tend to a greater social separation. I tell them they keep all the privileges they have and that they can continue to go to the white churches, but they do not want to understand it. A separate congregation is a trial, and I think here, where we have two-thirds of all the Colored Catholics in the United States, this ought to be given a fair trial. If we succeed, we will have far less difficulty with the following; and if we, after giving it a fair trial, fail, we will simply give it up for the future; and console ourselves with the thought that we tried, did our best and could do no better. If these reasons seem good to you, please lay them before Archbishop Ryan, saving me the trouble of writing the same thing twice. I hope I do not bother

44. Janssens to MKD, August 8, 1893.
45. Janssens to MKD, October 7, 1893.

you too much; you know I do it because I want to do my duty toward the Colored people.[46]

His was not the only diocese where black Catholics were requesting churches of their own. The usual practice in American Catholic churches called for racially mixed parishes, with certain pews reserved for African Americans. At the end of the nineteenth century, African Americans in larger cities were asking their bishops to establish parishes especially for them. Some bishops resisted the idea of separate parishes, but Bishop Janssens thought it was a reasonable request and sought to accommodate his black Catholics. He opened black parishes, as did the bishops in Cincinnati, Boston, and other dioceses. It was a measure that made sense given the social relations of the races at the time. Separate but equal facilities for the races would become, unfortunately, the law of the land with the 1896 Supreme Court decision on the Louisiana case *Plessy v. Ferguson*. While they may have been separate, the reality is that facilities for African Americans were never equal to those for whites. Educational standards for white students were appallingly low in the old Confederacy; they were abominable for blacks. In 1900, in one Louisiana parish (county) school district, white children reportedly went to school from four to eight months a year while black children went from three to six months.[47] In spite of this fact, Archbishop Janssens was sincerely trying everything he could to help the African Americans in New Orleans, and Mother Katharine was his natural friend and ally.

The Sisters of the Blessed Sacrament did not go into southern Louisiana for twenty-two years, but at last Janssens's successor, Archbishop James H. Blenk, had the perfect lure to entice them there. He pointed out that what was needed most in southern Louisiana was a normal school, or teachers' college, where young black men and women could study to become teachers. Because of the high level of education that Katharine Drexel insisted her sisters attain, a normal school, or college, was one thing the SBS could achieve that the Sisters of the Holy Family could not.

Mother Katharine gave her sisters rigorous training, both spiritual and practical, before they were allowed to leave the motherhouse to work in SBS schools and missions. In addition to their spiritual routine and basic housekeeping duties of their regular workday, sisters were also taught the basics of sewing, shoe making and shoe repair, housecleaning, gardening, food

46. Janssens to MKD, November 11, 1893.
47. Duffy, *Katharine Drexel*, p. 319.

preservation, and first aid. Other sisters had more intensive vocational training at the Drexel Institute, founded by Katharine's uncle, Anthony Drexel. Those destined for the classroom received professional teacher training at a time when such training was relatively new. Mother Katharine engaged Katherine T. Meagher, a graduate of the Normal College in Bridgewater, Massachusetts, to come to the motherhouse to teach the sisters. Meagher taught them psychology, Church history, plane geometry, and methods of teaching; she also supervised their practice teaching in the classroom.

In the early years of the twentieth century, it was unusual for women to have college degrees, and even most teachers, especially in rural areas, did not have one. The Catholic University of America in Washington, D.C., to which the Drexel sisters had donated $50,000 in honor of their father, opened the Sisters' College in 1911 to provide a higher education to sisters in religious congregations during the summer months. Katharine attended the college in the summers of 1911, 1917, 1918, and 1920. Naturally, she also sent her sisters. In 1921, thirty-six of her sisters attended the institution. Catholic University also set up an extension at what would become Xavier University in Louisiana to help nuns attain degrees and certificates needed to be effective teachers at any level between first grade and college. Villanova University, another Catholic university, also created an extension at the SBS motherhouse in Pennsylvania to prepare the novices for service in the order's schools and missions. In practical virtues as well as in spiritual ones, Katharine always led by example. For someone who had never once set foot in a real schoolroom as a young girl, she led the way by becoming a student in summer school at the Catholic University of America at the age of sixty-two. Even today, sixty-two is a little superannuated for a university student, and it was all but unheard of in Katharine's day. When the call came to found a college for black students in New Orleans, both she and her sisters were ready. Not only were they well educated, but, between the foundation of Immaculate Mother in 1905 and the opening of what would become Xavier University in 1917, they had also become experienced at creating new institutions, having opened and staffed thirteen other missions and schools in such places as Chicago, New York City, Washington, D.C., St. Louis, Macon, Cincinnati, and Montgomery.

Three Protestant colleges in New Orleans had been established for blacks after the Civil War: New Orleans University, originally the Methodist Episcopal Union Normal for Negroes; Straight University, sponsored by the American Missionary Association; and the Baptist Leland University. As was the custom in those days, all students, including Catholics, were required to attend the Protestant religious services of the colleges. "Straight University in New Orleans boasts in its catalogue of drawing Catholics from their faith. . . . Of course, young Catholics, boys and girls, go there from want of similar Catholic institutions."[48] There was, additionally, a state-supported land-grant university for black students, Southern University. As the area surrounding Southern University became populated with white middle-class citizens, pressure was put on the state to move the school to a distant location, which it did in 1913.

Consequently, the vacated campus and buildings of Southern University were put up for sale in 1915. Katharine was approached by a number of priests and laymen and, ultimately, Archbishop Blenk of New Orleans about acquiring the property and establishing a Catholic college for African American students. She made the purchase through Henry McInery, an influential businessman, who bought the property at a public auction for $18,000. When the real purchaser became known, a motion was brought before the New Orleans city council to ban the establishment of a "convent or a school for Negro educational purposes" on the grounds of old Southern University, but it failed.[49] The SBS voted a total of $23,000 to purchase Southern University and refurbish the buildings. The university auditorium was to serve as a temporary church for the newly established Blessed Sacrament parish. The SBS voted an additional $12,000 to build the parish church and school, which would be staffed by the Josephite Fathers. The Josephites, of the Society of Saint Joseph, the American branch of the Mill Hill Franciscan Fathers, were dedicated to the service of African Americans and worked closely in Louisiana and elsewhere in the country with Katharine Drexel to further their common mission.[50] St. Francis Xavier School served almost five hundred students in its first year in grades seven through twelve. The high school was called Xavier Preparatory School, and its first graduating class in 1916 consisted of twenty-six students. In 1918, the governor of Louisiana signed a bill that allowed Xavier University to award college degrees. The new university grew quickly, and by 1927 had four separate departments, the teachers' college, college of arts and sciences, premedicine, and the college of pharmacy.

48. Letter from Pierre O. Lebeau, SSJ, to MKD, September 15, 1906, quoted in Lynch, *Sharing the Bread,* 1:219.

49. Lynch, *Sharing the Bread,* 1:413 n. 67.

50. Louise Drexel Morrell and her husband Edward funded the building of Epiphany College in Baltimore for the Josephite Fathers, where priests could be educated who would then serve in their missions and schools for African Americans.

At a time when official Church teaching prescribed separate sex institutions for men and women, Xavier University was coeducational. When Pope Pius XI issued his 1929 encyclical, *The Christian Education of Youth,* which expressly disapproved of coeducational institutions for college students, Mother Katharine was concerned enough to turn to the papal legate, Archbishop Pietro Fumasoni-Biondi, for guidance. She was reassured that due to the peculiar circumstance of there being no other higher education available to black students and the need to encourage Catholic marriage among black youths she need not worry about Xavier's coeducation. While Xavier was indeed a Catholic coeducational university, it was never exclusively Catholic. Students of all faiths, or no faith, were accepted to Xavier. By 1933, it boasted 396 students and a faculty of two Josephite Fathers, twelve Sisters of the Blessed Sacrament, and twenty-one laymen and laywomen.

Mother Agatha Ryan, SBS, the institution's first president, was clear about the mission of Xavier University. The goals of which she writes are, not surprisingly, both this-worldly and otherworldly.

> The education of little ones is important, as important as the foundation of any structure of beauty, but the philosophical training of youth is most important if permanent covering and protection are to be given those foundations. The missionary must not only convert souls, but he must raise up among the people for whom he labors, leaders of their own flesh and blood who can guide and direct their own in a way that even the missionary is powerless to do. . . . The Sisters firmly believe that from the growing student body would come undoubtedly the race leaders who will do much to mold the opinions of Colored America.
>
> It is the missioner's hope that these young men and women[,] deeply imbued themselves with the life giving principles of the Faith of God[,] will strengthen the faith in others and, as lay apostles in their respective fields and professions, carry on the glorious work of extending the kingdom of Christ in the souls of Colored men and women.[51]

The influence of Katharine Drexel and the Sisters of the Blessed Sacrament through Xavier University cannot be overstated. In 1987, 40 percent of the New Orleans public school teachers were Xavier graduates. Moreover, in New Orleans public schools alone, "four out of six high school principals, seven out of eight junior high school principals and thirty out of forty-two

51. Lynch, *Sharing the Bread,* 1:226.

elementary principals" were Xavier graduates.[52] The impact of the university was immediately felt in the black communities in New Orleans and southern Louisiana. Today there are approximately four thousand students at Xavier, and the university is run by an independent board of directors. Many Sisters of the Blessed Sacrament serve on the board and on the faculty.

Archbishop Blenk had in mind at least six new parochial schools for African American children when he invited Mother Katharine to settle her sisters in New Orleans, and she quickly fell in with the bishop's plans. After the purchase of the grounds of Southern University, Mother Katharine wrote to the SBS at the motherhouse in Pennsylvania: "O Sisters! This is a grand field. It is teeming with souls, and all should be Catholic. . . . We could easily use fifty Sisters right here in New Orleans."[53] The order boasted approximately 150 sisters when she wrote that statement.

Essential to the establishment of the new parishes for black Catholics was the establishment of parish schools to educate their children. From their convent at Xavier University, the sisters fanned out across the city to staff the schools at the new black parishes of "Holy Ghost (1916), St. Louis School (1917), Blessed Sacrament (1918), Corpus Christi (1919), St. Peter Claver (1921), and St. Monica (1924). Sisters from the St. Francis Xavier Convent taught catechism in the various parishes as they were established. When it was possible to start a school, the SBS faculty remained at the [Xavier] Prep[aratory] convent until a convent was built in the new parish, something which often took years."[54] Not only did the SBS staff the schools, but also Drexel money built the churches and the schools and helped pay the salaries of lay teachers.

Of the six parish schools established and maintained by the sisters, all but one lasted until the latter half of the twentieth century. The order was unable to provide sufficient sisters to maintain all its schools, so in 1933 it withdrew from St. Louis School and turned it over to Holy Ghost sisters. The largest of the New Orleans schools was Corpus Christi. In 1939-1940, 1,133 students were taught by twenty teachers, for a student-teacher ratio of 60 to 1. In 1942 the sisters gave religious instructions to an additional 1,250 public-school children, who attended Corpus Christi in the late afternoon one day a week.[55] This was an unusually large school for the SBS. By 1973,

52. Duffy, *Katharine Drexel*, p. 330.
53. Quoted in Lynch, *Sharing the Bread*, 1:226.
54. Lynch, *Sharing the Bread*, 1:227.
55. Lynch, *Sharing the Bread*, 1:234.

declining vocations forced the SBS to withdraw from the Corpus Christi school and the school in the Blessed Sacrament parish. Holy Ghost school lost its sisters in 1989, and St. Peter Claver lost them in 1991.

St. Monica, which began as a mission from Holy Ghost parish, was able to hold on to its SBS faculty for a few years longer, into the 1990s. At St. Monica, which was in a very poor neighborhood, the sisters organized a social service apostolate in 1978 and ran it out of the rectory garage. The social service center eventually served approximately seventy families on a monthly basis, and regularly provided food boxes for ninety senior citizens. The center kept in daily telephone contact with over two hundred people, and it provided emergency services to those without food or shelter. This type of outreach was typical of the Sisters of the Blessed Sacrament, while at the same time they maintained their educational emphasis. In some ways, the success of the SBS was also the cause of its decline in New Orleans. The pattern was for Katharine Drexel's order to build and staff parishes and schools and then to turn them over to other orders of sisters or to lay faculty, while the SBS moved on to establish other schools in new or developing parishes somewhere else. From New Orleans, Katharine moved her sisters into rural southern Louisiana, where she established more than twenty schools. In most cases, she would provide two sisters to open the school and hire Xavier graduates as lay teachers. It was an ingenious system that provided employment for Xavier graduates and brought educational opportunities to rural blacks, where few or none had existed before. One of the rural black parish schools established by the SBS was St. Edward's. In 1968, a writer in the St. Edward's jubilee book noted of Mother Katharine, "No one will ever know the influence this one woman has had on the development — intellectual, spiritual, and otherwise — of the Colored People in Southwest Louisiana."[56]

As an order, the sisters were able to do so much for Native Americans and African Americans because of Katharine Drexel's large income, but her funds were seriously compromised with the introduction of a federal income tax in 1913. She paid an average of $10,000 a year in federal taxes until 1917, when a graduated income tax schedule was established that placed her income in the highest bracket. In 1918, she owed over $77,000 in federal taxes, while in 1921, approximately 50 percent of her income went to taxes. From 1917 to 1924, she paid almost $800,000 in taxes, while distributing $1.5 million to the missions and schools. Her brother-in-law, Walter Smith,

---

56. Quoted in Lynch, *Sharing the Bread,* 1:273.

convinced her to seek a tax exemption. As part of the petition to Congress, she pointed out that in the Sisters of the Blessed Sacrament "fewer than fifteen percent of the houses [convents] were self-supporting. The congregation was . . . relieving the public of over 15,000 dependents annually . . . employed '211 salaried lay teachers and 89 salaried lay service people, . . . erected buildings worth $2.5 million. . . . The Sisters contributed $54,000 annually to the support of Indian and Colored children in schools outside our own.' "[57] With the help of Senator George Pepper of Pennsylvania, Congress passed an amendment to the Internal Revenue Code that exempted from taxation income expended "for religious, charitable, scientific, literary, and educational purposes . . . if in the taxable year and in each of the ten preceding taxable years the amount . . . exceeded ninety percent of the taxpayer's net income for each year."[58] At the time, Katharine Drexel was the only person in the United States to benefit from the amendment. The newspapers labeled it the "Millionaire Nun Exemption." Katharine tried through the courts and Congress to make the exemption retroactive to the establishment of the tax code so as to gain a refund of the taxes she had previously paid. She lost in the courts, and in 1933 Congress nearly removed her exemption altogether. No tax refund would be forthcoming. It was a battle she could not win. To make matters worse for the Sisters of the Blessed Sacrament, Mother Katharine's income diminished by about 35 percent during the Great Depression.[59]

Social Justice/Social Action in the 1930s

Katharine Drexel put her name, resources, and the prestige of the SBS behind the growing movement to grant social justice to African Americans. In 1934, she joined the American Scottsboro Committee for the legal defense of the "Scottsboro Boys," nine black men between the ages of thirteen and nineteen who were tried and convicted of raping two white women. Eight of the men were condemned to death for the crime. Because they had been denied legal counsel, they were granted a second trial, where another all-white jury found them guilty, even though one of the alleged victims repudiated her previous testimony and denied the charge. Mother Drexel wrote to the president of the United States about the case and urged her sisters to write as well.

57. Lynch, *Sharing the Bread*, 1:275. No further reference given.
58. Pepper to MKD, December 28, 1924.
59. Lynch, *Sharing the Bread*, 1:275.

They also supported the National American Association of Colored People (NAACP) and were active in its antilynching campaign. In addition to aiding the NAACP financially, she and her sisters wrote letters to the president and to congressmen in all the districts where they had missions. Walter White, the first executive secretary of the NAACP, wrote this about Katharine Drexel and Catholic support for the organization:

> With the main body of Catholic opinion behind our efforts, along with assistance already given by other groups, our [antilynching] contest would be brief and successful. I am happy to tell you of the considerable aid given by Mother Katherine Drexel and her sister, Mrs. Louise Morrell, in this issue. They have also rendered valuable assistance in the work of Negro education and in the relief of Negroes in the area of the levee control project on the Mississippi. Mother Katherine's flaming spirit is a great inspiration to all of us who are working for the welfare of the Negro group in America.[60]

White visited Mother Katharine at the motherhouse to solicit her advice, help, and, of course, funding for the NAACP campaign for the black workers engaged in the Mississippi River Flood Project. Workers were building levees along the Mississippi, which had flooded its banks in 1927 and caused great destruction. The Army Corps of Engineers designed a system of levees to control future floods. Contract workers were housed and fed by local people in conditions that, according to Lynch, approached slavery. There were "70-100 hour work weeks, and various charges against wages that left the men ten cents an hour, an amount that was often kept from them."[61] Because of pressure from the NAACP, the Sisters of the Blessed Sacrament, and many others, conditions improved. "You and Mrs. Morrell through your generous contribution for this fight have given hope and opportunity to some 35,000 Negroes employed on this project. On their behalf and ours may I once again express our deep gratitude." He went on to regret that she would not "let the public at large know to whom we are indebted for the great accomplishment in getting decent working conditions and adequate wages for 35,000 workers."[62]

60. Quoted in Amy MacKenzie, "Walter White on Lynching," *Interracial Review,* September 1946, online.
61. Lynch, *Sharing the Bread,* 1:278.
62. White to MKD, May 20, 1937.

Unique for the sisters was their mission in Boston, because it was not centered on a school. Rather, it was a mission of social outreach to the local black community. Begun in 1914, it grew rapidly. The sisters there made more than 13,000 home visitations in 1924, in addition to their catechism classes for children and adults and preparation for the sacraments. By 1935, the order had built a large mission center in the Roxbury district of Boston. They averaged seventy-five to eighty conversions a year to the Catholic faith. They visited prisons, and during World War II they gave catechism classes to black conscientious objectors at the Miles Standish labor camp in Carver, Massachusetts.[63] In Boston, the SBS played the role of social workers who were also, and mainly, interested in the spiritual welfare of their clients.

In a social outreach of a different type, Mother Katharine and her sisters helped Father Sylvester Eisenman found the Oblate Sisters of the Blessed Sacrament, an order of Native American sisters, in 1935. The Oblates opened a mission outside of Marty, South Dakota. The SBS had staffed the mission at Marty after its inception in 1922, and the SBS encouraged and financially supported the new Indian order of sisters, supplying its first mistress of novices. The Oblates named themselves after the Sisters of the Blessed Sacrament in honor and appreciation of Katharine Drexel. The founding of this order of nuns confirmed Mother Katharine's belief in education as a means of uplifting not merely individuals, but whole peoples.

The Retirement of Mother Katharine

Larger classes of postulants joined the SBS in the 1930s than in any other decade. There were 134 newly professed sisters from 1931 to 1940. The country endured the worst of the Great Depression during this period, and the order served in an increasing number of important missions, so it is not surprising that young women would seek the security of convent life that also offered them interesting and significant work in evangelization and social justice.

The decade also saw the retirement of Katharine Drexel. In 1937, after forty-six years of actively leading her sisters in missions throughout the United States, the seventy-eight-year-old Mother Katharine retired from the active leadership of the congregation. When she suffered from typhoid and pneumonia, the doctor also detected some heart irregularity in the

---

63. Lynch, *Sharing the Bread*, 1:339-43.

founder. In 1920, she spent six weeks in the infirmary recovering from angina. In 1923, Mother Mary Agatha, SBS, wrote to Bishop Jules B. Jeanmard of Lafayette, Louisiana, that Mother Katharine "simply and utterly ignores herself. . . . She refuses [her body] the rest and nourishment which everyone but herself deems necessary."[64] Mother Katharine, however, considered herself "fine, fat, [and] splendid" and hoped that her sisters were "3/4 or 100% as well."[65] In fact, she was not well. She suffered two heart attacks in 1935 and a third in 1936. Her physicians warned her that to preserve her life, she must turn over the reins. She told her doctor, "Nobody is necessary for God's work. God can do the work without any of His Creatures." Her doctor replied, "Certainly, Mother, I agree with you, but ordinarily He does not."[66] Once the dictum was given and accepted, she cheerfully retired into the contemplative life she had originally desired. She briefly led the order during the period between the death of her immediate successor, Mother Mercedes, and the election of the third superior general, Mother Mary of the Visitation, in 1940. Her last communal act as the founder of her order was to lead the prayers for the congregation on September 27, 1940, when the sister in charge lost her place.

In 1941 the order celebrated its fiftieth birthday. "The little band of 13 which had left the Mercy Convent in 1891 had now swelled to over 500. Sisters of the Blessed Sacrament were serving in 25 dioceses, 49 elementary schools, 13 high schools, and Xavier University."[67] There was a large, public golden jubilee celebration that lasted for three days in April, but the order celebrated quietly on February 12, the actual date of Mother Katharine's profession. She addressed her spiritual daughters on that day.

> I just want to say this to the Sisters. I want to say that I thank God I am a child of the Church. I thank God it was my privilege to meet many of the great missionaries of the Church and to have had the prayers of those great missionaries like Monsignor Stephan and Bishop Marty. We have been reading about them in the refectory. . . . I saw them in their agony, those great souls! I thank God He gave me the grace to see their lives. They are a part of the Church of God, and I thank God like the great St. Theresa that I, too, am a child of the Church.

64. Mother Mary Agatha to Jeanmard, May 2, 1927.
65. MKD to motherhouse, October 7, 1930.
66. ASBS, vol. 29, p. 141, 1936.
67. Lou Baldwin, *A Call to Sanctity: The Formation and Life of Mother Katharine Drexel* (Philadelphia: Catholic Standard and Times, 1987), p. 80.

Scores of priests and bishops either attended the larger celebration or sent their best wishes. Cardinal Denis Dougherty wrote about Mother Katharine in his foreword to the jubilee booklet:

> If she had done nothing else than set such an example to a frivolous, self-seeking world, she should be regarded as a benefactress to the human race. . . . She had won it all without the blare of trumpets; her picture never appears on the front page of our papers; her name is not to be found in the lists of great women . . . for the world knows only its own. . . . Whilst others persecute and revile Indians and Negroes as if they are mere hewers of wood and drawers of water, rather than God's children for whom our Savior's Blood was shed, she, a refined lady of culture, takes them into her heart and makes their cause her own.[68]

Mother Katharine took an active interest in her sisters and their missions as long as she was physically able. She continued to write and to see occasional visitors throughout World War II. One item that caught her attention during the war was a safe the sisters had constructed to protect the consecrated hosts of the Blessed Sacrament, lest Jesus be injured in an air raid on the American homeland.[69] The presence of Christ in the Eucharist was real to Katharine. Because of her devotion to Jesus in the Blessed Sacrament, she prayed for everyone in the war. Her nocturnal adoration for June 29, 1944, even included Hitler:

> The altar of the Sacred Heart is in this room where my Jesus, both priest and victim, offers Himself up six times each week and is as really offered as upon the Cross on Calvary. There on the Cross, He looks out over all the world and sees only souls to save. I have the immense privilege of having the priest offer it up for all our valiant soldiers, their salvation, their chaplains, and for all those who die now by being bombed, for all the Germans, even for Hitler, even for myself. Father, forgive them.[70]

In 1946, Mother Katharine wrote what would be her last Christmas letter to her sisters. She commented on the deaths of three of the older sisters

---

68. Denis Dougherty, foreword to the *Golden Jubilee Booklet, 1891-1941,* by the Sisters of the Blessed Sacrament (Cornwells Heights, Pa.: Sisters of the Blessed Sacrament, 1941), p. 3.

69. Lynch, *Sharing the Bread,* 2:387.

70. Duffy, *Katharine Drexel,* p. 371.

and the need for the younger sisters to come to the fore "to continue the work of those who have gone on before them." She exhorted them: "Lean on your Guardian Angels, for God has given them charge of you 'to guide you in all your ways.' "[71] "Holy Angels!" is what she would say when she was particularly pleased or even vexed. Until her death, she worried about the children of the missions. In 1935, she wrote to her sisters about their care. "Keep the children happy. If they love the school and all the Sisters, you will have done much towards winning them to the Church. Keep the children happy. God wants it."[72] As she lay dying twenty years later, it was still the children she was thinking about. Looking vacantly about, she asked the sister who was sitting with her during the night, "Did you see them? The children. Oh all the children were there, all going past, so many of them. And the Pope was there too in all his regalia, and so many children."[73] The founder of the Sisters of the Blessed Sacrament died on March 3, 1955.

By the Numbers: Peak and Decline

The Sisters of the Blessed Sacrament, despite the enthusiasm and obvious strength of their founder and the value of their apostolate, did not share in the impressive growth of other orders of nuns in the United States in the 1940s and 1950s.[74] The order finally opened its novitiate doors to African American applicants, perhaps in response to the low numbers of new postulants. The first two African American women to enter the novitiate were graduates of Xavier University. They joined in 1950 and were followed over the years by no fewer than twenty black women. Mother Mary of the Visitation was the SBS superior general at the time the first black sisters entered. She had been with Mother Katharine many years earlier in New Orleans when the superior general of the Holy Family Sisters asked Mother Katharine not to accept black applicants into the SBS because she "believed it would hurt the Negro congregations."[75] More than fifty years later, such promises could no longer be kept. The first black member of the order,

---

71. Baldwin, *St. Katharine Drexel,* p. 190.

72. ASBS, vol. 38, p. 138.

73. The sister was Consuela Marie Duffy, who recorded it in her biography, *Katharine Drexel,* p. 376.

74. See chart on p. 142 for a decade-by-decade count of the Sisters of the Blessed Sacrament in relation to the total number of American sisters.

75. Lynch, *Sharing the Bread,* 2:7.

Sr. Juliana Haynes, made her first vows the year the founder died and was the president of the SBS at the time of Katharine's beatification. In an interview, she said she really had not known who Katharine was and that it was the order's devotion to the Blessed Sacrament that first attracted her to the SBS. "And then, when I heard the work of the congregation, that is when I knew it was for me."[76] It was not until the founder died that she realized her importance.

At the time of Mother Katharine's death, there were 501 SBS, including Sr. Juliana, in 51 convents. They staffed 49 elementary schools, 12 high schools, 1 university, 3 houses of social service, and 1 study house. Additionally, they staffed 37 missions in 20 states and the District of Columbia.[77]

With the passing of Katharine, the Sisters of the Blessed Sacrament no longer had the income from the Drexel estate to fund their activities. The income for 1955 had been $410,000. Adjustments would have to be made, even though Archbishop John F. O'Hara of Philadelphia arranged with the beneficiaries of Francis Drexel's will and the diocese to help fund the SBS for the next ten years. In 1965, all diocesan financial support of Katharine Drexel's order ceased.

Perhaps one of the most controversial decisions the founder ever made was not to secure her order financially through an endowment and not to challenge the stipulations of her father's will. Early on she had decided not to endow the order while she was still receiving an income from the Drexel estate. She took seriously her vow of poverty, and she fully believed in divine Providence to sustain her apostolate; if it be the will of God, her order would endure. Furthermore, she feared that the larger Catholic Church would relinquish any responsibility for the blacks and Native Americans if it was perceived that she was fully supporting the missions herself. The decision not to challenge her father's will had a similar logic. Her father's will stipulated that should all his daughters die without issue, his estate would be distributed to the original twenty-nine specified beneficiaries. Naturally, he had no knowledge of the course of his second daughter's life. Had he known that she would found an order of nuns, it is reasonable to assume that he would have wanted her order to receive at least that portion of his estate that had been hers. It is also reasonable to assume that a competent estate attorney could have convinced a judge to set aside her father's will so the SBS could inherit his estate after her death. Her decision not to challenge the will is not

76. Baldwin, *A Call to Sanctity*, p. 95.
77. Duffy, *Katharine Drexel*, pp. 271-72.

detailed in the archives. The chapter meeting when it was discussed, immediately after Katharine retired, was considered confidential, and its debates and proceedings went unrecorded. Her decision was a complex one that hinged on her always obedient stance toward her father and his wishes, her understanding of the importance of communal poverty for the congregation, and, again, her utter dependence on the providence of God. She wrote to her sisters, "You will have no peace of soul until you arrive at total abandonment of self and all things into the Hands of God."[78]

The apostolate of the SBS continues today with the fees and tuitions the order charges for their schools, retreats, and conferences; donations; professional fund-raising since 1967; a small endowment set up by Louise Drexel Morrell for the order; funds from the United States Conference of Catholic Bishops' Committee on Home Missions; the sale of properties, particularly of St. Michel, the old Drexel summer home in Torresdale that had been the first convent and novitiate for the sisters; and, since 1966, Social Security payments for sisters over sixty-five years of age.

Between 1964, when there were 551 sisters, and 1991, when there were only 328 professed sisters, the order still managed to open forty-one new convents and missions or schools. Many older convents and schools closed during this period, and not even all the forty-one new undertakings survived the period. The number is partially explained by the fact that after the Second Vatican Council, the General Council of the SBS allowed for individual apostolates. Sisters, individually or in very small groups, would open missions in urban areas to serve the poor African Americans there. These individual apostolates are counted in the order's records as SBS missions. The declining number of sisters in the order and the ever diminishing number of missions must have created a circular problem for the order. Less money and fewer sisters meant fewer missions. Fewer missions meant fewer opportunities for the sisters.

The number of vocations fell off not only for the SBS but also for all orders following Vatican II. From 1966, when the total number of women religious in the United States reached its height of 181,421, until 1990, when there were 103,269 women religious in the country, a decline of 44 percent, the SBS suffered a decline of 40 percent.[79] By comparison, according to the

78. MKD, *Conferences, Counsels, and Maxims of a Missionary Foundress,* p. 44, in the archives of the motherhouse, 1935.

79. Thomas C. Reeves, *Twentieth Century America: A Brief History* (New York: Oxford University Press, 2000), p. 158; Roger Finke and Rodney Stark, *The Churching of America,*

figures supplied by George Stewart in *Marvels of Charity,* from 1965 to 1990 the Franciscan sisters lost 48 percent, the Benedictines 44 percent, and the Dominicans 49 percent.

The Rise and Fall of the Number of Sisters in the United States			
By Date Ending In	Total U.S. Sisters[a]	New SBS	Total Professed SBS[b]
1900	46,583	67	64
1910	61,944	52	108
1920	90,558	108	207
1930	134,339	96	284
1940	164,273	134	379
1950	179,657	104	456
1960	184,353	61	476
1965	209,000		551
1970	194,941	41	446
1980	141,115	12	390
1990	111,481	10	328
2000	78,094[c]	6[d]	255[d]
2006	68,634[f]	2[d]	183[d]
2012	54,018[f]	0[e]	124[e]

a. Except where otherwise indicated, figures taken from Stewart, *Marvels of Charity,* pp. 564-65.

b. Except where otherwise indicated, SBS numbers based on data supplied by Lynch, *Sharing the Bread,* 2:297-303.

c. Kathleen Sparrow Cummings, "Change of Habit," *Notre Dame Magazine Online,* Autumn 2003 (accessed August 1, 2006).

d. Figure supplied by the Public Relations Office of the SBS to the author on August 1, 2006.

e. Figure supplied by the SBS archivist, Stephanie Morris, Ph.D.

f. Figure supplied by the online services of the Center for Applied Research in the Apostolate at Georgetown University, February 14, 2013.

Various reasons can be given for the decline in vocations. The general secularization in society and the crisis in the Church following Vatican Coun-

---

1776-1990 (New Brunswick, N.J.: Rutgers University Press, 1992), p. 259; Lynch, *Sharing the Bread,* 2:108; Stewart, *Marvels of Charity,* p. 461.

cil II are primary. Growing prosperity and the women's movement brought important economic and social gains to all women. As more middle-class women gained higher education and entered the general U.S. workforce, the sisterhood no longer seemed an attractive "career." Other avenues were open besides the traditional teaching and nursing. If one were inclined, one could do the same kind of work among the poor without suffering the limitations imposed by vows of poverty, chastity, and obedience. Many women no longer found the idea of the religious life appealing or relevant. For some, the post–Vatican II Church was not moving fast enough. Indeed, it was not just a problem of attracting new vocations; many sisters were leaving the order.

Twenty-three percent of the nuns who were members of the SBS in 1964 left the order.[80] For the seventy-three years preceding Vatican II, only 10 sisters who had made perpetual vows had departed. In the first ten years after the council, 61 women who had made their perpetual vows received Indults of Secularization, and 34 of the sisters in temporary vows withdrew before making their final vows. In June 1970, there were 446 sisters in the order, including those in temporary vows. By 1980, the number had dropped to 390 through deaths and withdrawals. By 1990, the SBS had lost another 79 women, for a total of 309 professed sisters. While priests who were laicized after Vatican II usually married, ex-sisters did not. Most found work as teachers and social workers.[81]

Another plausible reason for the decline in the number of women attracted to the SBS is the change in the social and political climate of the country during the 1960s and 1970s. A more militant African American social and political agenda was promoted by the less moderate leaders of the black power movement. This militancy drove a wedge in the ranks of those who had supported the earlier civil rights movement.

In the spirit of their founder, the SBS continued to support civil rights for blacks and to be active in the civil rights movement. In 1959, Sister Consuela Marie Duffy, SBS, was a witness in a U.S. civil rights suit against Harrison County, Mississippi, after police officers would not allow her Xavier University History Club to picnic on a public beach. Sisters of the order supported African Americans in their struggle for civil rights. They prayed with black Americans, and they marched in the streets with them in the 1950s and 1960s.

---

80. Lynch, *Sharing the Bread*, 2:108.
81. Jay P. Dolan, *The American Catholic Experience: A History from Colonial Times to the Present* (Garden City, N.Y.: Doubleday, 1985), p. 438.

However, by the mid-1960s, race relations in the country were taking a turn many white citizens could not understand. In August 1965, the predominantly African American community of Watts in Los Angeles erupted into a full-scale riot. It may have been the first race riot in the country begun by blacks, and it left thirty-four dead and over one thousand injured. In July 1967, Detroit was the scene of an ugly race riot that left forty-two dead. After the assassination of Martin Luther King in April 1968, riots broke out in over 168 U.S. cities and towns. At the time, the leader of the United Black Front, Lincoln Lynch, was quoted as saying, "It is imperative to abandon the unconditional non-violent concept expounded by Dr. King and adopt the position that for every Martin Luther King who falls, 10 white racists will go down with him. There is no other way — America understands no other language."[82] These actions and this rhetoric were no longer seen by many as emblematic of a race riot, but of a race war. Many who had been part of the cadre willing to support civil rights no longer could do so. Indeed, legal structures were in place to ensure civil rights for blacks, such as voting rights, fair housing practices, and the legal integration of schools. The political obstacles African Americans had faced in the initial years of the SBS mission no longer existed. In the face of civil unrest and violent demands, fewer and fewer young women were interested in the apostolate of the order. They could put up with being called "nigger sister" when the cause seemed just, but in the late 1960s events changed the racial climate in the United States. For many, it was not a fight they wanted to join.

Of course, what happened to Native Americans in all this racial uproar is more difficult to establish. They traditionally have been a much more invisible and smaller population in the United States. The Indians were the first to benefit from Katharine Drexel's vision, and they too had their moments of public struggle. Native Americans are members of separate nations or tribes. There had been no successful pan-Indian movement for civil rights until the late 1960s, when Native Americans began to borrow tactics from the civil rights movement. The American Indian Movement (AIM) made national headlines when it seized Alcatraz Island in the middle of San Francisco Bay in 1968. AIM successfully occupied the offices of the Bureau of Indian Affairs in Washington, D.C., in 1972. Most spectacularly, AIM supporters had a standoff with federal law enforcement officers at Wounded Knee, South Dakota, in 1973. Wounded Knee was the site of the last armed conflict of the nineteenth-century Indian wars. On December 29, 1890, an overwhelmingly

82. BBC online, April 6, 1968.

superior force of the U.S. cavalry killed 153 Lakota Sioux men, women, and children in what has been called the Massacre at Wounded Knee. While the Wounded Knee incident of 1973 was undoubtedly a symbolic struggle, it did not symbolize the same thing to all. Again, like the African Americans in Watts, Chicago, and Washington, D.C., Native Americans lost a great deal of sympathy by their actions, however honorable their intentions. Some of the losers in these racial conflicts were the Sisters of the Blessed Sacrament, whose founder had pledged herself to be "as a mother to the Indians and Colored People." It was a pledge that no longer made sense to a number of people.

One can imagine that young women of the last decade of the nineteenth century or of the early decades of the twentieth century could romanticize and idealize the plights of peoples largely unknown and unseen by them. When frightful images of death and destruction and jarring confrontational rhetoric become nightly fare on the television news, it is easy to understand why young women might wish to put their talents in other places than the Sisters of the Blessed Sacrament.

However, Katharine Drexel and her sisters were never dedicated only to civil rights, education, and social work. Their goal was, and is still, directed toward the spiritual well-being of those of their apostolate. While Native Americans and African Americans have a special place in their ministry, the Sisters of the Blessed Sacrament are now open to the needs of those of all races. Their present mission statement reads as follows: "As Sisters of the Blessed Sacrament, we believe God calls us to be a sign in the world of the power of the Eucharistic Christ to effect unity and community among all peoples. Guided by the spirit of Katharine Drexel we are called to share the gospel message with the poor, especially among the Black and Native-American peoples and to challenge the deeply rooted injustice in the world today."[83]

They are called Sisters of the Blessed Sacrament because they find sustenance in the Sacrament for themselves and desire to bring others to Jesus in the Sacrament. The greatly reduced number of sisters has in some ways brought the SBS back to where it started. The order presently maintains only three schools, including Xavier Preparatory School in Louisiana and St. Michael's Indian High School and Grammar School in Arizona. The rest of the sisters are either in apostolates across fifteen states or at the motherhouse, where there are approximately 100 sisters, including 55 who are

83. SBS Web site.

retired.[84] There are, at the time of this writing, 124 sisters and no novices. As in the days of Katharine Drexel, the SBS supports the missions of bishops and other orders by distributing nearly $150,000 annually. However circumscribed and reduced their actual missionary field has become, the sisters continue to be faithful to the vision of their founder and the vows they made to serve the Church by serving blacks and Indians. In 1990, they even managed to open a small mission outside the country, in Haiti, to serve the people there. They may be daunted but are not defeated by their present situation.

Like Mother Teresa of Calcutta, faithfulness, not success, is what the Sisters of the Blessed Sacrament pray for, and is the quality by which they want to be judged. Indeed, as previously quoted, Mother Katharine wrote to her sisters, "Success is not the criterion of the spiritual life."[85] Her order's very existence and its continuing apostolate serve as a legacy to Katharine Drexel's kenotic and eucharistic spirituality. But it would be wrong to maintain that the order was all of her legacy; in fact, her order may cease to exist one day. Katharine Drexel was granted a much larger legacy by Pope John Paul II when he canonized her. Her spirituality, the subject of the next chapter, is what sustained her throughout her life, and, in canonizing her, the pope suggested that her spirituality could serve as a model for other Christians.

84. The number of states varies from year to year. Presently, there are SBS in Alabama, Arizona, California, Colorado, District of Columbia, Florida, Illinois, Indiana, Louisiana, Massachusetts, New Mexico, New York, Oregon, Pennsylvania, Tennessee, and Virginia.

85. MKD, *Reflections on Religious Life* (Bensalem, Pa.: Sisters of the Blessed Sacrament, 1983), p. 25.

FIGURE 1. Francis Martin Drexel, grandfather to Katharine (Archives of the Sisters of the Blessed Sacrament)

FIGURE 2. Hanna Langstroth Drexel, Katharine's birth mother (Archives of the Sisters of the Blessed Sacrament)

FIGURE 3. Francis Anthony Drexel and Emma Bouvier Drexel, Katharine's father and stepmother (Archives of the Sisters of the Blessed Sacrament)

FIGURE 4. Katharine and Elizabeth
Drexel (ca. 1860) (Archives of the Sisters of
the Blessed Sacrament)

FIGURE 5. Katharine at about age eight
(Archives of the Sisters of the Blessed Sacrament)

FIGURE 6. The "All
Three," Katharine,
Louise, and Elizabeth
(ca. 1867) (Archives of the
Sisters of the Blessed Sacrament)

FIGURE 7. St. Michel's Sunday School, taught by Elizabeth and Katharine
at the Drexel family summer home in Torresdale, Pennsylvania
(Archives of the Sisters of the Blessed Sacrament)

FIGURE 8. Katharine, driving her horse, Roland, at the family's summer home
(Archives of the Sisters of the Blessed Sacrament)

FIGURE 9. Elizabeth Drexel in Paris
(ca. 1875) (Archives of the Sisters of the
Blessed Sacrament)

FIGURE 10. Pope Leo XIII.
In 1883 he suggested to
Katharine that she become
a missionary (Courtesy of
Creative Commons)

FIGURE 11. Katharine at Rosebud Mission. She is in a tall black hat in the right rear (1887). (Archives of the Sisters of the Blessed Sacrament)

FIGURE 12. Bishop Martin Marty, vicar apostolic of northern Minnesota. He appealed to Katharine in 1885 for funds for a school on the Rosebud Reservation (Department of Special Collections and University Archives, Marquette University Libraries)

FIGURE 13. Msgr. Joseph A. Stephan, director of the Bureau of Catholic Indian Missions and a close collaborator with Katharine. He was with Bishop Marty when he first met Katharine in 1885 (Department of Special Collections and University Archives, Marquette University Libraries)

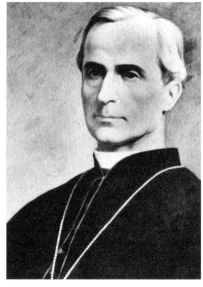

FIGURE 14. Katharine as bridesmaid for Louise (1885) (Archives of the Sisters of the Blessed Sacrament)

FIGURE 15. Bishop James O'Connor, spiritual adviser to Katharine. He first suggested to her that she found an order of sisters to serve Native Americans and African Americans (Archives of the Archdiocese of Omaha)

FIGURE 16. Katharine, after her first profession of vows at the Sisters of Mercy convent in Pittsburgh (1891) (Archives of the Sisters of the Blessed Sacrament)

FIGURE 17. Mother Mary Katharine Drexel, after her final profession of vows (1895) (Archives of the Sisters of the Blessed Sacrament)

FIGURE 18. St. Michel, the Drexel family summer home, became the temporary motherhouse for the Sisters of the Blessed Sacrament. The Drexel home is in the center, above the added church and novitiate. (Archives of the Sisters of the Blessed Sacrament)

FIGURE 19. St. Elizabeth Convent, motherhouse of the Sisters of the Blessed Sacrament, Bensalem, Pennsylvania (Archives of the Sisters of the Blessed Sacrament)

FIGURE 20. SBS novices in white veils at the motherhouse
(Archives of the Sisters of the Blessed Sacrament)

FIGURE 21. St. Catherine's Mission for Pueblo Indians, Santa Fe, New Mexico,
the first SBS mission. Students with Sr. Kateri Dunn (1894)
(Archives of the Sisters of the Blessed Sacrament)

FIGURE 22. St. Michael's Mission, Arizona, still under construction circa 1900.
Opened in 1902 (Archives of the Sisters of the Blessed Sacrament)

FIGURE 23. St. Michael's Mission. Navajo girls performing traditional dances
(Archives of the Sisters of the Blessed Sacrament)

FIGURE 24. St. Michael's Mission football team and band
(Archives of the Sisters of the Blessed Sacrament)

FIGURE 25. Mother Katharine
with her sister Louise Morrell
(Mrs. Edward Morrell)
(Archives of the Sisters of
the Blessed Sacrament)

FIGURE 26. Mother Katharine, second from left, visiting Hopi Indians (1927)
(Archives of the Sisters of the Blessed Sacrament)

FIGURE 27. Mother Katharine, far right, visiting Navajo Indians
(Archives of the Sisters of the Blessed Sacrament)

FIGURE 28. Bishop Patrick John
Ryan, adviser to St. Katharine
after death of Bishop O'Connor
(1886) (Philadelphia Archdiocesan
Historical Research Center)

FIGURE 29. Graduates of St. Francis de Sales School, Rock Castle, Virginia (1923)
(Archives of the Sisters of the Blessed Sacrament)

FIGURE 30. Boys of the lower grades, Immaculate Mother School, Nashville, Tennessee, opened in 1905 (Archives of the Sisters of the Blessed Sacrament)

FIGURE 31. Old Xavier University on Magazine Street in New Orleans. The building had been bought by Mother Katharine from Southern University. Later it housed Xavier Preparatory School. The university opened in 1917 (Archives of the Sisters of the Blessed Sacrament, with permission from Xavier University Archives and Special Collections, New Orleans)

FIGURE 32. Some early graduates of Xavier University (1929)
(Xavier University Archives and Special Collections, New Orleans)

FIGURE 33. Xavier University was famous for its fine arts, including grand opera. Opera students in costume with Sr. Elise Carmen, head of the opera program
(Archives of the Sisters of the Blessed Sacrament)

FIGURE 34. Mother Katharine with families of Xavier graduates
(Archives of the Sisters of the Blessed Sacrament)

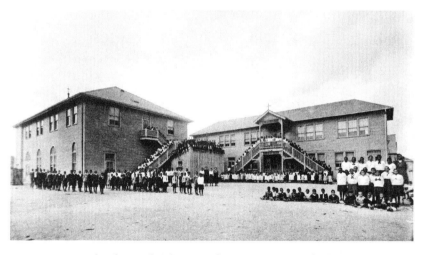

FIGURE 35. Holy Ghost School, New Orleans. At one time this was the largest
parochial school in the United States (Archives of the Sisters of the Blessed Sacrament)

FIGURE 36. Mother Katharine on the Mississippi River. She was preparing
to go into the bayous to establish schools for African American children
(Archives of the Sisters of the Blessed Sacrament)

FIGURE 37. Mother
Katherine in Pawhuska,
Oklahoma. She regularly
made the rounds of
schools she had funded
or founded (Archives of the
Sisters of the Blessed Sacrament)

FIGURE 38. St. Patrick's School in Anadarko, Oklahoma.
Not an SBS school, but funded by Mother Katharine

(Department of Special Collections and University Archives, Marquette University Libraries)

FIGURE 39. St. Teresa's Institute for Creek Girls in Tulsa, Oklahoma. (1899).
Not an SBS school, but funded by Mother Katharine

(Courtesy of Holy Family Cathedral Archives)

FIGURE 40. St. Mary's Academy outside of Sacred Heart, Oklahoma. Funded by Mother Katharine, who helped fund all seventeen Indian Catholic schools and missions in Oklahoma (Department of Special Collections and University Archives, Marquette University Libraries)

FIGURE 41. Pope John Paul II, the pope who canonized St. Katharine, October 1, 2000

FIGURE 42. St. Katharine Drexel: "We must attract them with joy"
(Archives of the Sisters of the Blessed Sacrament)

CHAPTER 4

The Kenotic and Eucharistic Spirituality of Katharine Drexel

Katharine Drexel chose a very difficult vocation for her life's work, but what sustained her throughout was her deep spirituality. Christian life is life lived with Christ in the Spirit. Christian spirituality, in this sense, is the lived experience of the individual. It is the means by which the Christian opens herself up to God and makes herself present to God or, rather, allows God to be present to her. Spirituality constitutes a continuing, lived effort to hear the word of God and to be docile to his Spirit. It is the Christian's spirituality that prepares the believer both to hear the word of God and to do his bidding. Because the individual's relationship is with a transcendent God, Christian spirituality also contains something of mystery. Relationships are as varied as the persons involved. There are, therefore, many ways of living out one's Christian spirituality. Additionally, an individual's lived Christian experience may change with differing circumstances. There are different paths of Christian spirituality, and the individual Christian may engage many different kinds of spiritualities simultaneously and seriatim. Specific spiritualities are associated with certain religious orders, such as Jesuit, Franciscan, or Benedictine spiritualities; other specific spiritualities are, for instance, Trinitarian or Marian in focus. Katharine's lived experience of Christ in the Spirit was both kenotic, or self-emptying, and eucharistic. This chapter will explore the kenotic and eucharistic spiritualities through which she was able to conform herself to Christ, to endure, and even to flourish in her vocation as a missionary founder.

Kenotic Spirituality

Kenosis comes into the Christian consciousness most emphatically in St. Paul's letter to the Philippians: "Let the same mind be in you that was in Christ Jesus, who, though he was in the form of God, did not regard equality with God as something to be exploited, but emptied himself, taking the form of a slave, being born in human likeness. And being found in human form, he humbled himself and became obedient to the point of death — even death on a cross" (2:5-8). The Greek word employed by St. Paul in this passage is *ekenōsen,* the aorist form of the verb *kenoō.* According to Albrecht Oepke, the verb *kenoō* in Philippians 2:6 implies "to make empty" or "to deprive of content or possessions."[1] In the context of Christian spirituality, *kenosis* has come to mean the self-emptying of the believer in imitation of Christ as described by St. Paul: "Kenosis is at the heart of Christian life as well as at the core of ministry. Kenosis is the resolute divesting of the person of every claim of self-interest so as to be ready to live the Gospel of Christ in every aspect of living, freed from the dictates of personal preference."[2] Naturally, kenotic spirituality takes many forms. It can mean something as simple as personal humility, as trivial as denying oneself sugar, wine, or other pleasurable foods, or as horrific as freely embracing a martyrdom of the most gruesome sort. The Christian kenotic empties herself of her own desires and will, and takes on the will of God and does his work on earth. As directed by St. Paul, she takes Christ as her exemplar in all things.

This use of *kenosis* in spirituality is not to be confused with the christological controversy surrounding St. Paul's use of the term in Philippians 2:7. Some nineteenth-century theologians argued that at the incarnation Christ gave up all or some of his divine powers and attributes to live as a mere man. If this were the correct understanding of *kenosis,* then the divinity of Christ would be undermined and, thus, the integrity of his sacrifice would be destroyed, along with the immutability of God. According to Reformed theologian Louis Berkhof, "The Christ of the Kenotics is neither God nor man."[3]

The father of nineteenth-century christological kenoticism was Gottfried Thomasius (1802-1875), who taught at the University of Erlangen in

---

1. Albrecht Oepke, "Kenoō," in *Theological Dictionary of the New Testament,* ed. Gerhard Kittel, 8th ed., vol. 3 (Grand Rapids: Eerdmans, 1981), pp. 659-62.

2. Kevin M. Cronin, OFM, *Kenosis: Emptying Self and the Path of Christian Service* (Rockport, Mass.: Element Books, 1992), p. 1.

3. Louis Berkhof, *Systematic Theology* (Grand Rapids: Eerdmans, 1941), p. 327. See part 3, chapter 3, "The Unipersonality of Christ," for a complete discussion.

Germany. Thomasius wrote: "I cannot maintain on the one hand, the full reality of the divine and human natures of Christ, particularly the full truth of the natural development of his human life, and on the other hand, the full unity of his theanthropic person unless I assume a self-limitation of the divine Logos, which took place in the Incarnation, for without this assumption, I cannot conceive of the unity affirmed on the subject."[4] Another of the christological kenoticists wrote: "The Son of God became man, that is, he renounced his self-conscious divine personal being and took the form of a spiritual potence, which self-forgotten, as unconscious formative power worked in the womb of Mary, and formed a body that was fitted so to serve the development of this spiritual potence that it could use it as its own property and become conscious, could develop itself therein, and by means thereof put forth its energy."[5] This understanding of Philippians 2:7 came about in light of the development of the historical-critical method of studying the Bible, the search for the historical Jesus, and the widespread application of the Hegelian dialectic. It had its proponents in both Lutheran and Anglican circles into the early twentieth century and is held in some U.S. evangelical circles today. This christological understanding of *kenosis* is rejected by more orthodox scholarship. The *kenosis* important to Katharine was spiritual *kenosis*.

Katharine would not have applied the term to her own spirituality, because in her day it was not applied to ascetic theology. However, many of her spiritual devotions and activities are most aptly described and identified by it as it has come to be employed in present-day Christian spiritual theology. It is a term that covers the broad range of activities and attitudes that constitute an expressed or implied emptying out of self. Other terms or phrases more often encountered in earlier spiritual writing are "die to self," "lose one's life in order to save it," "self-abasement," "self-surrender," "humility," "self-forgetfulness," "self-annihilation," "renounce self," "entrust oneself to God," "give oneself over to God," "relinquish oneself," "offer oneself," "desire less," and "powerless."[6] A cruci-centric and kenotic spirituality is expressed

---

4. Quoted in John M. Drickamer, "Higher Criticism and the Incarnation in the Thought of I. A. Dorner," *Concordia Theological Quarterly* 43, no. 3 (June 1979): 200. Also see Thomasius, "Against Dorner," in *God and Incarnation in Mid-Nineteenth-Century German Theology: G. Thomasius, I. A. Dorner, A. E. Biedermann*, trans. and ed. Claude Welch (New York: Oxford University Press, 1965), p. 89.

5. Drickamer, quoting Schneider, without further reference or identification, "Higher Criticism and the Incarnation," p. 200.

6. See Sarah Coakley, "Kenosis and Subversion: On the Repression of 'Vulnerabil-

by this meditation from Katharine: "Plunge me with thyself into the Heart of Jesus crucified in order that my poor nature may be consumed in the flame and my life may become pure and holy with Thee!"[7]

Kenosis is controversial among feminist theologians because many believe that it puts one inherently in a position of powerlessness in a patriarchal Church that has historically denied hierarchical power to women. Daphne Hampson's critique of *kenosis* is typical. She maintains that self-emptying and self-abnegation could not have a place in the feminist principles of self-actualization and equality.[8] She insists that the vast majority of women, both those who leave patriarchal religions and those who stay within them, find the notion of sacrifice an alienating concept.[9] On the other hand, Sarah Coakley and Rosemary Radford Ruether support kenotic spirituality for women as transformative. Ruether advances a theory of power expressed in her description of the *kenosis of patriarchy,* or the "self-emptying of power as domination." To exercise power as a means of liberation rather than domination could challenge, she argues, patriarchal constructions of power. "Service to others does not deplete the person who ministers," she contends, "but rather causes her (or him) to become more liberated."[10] Coakley challenges those who, like Hampson, would critique Ruether's use of *kenosis,* by arguing that they reduce the idea of *kenosis* to only "self-destructive subordination" for women. This way of thinking, Coakley contends, neglects a vital element of what constitutes Christian feminism, in effect, engaging with the paradox of losing one's life in order to find it.[11] In contrast, she distinguishes

---

ity' in Christian Feminist Writing," in *Swallowing a Fishbone? Feminist Theologians Debate Christianity,* ed. Daphne Hampson (London: SPCK, 1996), pp. 82-111. The following are seminal works in feminist theology that address women and power within Christianity: Mary Daly, *The Church and the Second Sex* (London: Geoffrey Chapman, 1968); Mary Daly, *Beyond God the Father: Towards a Philosophy of Women's Liberation* (Boston: Beacon Press, 1973); Rosemary Radford Ruether, *Sexism and God-Talk* (London: SCM, 1983); Elisabeth Schüssler Fiorenza, *In Memory of Her: A Feminist Theological Reconstruction of Christian Origins* (London: SCM, 1983); Letty M. Russell, *Human Liberation in a Feminist Perspective: A Theology* (Philadelphia: Westminster, 1974); Letty M. Russell, *Becoming Human* (Philadelphia: Westminster, 1982).

7. MKD, Meditation Slips, 11, pp. 4-5, July 1943.

8. Daphne Hampson, *Theology and Feminism* (Oxford: Basil Blackwell, 1990), pp. 153-55; Daphne Hampson, *After Christianity* (London: SCM, 1996), pp. 141-46.

9. Hampson, *After Christianity,* p. 141.

10. Ruether, *Sexism and God-Talk,* pp. 137-38, 207.

11. Coakley, "Kenosis and Subversion," pp. 82-83. "Whoever finds his life will lose it and whoever loses his life for my sake will find it" (Matt. 10:39).

what she calls a "right" *kenosis* or "power-in-vulnerability," grounding this in the practice of contemplative prayer, where a "*special* form of vulnerability or self-effacement" and "personal empowerment" are held together in the space where a "non-coercive divine power" manifests itself.[12] Lamenting what she calls the "*repression* of all forms of vulnerability" within Christian feminism, she calls for a feminist rereading of the power of the dynamic of the cross and resurrection. In true *kenosis,* the Christian woman, or man, responds to the divine; the self makes "space," which leads not to self-loss and silencing of the self, but rather to its "transformation and expansion into God."[13] This is the *kenosis* recognizable in Katharine. Putting aside the question of exactly what Paul meant when he wrote that Christ emptied himself, it is somewhat paradoxical that Christ emptied himself to become man, and Christians empty themselves to become more like Christ, more divine. Katharine sought ways to make "space" to transform and expand herself into God.

There are quite naturally many ways of being kenotic or expressing kenotic spirituality, and it is reasonable to reinterpret her thoroughly traditional Catholic spirituality in kenotic terms along these same lines. Katharine favored mortification of her flesh and the living out of the evangelical counsels as ways to surrender herself completely to God, to empty herself out in order to be filled with Christ, especially the Christ she found in the Eucharist.

Kenosis through Mortification of the Flesh

Even as a child, Katharine Drexel was aware of the importance and the difficulty of limiting one's gustatory intake for spiritual reasons. In her childhood spiritual journals, alongside her assessment of her virtues and vices, she constantly mentioned her intention to give up such foods as jams, sugar, butter, fruits, and desserts. That she made vow after vow to give up the same foods indicates that her attempts to be abstemious were most often failed attempts, and that the foods from which she chose to refrain were indeed foods that she enjoyed, and therefore, that their loss was a real sacrifice for her. Her desire to come down to "convent rations" was part of her spiritual development during the period of her vocational discernment. Her eating habits were part of an intuitive self-emptying self-abnegation.

12. Coakley, "Kenosis and Subversion," p. 84.
13. Coakley, "Kenosis and Subversion," pp. 106-8.

Of course, Catholic Christians of her day regularly practiced fasting and abstinence from meat as part of church discipline. Lent, Fridays, and holy days were days of fasting and/or abstinence.[14] The family table was the place where a Catholic child would first learn to discipline the body for the sake of the spirit. From the family table to the refectory table of the convent, Katharine continued her eating habits. When she was the head of her order, her sisters noted that she was fasting to excess. "Finally, the Sisters, fearing for her health, told the Archbishop [Ryan]. He put her under obedience to take regular meals, and she immediately obeyed. For some years the Archbishop was watchful of her external penances, especially in the matter of fasting and denying herself nourishing food."[15] The Annals for 1892 noted the appointment of Rev. John Scully, SJ, as Extraordinary Confessor of the SBS. Father Scully

> evidently belonged to the more severe school of spiritual directors, and leaned more to the severer form of observance of the spiritual life, in consequence of which he was using this way of guiding our Mother. She, herself, was very much inclined to the practice of external mortification, and under the direction of Father Scully, she adhered to an extremely severe regimen and her bodily mortifications were excessive. She observed a strict Lenten fast every day and curtailed her food in every way, so much so that the Sisters began to fear that she would undermine her health and thus shorten her days which were so much needed by the little congregation. The matter was brought to the attention of the Archbishop, and he was horrified and immediately put Mother under obedience to take her regular meals and after that for some years, in the matter of the practice of external penance, His Grace was most watchful in regard to Mother.[16]

Though she obeyed the archbishop in the amount she ate, she still neglected to take butter or to use condiments that might have made her food more enjoyable.[17] When she traveled, she took her eating habits on the road with her. She insisted on carrying what the sisters referred to as her "poverty bag," which contained cold sandwiches, fruit, and jars of water or coffee to drink. Finally, the archbishop ordered her to take at least one hot meal a day when traveling. Her self-denial of nutrition was a constant theme throughout

14. Since 1983, Catholics in the United States no longer must fast or abstain from meat except on Ash Wednesday and Good Friday.

15. *Positio*, 1:521-22.

16. ASBS, vol. 3, p. 242, 1892.

17. ASBS, vol. 3, p. 77.

her life, even after she had recovered from her youthful anorexia. She quite literally emptied herself of nutrition her entire adult life. Had she been able to get away with nothing but hard bread crusts and water like some of the medieval hermits, she probably would have. But hers was a life in community, and a community has eyes to see and ears to hear everything that goes on within its walls. There was little of her kenotic life that was not known. What happened at table was the least of her kenotic practices.

For Katharine, the essence of holiness was to become a "victim of love," to empty oneself so that Christ might live within: "Let Christ live within us, that is really the sacrifice of self. . . . That is the privilege of the true religious — to be a victim of love in whatever we have to do. . . . To give is to love. That is the idea of the Mass — to give our elder brother, Jesus Christ."[18] She taught her sisters to imitate the self-giving, self-emptying of Christ, and she modeled that behavior: "Self has no place in perfect love . . . self-sacrifice, self-immolation are the fitting expressions in daily life of the love of the soul for the Divine Victim of the Tabernacle."[19] As early as 1881 and ten years before entering the convent, Katharine wrote in her retreat notes, marked front and back in her hand as "Strictly Private,"

> The End for which God made us. What was that end? That I might know & serve my God, my Creator & Maker here on earth and afterwards see Him & enjoy Him forever in Heaven, I was therefore not created to shine in society, to enjoy myself, to do my own will, to follow my own inclinations, to be loved by creatures. Away, away with such thoughts, annihilate them, drive them, drive them not only now, but forever from your mind, O my soul. To know, love and serve God, that is your immediate end, that is why you exist. I must, then, strive year by year, month by month, week by week, day by day, hour by hour, second by second to know, to love, to serve God more & more. *"Amplius et amplius"* [more and more] God Himself will be my teacher in this knowledge.[20]

Indeed, she calls self-love one's greatest enemy: "To die to self-love that I may live in God alone is the great business of Spiritual Life."[21] As self grows in

---

18. MKD, *Reflections on Religious Life* (Bensalem, Pa.: Sisters of the Blessed Sacrament, 1983), p. 9.

19. MKD, *A Call from Jesus Dwelling in the Blessed Sacrament* (Bensalem, Pa.: Sisters of the Blessed Sacrament, 1912), p. 17.

20. MKD, Retreat Notes, 1881.

21. MKD, Meditation Slips, 1, p. 53.

importance, the love of God and fellow man decreases. The opposite is equally true; therefore, she exhorted her sisters, whom she looked upon as both sisters and spiritual daughters, "Arise [from Holy Communion] and go out of your-selves, empty yourselves of all self — all self-seeking. There should not be an interest for you but for Jesus, and the interests of Jesus, and Jesus is Savior and comes little and emptied of Self to save that which is lost. Help him."[22] Katha-rine practiced *kenosis* in many small ways common to Christians throughout the ages; she was humble and self-sacrificing, and she fasted and prayed.

She also practiced *kenosis* in a very radical, indeed, shocking way. She indulged in extreme mortification of her flesh. Mother M. Mercedes, SBS, the second superior of the order and one of the original three sisters to join with Katharine in the Mercy Convent, wrote in her memoirs of a disturbing discovery she made as a young novice.

Reverend Mother always impressed me as a soul who practiced morti-fication in an heroic degree. In the early years, or rather in the first year of my Novitiate, having charge of the cleaning of her cell and office at St. Michael, I accidentally stumbled on a heavy discipline [an instrument of flagellation] all blood stained. Later on in the same year, having occasion to be sleeping in the same part of her house in which her cell was located, I was many times awakened by fearful scourging which was kept up with some vigor and strength for such a long time that it fairly sickened me. Later on, the Vicar General, Mother M. James, showed me a discipline which she had surreptitiously abstracted from Mother's drawer, which was filled with small iron points and the whole almost saturated through and through with blood. I knew she practiced kneeling on her fingertips behind the main altar after night prayers from 15 to 20 minutes at a time, also with arms outstretched for like or longer periods. . . .

Then again, she wore iron chains round [her] waist and arms and the hair shirt quite frequently. At meals she was most abstemious. For over thirty years she was never known to take a dessert or anything that was unusually palatable, such as the community had on Feast days. When a dish was presented to her, it was noticed that she always took the toughest or worst portion of meat, saying she liked that the best. Until forbidden by the Cardinal, or her Spiritual Director, I do not know which, she fasted very severely all the Lenten season and during the fast and abstinence days of the Church. . . .

22. MKD, Meditation Slips, 1, p. 56.

In kneeling she very seldom used any support, even during Mass or during the half-hour's adoration before the Blessed Sacrament. In sitting she nearly always placed herself on the extreme edge of the chair and very seldom reclined against its back.

In traveling, no matter how young or robust was the Sister companion she [MKD] invariably insisted on carrying the heaviest bag or suitcase, and never unless absolutely under obedience to do so would she travel in any but the cheapest way, saying that she preferred the day coaches that were crowded to their utmost capacity.[23]

Other sisters also testified to Mother Katharine's severe penitential practices. Mother M. Agatha Ryan, a member of the SBS Council in 1918 and a traveling companion of Mother Katharine in the 1920s and 1930s, remembered that sisters who had been in the order in the earliest days had commented on the severity of her practices. She testified, "I saw the chains which she used on herself. I also saw the hair shirt that she used on herself."[24] Sr. M. Frances Buttell, the dean of Xavier University, also testified to the ascetic practices of the founder:

> She did use the discipline and she used the chain. In the early days of the community Mother Katharine encouraged the discipline be used, but always with permission of the [priest] confessor. I am positive she would not have encouraged it [the use of the discipline] if she did not use it herself. Her method of penance was a constant deprivation in small things, no one of which would attract notice. For example, she herself would never take dessert or sweets unless she was dining out. She herself prayed in uncomfortable positions — with arms outstretched or on her fingertips. She did these privately. I remember her giving the latter to me for a penance. . . . She seemed to be in constant communion with God.[25]

It was her practice of mortification of her flesh with the metal-tipped discipline that shocked Mother Mercedes and the other sisters. Their distress over their superior's spiritual practices was recorded in the order's annals: "Mother naturally turned to the practice of mortification and bodily

---

23. Quoted in Kenneth L. Woodward, *Making Saints: How the Catholic Church Determines Who Becomes a Saint, Who Doesn't, and Why* (New York: Simon and Schuster, 1990), p. 240.

24. *Positio*, 2:10.

25. *Positio*, 2:24.

penance. It was always a subject of worry to those whose duty it was to watch Mother and persuade her to be at least moderate in the practice of mortification."[26] Lynch, in her history of the SBS, wrote, "Father Scully, who was strong and energetic, believed in the penitential life for religious and had the Sisters, especially Mother Katharine who tended to that way herself, fasting and using disciplines and hair shirts."[27] Fr. Scully wrote to Mother Katharine on the use of the discipline in the Jesuit novitiate at Old St. Joseph's:

> Yes, the discipline is used in common in our novitiates after the lights are lowered in the dormitories on Wednesday and Friday night during the time that the head of the dormitory recites slowly the Hail Mary; a small bell is used to give the signal for commencing and ending. In public no one does more than this, and for beginners it is a good deal when the discipline is taken on the soft parts of the body and is well laid on. And the permission to do even more so is given very reluctantly, and of course, leave to use it at other times and to a greater extent — a request often prompted by vanity and self love, is with difficulty given.[28]

According to Lynch, under the direction of Fr. Scully, Mother Katharine put aside "all the moderation in pursuit of virtue she had learned from Bishop O'Connor."[29] Whether her excessive and extreme use of the discipline originated with her or with Fr. Scully cannot be known at this distance, but that it shocked and distressed her sisters is obvious. That it was an assigned "duty" to watch over Mother and try to dissuade her from her excesses indicates how out of the ordinary her practice was. However, to Katharine's mind, moderation in pursuit of holiness was no virtue.

What obviously disturbed Mother M. Mercedes as a novice, and was apparently still disturbing to her in retrospect, is even more disturbing to those of the twenty-first century for whom well-being and filling up, not emptying out, are the highest goods. It is far easier to accept abstemious habits at the dinner table than to countenance self-inflicted pain. Those who have seen Mel Gibson's film *The Passion of Christ* have a clear image of scourged flesh, albeit a Hollywood image manipulated for the sake of dramatic effect. Nonetheless,

26. ASBS, vol. 3, p. 243, 1892.

27. Sr. Patricia Lynch, SBS, *Sharing the Bread in Service: Sisters of the Blessed Sacrament, 1891-1991*, 2 vols. (Bensalem, Pa.: Sisters of the Blessed Sacrament, 1998), 1:54.

28. Scully to MKD, September 29, 1893.

29. Lynch, *Sharing the Bread*, 1:54.

it is difficult to imagine voluntarily inflicting that sort and degree of pain on oneself. It seems medieval. The very idea brings to mind images of flagellation like the famous scene in Ingmar Bergman's film *The Seventh Seal*. Indeed, a medieval monastic handbook reads: "Brother, it is necessary for thee to be punished in this life or in purgatory: but incomparably more severe will be the penalty of purgatory than any in this life. Behold, thy soul is in thy hands. Choose therefore for thyself whether to be sufficiently punished in this life according to canonical and authentic penance, or to await purgatory."[30] Mortification of the flesh is still acceptable within the Catholic Church, but self-scourging with an iron-tipped discipline is a rare practice indeed. Studies of pain, whether inflicted by others or by oneself, show that under the influence of pain the individual loses himself. In her article "Sacred Pain and the Phenomenal Self," Ariel Glucklich wrote, "Prolonged and unremitting pain has the effect of destroying the victim's ability to communicate and finally shatters his or her entire world, including even the victim's innermost self." Glucklich adds, "Pain, in short, unmakes their profane world and leads the mystics to self- and world-transcendence."[31] Maureen Flynn says much the same in an earlier article: "For the mystic seeking to chain the human mind in order to acquire a higher, more perfect form of understanding, pain provided the necessary psychic shackle. This is why we see mystics conscientiously intensifying pain, on the surface of their bodies through vigorous scourging and within their bodies through concentration on the Crucifixion, until finally the contents of the world (including themselves) were canceled out in their minds."[32]

---

30. John Thomas McNeill and Helena M. Gamer, eds., *Medieval Handbook of Penance* (New York: Columbia University Press, 1938), p. 223.

31. Ariel Glucklich, "Sacred Pain and the Phenomenal Self," *Harvard Theological Review* 19, no. 4 (October 1998): 391-92. There are many other aspects of sacred pain, such as the close self-identification with the suffering of Christ and penance for sin, but I do not believe they apply to Katharine's practice. She was too humble to identify herself in that way with Christ, and while she had to deal with scrupulosity as a teenager, she overcame that as an adult. For other approaches to the roles of sacred pain, see Mircea Eliade, *Rites and Symbols of Initiation: The Mysteries of Birth and Rebirth* (New York: Harper Torchbooks, 1958); Lawrence P. Sullivan, *Icanchu's Drum: An Orientation to Meaning in South American Religions* (New York: Macmillan, 1988); Bruce Lincoln, *Emerging from the Chrysalis: Studies in Rituals of Women's Initiation* (Cambridge: Harvard University Press, 1981); on *kenosis* see Elaine Scarry, *The Body in Pain: The Making and Unmaking of the World* (New York: Oxford University Press, 1985); Maureen Tilley, "The Ascetic Body and the (Un)Making of the World," *Journal of the American Academy of Religion* 59 (1990): 467-79.

32. Maureen Flynn, "The Spiritual Uses of Pain in Spanish Mysticism," *Journal of the American Academy of Religion* 65 (1995): 274.

Thus extreme pain becomes the ultimate tool for *kenosis,* one that Katharine did not hesitate to employ.

The use of the discipline is largely unmentioned in the literature on convent life. However, the lives of saints are replete with disciplines, hair shirts, and chains about the waist. It is known that St. Catherine of Siena, Katharine Drexel's patron saint, wore the hair shirt and chains. She also famously drank the pus from the sores of someone she was nursing.[33] St. Peter Damian (d. 1072), the prior of Fonte-Avellana, introduced the use of the discipline to Monte Cassino: "There was much opposition outside his own circle to this practice [use of the discipline], but Peter's persistent advocacy ensured its acceptance to such an extent that he was obliged later to moderate the imprudent zeal of some of his own hermits."[34] When Sister Claire Spellman entered the novitiate of the Sisters of Notre Dame De Namur in 1946, each novice was given a discipline and an armband, "the bracelet," which she described as being made out of metal and looking like a pot scrubber with points on the inside. "That was a common practice in all the orders. . . . These [types of mortification] were private practices, conducted in private. Some felt a need for their own penance and some did penance on behalf of others. I hated the idea of the discipline. Most of us just stopped doing it."[35] As late as 1949, the Sisters of Notre Dame in the California Province were reminded to wear the bracelet on the left arm. "The 'bracelet' resembled a row of interlocking links of a chain fence. The points of the links put pressure on the arm but did not pierce the skin. Any flexing of the muscles would bring a sharp reminder of its presence. [The sister] and the superior decided on frequency and duration of use."[36] However, according to Sister Spellman, the bracelet did indeed pierce the skin to the point that one sister's doctor, upon seeing her severely pierced arm, forbade her to wear it.[37] At any rate, the sisters were to wear the bracelet on the left arm so as to leave the right arm free for meals. Novices of the Sisters of Notre Dame are no longer given a discipline or bracelet upon entering, yet presently, members of Opus Dei are known to use the discipline and the cilice: "The cilice is a chain, or strap

33. Maiju Lehmijoki-Gardner, ed. and trans., *Dominican Penitent Women* (New York: Paulist, 2005), p. 95.

34. *Catholic Encyclopedia,* 1907, online (accessed July 18, 2005).

35. Personal interview with the author, August 4, 2005. Spellman noted that the Sisters of St. Joseph of Carondelet employed the discipline as a group exercise in a darkened room.

36. Patricia Curran, SND, *Grace Before Meals: Food Ritual and Body Discipline in Convent Culture* (Chicago: University of Illinois Press, 1989), p. 37.

37. Personal interview with the author, August 4, 2005.

with small spikes in it. Numeraries and associates [members of Opus Dei] wear it around their thigh for 2 hours a day. It has also been described as a wire mesh, with the ends of the wires pointing inward. Sometimes the points are filed down."[38] The bracelet of the Sisters of Notre Dame must have been similar to the cilice of Opus Dei. Mortification of the flesh is a time-honored aid to the spiritual life, and not just for Christians. It is common among Buddhists.

It is clear from reading Frederick William Faber's *Spiritual Growth* that mortification of the flesh was a practice that needed defending to mid-Victorian, English-speaking Catholics. Painful mortification was considered outdated on both sides of the Atlantic. Yet Faber maintained that mortification, including that which inflicted real pain, was not simply ancillary to the growth and development of Christian spirituality but essential to it: "There can be no interior mortification without exterior; and this last must come first." One aspect of mortification would have appealed to Katharine: it intensifies love and prepares the heart for the emotion of love. "And where the object loved and contemplated is one of sorrow and suffering, as Jesus is, love impels us more or less vehemently to imitation."[39] Another important aspect of mortification for her would have been its connection to prayer. Faber called mortification the single means by which prayer succeeds, and he insisted that it be carried out only under obedience to a spiritual adviser or confessor, lest the pain itself become its own end.[40] Katharine, as a reader of Faber's works from her early teen years, would have been familiar with his recommendations on mortification of the flesh and its importance to one's progress in spiritual development and, indeed, one's salvation. Modern readers are nonetheless distressed, while at the same time fascinated, by those who would give pain to the body for the sake of the soul.

Yet many people severely restrict their diets or run miles a day through heat, cold, rain, and snow for bodily fitness. Were this done for the sake of the soul, it would be mortification of the flesh and cause many to look askance at it. There are runners and other athletes who have run through shin splints, plantar fasciitis, and broken bones. Medical patients endure various noxious and painful therapies and surgeries to regain health. Women undergo Botox injections and the surgeon's knife for the mere sake of per-

38. Matthew G. Collins, "Matt's Opus Dei FAQ," online (accessed March 3, 2005). Also see the Opus Dei Web site at opusdei.org.

39. Frederick W. Faber, *Spiritual Growth: The Progress of the Spiritual Life*, 15th ed. (Baltimore: John Murphy, n.d.), pp. 163, 172.

40. Faber, *Spiritual Growth*, p. 175.

ceived physical beauty. Most people believe that such painful behavior for the sake of the body is sane, productive, and even worthy of praise; yet, these same people find the idea of undergoing pain for the health and purity of one's soul to be repugnant, illogical, and medieval. To the religious individual of a certain tradition and cast of mind, mortification of the flesh is but one means of practicing kenotic spirituality. Even Mother Teresa of Calcutta, perhaps one of the most recognized, respected, and admired women of her time, routinely used the cilice and discipline. She told her sisters in the Missionaries of Charity, "If I feel sick, I take five strokes (of the discipline). I must feel its need in order to share in the Passion of Christ and the suffering of our poor."[41] Fr. Clementin Wottle, a Franciscan missionary to Native Americans, quoted Mother Katharine as saying, "I wish I could take part and have the Lord give me those pains they made him suffer. I wish He would let me do it."[42] This was a desire she shared with St. Paul: "I am now rejoicing in my sufferings for your sake, and in my flesh I am completing what is lacking in Christ's afflictions for the sake of his body, that is, the church" (Col. 1:24).

This type of *kenosis,* or self-emptying through pain, is for the sake of the Church, that one may be able to bring others to Christ through the Church. One's spiritual progress "tends toward ever more intimate union with Christ."[43] "More intimate union" here refers to intimate love between Christ and his disciple, but something is not owned unless it can be shared with others; the love between Christ and his disciple must be shared by the disciple with her fellow beings in and through the Church.

Kenosis through the Evangelical Counsels

The apostle Paul puts *kenosis* in this manner, at once straightforward and mysterious: "It is no longer I who live, but it is Christ who lives in me" (Gal. 2:20). The Second Vatican Council puts its effects in this way:

> This love, this holiness, this self-emptied person now filled with Christ is expressed in many ways in individuals, who in their walk of life tend to the perfection of charity [or love], thus causing the edification of others; in a very special way this [holiness] appears in the practice of the counsels,

41. Quoted in Peter J. Boyer, "Hollywood Heresy," *New Yorker,* May 22, 2006, p. 35.
42. *Positio,* 2:278.
43. *Catechism of the Catholic Church* (Washington, D.C.: United States Catholic Conference, 1994), p. 2014.

customarily called evangelical. The practice of the counsels, under the impulsion of the Holy Spirit, undertaken by many Christians, either privately or in a Church-approved condition or state of life [as priests, nuns, brothers, and the like] gives and must give in the world an outstanding witness and example of this same holiness.... The Lord Jesus ... himself stands as the author and consummator of this holiness of life: "Be you therefore perfect as your heavenly Father is perfect" [Matt. 5:48].... The followers of Christ are called by God, not because of their works, but according to his own purpose and grace.... They are warned by the Apostle to live "as becomes saints" [Eph. 5:3] and to put on "as God's chosen ones, holy and beloved, a heart of mercy, kindness, meekness, patience" [Col. 3:12] and to possess the fruit of the Spirit in holiness [cf. Gal. 5:22; Rom. 6:22].[44]

Kenosis is a path toward holiness that is not to be grasped for itself alone. It is but a means to an end, to holiness. Mother Katharine shared the spirit of *kenosis* with her sisters, who had answered the call of Jesus to serve him. Christ initiates the call, and, moved by the Holy Spirit, the disciple discerns its authenticity and obeys. In "renouncing the world [religious] may live for God alone. They have dedicated their entire lives to his service. This constitutes a special consecration that is deeply rooted in that of Baptism and expresses it more fully.... In such a way they share in Christ's emptying of himself [cf. Phil. 2:7] and in his life in the Spirit [cf. Rom. 8:1-3].... Religious are to follow him as the one thing necessary [cf. Luke 10:42]. They fix their minds and hearts on him."[45] Their complete commitment to Christ in this life foreshadows and provides a pretaste of their complete unity with Christ in the perfection of love in the world to come. Here is a prayer from Katharine that demonstrates her understanding of the connection between serving Christ completely in this life and at the same time looking forward to the next. Self-abandoned, she no longer belonged to herself but to Christ alone — absolutely. "Yes, my Lord, and my God Jesus, to you I commend my spirit, my soul with its faculties, my body with its senses, my heart with its affection, all that I have, and all that I am. Dispose of me absolutely, in everything, according to Your will. Henceforth, dearest Jesus, may everything outside You be a matter of indifference to me, provide only I accomplish

---

44. *Lumen Gentium,* November 21, 1964, in *The Sixteen Documents of Vatican II,* introduced by Douglas Bushman, gen. ed., Marianne Lorraine Trouvé (Boston: Pauline Books and Media, 1999), pp. 39-40.

45. *Lumen Gentium,* 5.

Your will and advance Your love. O Jesus, I love You and Your Mother and abandon myself to Your love for time and eternity."[46]

In answering the call to become consecrated missionaries for Christ, Katharine and her sisters took the vows of the evangelical counsels of obedience, poverty, and chastity. These vows form a type of continuous kenotic exercise because they require the individual to empty herself of will, so that the will of Christ and her superiors may be fulfilled through her; of temporal goods, so that she may be filled with spiritual graces and complete dependence on the providence of God; and of personal comfort and human attachment, so that nothing will distract her from the care of her soul and those of others. Katharine and her sisters became the willing "victims of love."

Obedience Primary among the counsels is obedience. Obedience is so primary to the religious life that it is the only vow that the Benedictine sisters take. According to Katharine Drexel, "Love is surrender, surrender of the will."[47] To accept Christ's call to the religious state of life is to make an assent of the intellect and will. The call comes to be obeyed or not. It is never a forced choice but one to be taken of one's free will. The religious woman accepts the call joyfully and willingly. Jesus, the Bridegroom, "stands at the door and knocks." The suitor may be rejected, or the prospective bride may run to the door and throw it open exclaiming, "My Jesus, my Spouse! My God and my All!"[48]

> In professing obedience, religious offer the full surrender of their own will as a sacrifice of themselves to God and so are united permanently and securely to God's salvific will.
>
> After the example of Jesus Christ who came to do the will of the Father [cf. John 4:34; 5:30; Heb. 10:7; Ps. 39:9] and "assuming the nature of a slave" [Phil. 2:7] learned obedience in the school of suffering [cf. Heb. 5:8], religious under the motion of the Holy Spirit subject themselves in faith to their superiors who hold the place of God. Under their guidance they are led to serve all their brothers in Christ, just as Christ himself in obedience to the Father served his brethren and laid down his life as a ransom for many [cf. Matt. 20:28; John 10:14-18]. . . .

46. MKD, *Praying with Mother Katharine Drexel* (Bensalem, Pa.: Sisters of the Blessed Sacrament, 1986), p. 22.

47. MKD, *Reflections on Religious Life*, p. 10.

48. MKD, *Conferences, Counsels, and Maxims of a Missionary Foundress*, p. 95.

> Realizing that they are contributing to building up the body of Christ according to God's plan, they [religious] should use both the forces of their intellect and will and the gifts of nature and grace to execute the commands and fulfill the duties entrusted to them. In this way religious obedience, far from lessening the dignity of the human person, by extending the freedom of the sons [and daughters] of God, lead it to maturity.[49]

As consecrated women, they can only give to God, and his vicars in authority, that which is theirs to give. Katharine noted:

> The only thing we can give back to our Lord is our will. Other things He has given us He can also take back — our lives even. But our free will God does not take from us. . . . Tomorrow, of your own free will, you will renew your vows for one year with the intention (do not forget it) of persevering until death. You give your free will by that free act to God, and your will says: "We offer up the Host," and by your own free act, you are united to the Host in that offering. Let us offer ourselves every day to live our offering more and more perfectly.
>
> What is that act that we offer to God? It is submission. It is to offer yourselves on the altar, joined to Christ. What does this mean? It means we offer our submission, or obedience to God. That is what makes our Mass so important for us as consecrated beings, as it did for our Lord. Once I thought our Lord was a victim only when He died on the cross. I now know that He was a victim all His life. Every day of your life you, as a religious consecrated to God by your vows, are a victim of submission and obedience.[50]

Even Mother M. Katharine Drexel, the superior general of the Sisters of the Blessed Sacrament, was called to obedience. Her duty was to obey the bishop. She had to be reprimanded constantly by her spiritual director, Bishop O'Connor, to avoid excessive deprivation of nourishment.

With the irony of hindsight, one may read her letters and her retreat notes. One particular instance relates to obedience due superiors. While she was the superior and mother general of the order, each mission and each convent had its own superior. She wrote about herself and other superiors:

---

49. *Perfectae Caritatis,* October 28, 1965, 14, in *The Sixteen Documents of Vatican II.*

50. MKD, *Reflections on Religious Life,* p. 9. Also see, *Conferences, Counsels, and Maxims,* p. 53.

"I do not want you to consider your superior from a natural viewpoint, for naturally you may like her and naturally you may not. I know of no religious order of which it could be said that their superiors immediately became saints upon becoming superiors. If such were the case, would we not all scramble for the job?"[51] Furthermore, she did not want any down-faced, toe-dragging obedience: "Obey cheerfully because our Lord loves a cheerful giver. Obey courageously."[52]

Chastity One must be courageous indeed to give up the joy, comfort, and companionship of marriage or the relative liberty entailed in the single state to become a nun. By emptying herself of emotional and physical attachment to others through the vow of chastity, the religious woman, Katharine Drexel, for example, gave herself totally to Christ, her spouse, with an undivided love: "O happy indeed shall you be if your divine Spouse, Who is all love for you, finds you generously devoted to Him and so in love with Him that you no longer live, but He lives in you."[53] In renouncing human love, Katharine wholly accepted the more perfect acquisition of the divine love of Christ. She called chastity "the most angelic virtue consecrated in the Person of Jesus Christ and exalted in His teachings. Sisters, therefore, shall esteem nothing more precious than this heavenly gift and shall exercise constant vigilance to keep the purity of their hearts untarnished."[54] The Church also recognizes and honors holy chastity for the love of God. "Chastity 'for the sake of the kingdom of heaven' [Matt. 19:12] which religious profess should be counted an outstanding gift of grace. It frees the heart of man [or woman] in a unique fashion [cf. 1 Cor. 7:32-35] so that it may be more inflamed by love for God and for all [people]. It . . . symbolizes in a singular way . . . the most suitable means by which religious dedicate themselves with undivided heart to the service of God and the apostolate."[55]

The words "inflamed by love" call to mind Katharine's exhortation to her sisters on the need to immolate self, to die to self so that Christ may live within. It was a favorite trope of hers, as in this prayer: "May our own will, desires and self-will be annihilated so that we may burn with His love."[56]

---

51. MKD, *Conferences, Counsels, and Maxims*, p. 54.

52. MKD, *Reflections on Religious Life*, p. 10.

53. MKD, *Reflections on Religious Life*, p. 10.

54. Holy Rule of the Sisters of the Blessed Sacrament for Indians and Colored People, 1913, p. 110.

55. *Perfectae Caritatis*, 12.

56. MKD, Meditation Slips, 1, #102.

Lumen Gentium repeats the idea of self-sacrifice that is found throughout Katharine's writings, and it includes the same image of the "undivided heart" that is also found in the language of *Perfectae Caritatis.*

> The holiness of the Church is fostered in a special way by the observance of the [evangelical] counsels proposed by our Lord to his disciples. An eminent position among these is held by virginity or the celibate state [cf. 1 Cor. 7:32-34]. This is a precious gift of divine grace given by the Father to certain souls [cf. Matt. 19:11; 1 Cor. 7:7], whereby they may devote themselves to God alone the more easily, due to an undivided heart. This perfect continency, out of desire for the kingdom of heaven, has always been held in particular honor in the Church.[57]

In writing to one of her sisters on making her final vows, Katharine congratulated the young woman, calling the appointed day the happiest in her life, excepting the day of her initial vows. She added, "Our Final Vows may be considered as a consummation of that happiest Day which consecrated us a chalice to Our Lord. Now this consecration, thank God, is forever if you are faithful to Our Lord with that fidelity with which we are <u>sure</u> He will be faithful to you."[58] This type of nuptial language is proper to the concept of the professed religious as a bride of Christ. The language of *kenosis,* of emptying oneself to be filled by the bridegroom and of the virginal chalice also to be filled by the bridegroom, is symbolic of a type of holy, mystical intercourse consummating one to the other in a marriage of eternal fidelity. However, the vow of chastity is often narrowly construed to mean simply refraining from sexual activity and repression of any sexual thoughts or desires.

It is far more than that, as demonstrated by a rather lengthy quote from Katharine's writings. To be chaste is to be pure in everything one does, thinks, or expresses. It is both an interior and an exterior disposition of purity. It takes in everything from one's modesty and cleanliness of dress, to how one sits and walks, to thinking or saying evil of another, even if it is true. Not only what is said, but also the manner in which it is expressed, is subject to the rule of chastity.

> It is by the vow of chastity that the religious acquires the inestimable honor of becoming the spouse of the King of Kings. This exalted dignity

---

57. *Lumen Gentium,* 42.
58. MKD, Meditation Slips, 1, #1011.

is assigned to her by the Fathers of the Church who teach that the veil and the ring serve as exterior reminders of this sublime espousal. Truly do we say on that day of our profession "He has placed His seal on my forehead that I should admit no other lover but Him," and "I am espoused to Him whom the angels serve at whose beauty the sun and moon stand in wonder." With regard to the virtue of chastity, our Constitutions are explicit as to the means which are to be employed for reserving "the most angelic virtue." One of the means mentioned is religious modesty which is a precious help to chastity. Religious modesty is not an austere, unrelaxed seriousness, nor is it a repulsive coldness or indifference of manner which is calculated to repel others rather than to attract them to God. It is a manner and deportment which render it evident to all that the religious tends with her whole being to Him in Whom all her designs are centered and to Whom she would attract as many others as she can. Religious modesty is also the enemy of all affectation, singularity, and display. It leads to the practice of the hidden life in which the religious seeks only the pleasure of her Divine Spouse and finds all in Him. A truly modest religious would be ashamed and pained rather than pleased or flattered at being distinguished or particularly remarked in any way, for has she not "chosen to be an abject in the house of the Lord"? "We are dead and our life is hidden with Christ in God." Any apparent levity or want of self-control and amiable reserve which should ever characterize the religious would be a flaw in the chaste resemblance a Sister should bear to her Divine Spouse and Model. Modesty exercises its control over the whole exterior, restraining and moderating every movement and use of the senses. It regulates the manner of walking and retrenches everything in the deportment that would be unsuitable in a religious. It admits of no unnecessary gestures or movements. It excludes unbecoming postures in sitting. It preserves as much tranquility and repose as are consistent with each duty; one who indulges in a restless, fidgety manner is almost perpetually breaking the rules of religious modesty. Modesty controls the tone of the voice and the manner of speaking. It permits no words unsuitable to our state to escape us. Modesty teaches its possessor to listen with respect to the opinions of others and not to be too forward in expressing her own. It prevents her giving opinions in a decided manner, monopolizing a conversation, interrupting others, uttering words of self-praise, contradicting, complaining of heat or cold, or indulging in gossip.

The Sisters should speak and act in such a manner as will edify all those with whom they come in contact. They should act with childlike simplicity and always regulate their manner by rules of refinement and religious politeness.

Curiosity, which is also contrary to religious modesty, is the capital enemy of recollection and union with God. The two cannot co-exist. The necessity of hearing and seeing what our duties impose is incumbent, but we should mortify our curiosity in what is not necessary for the discharge of our duties nor conducive to our sanctification. . . .

The Sisters should not use slang words or phrases, which are most unbecoming to a religious and more particularly to us, dedicated as we are to Jesus in the Blessed Sacrament. The Sisters should ever appear as refined, dignified ladies in manner and speech.[59]

In many ways, the last sentence of this quotation reveals Katharine's understanding of what it means to be modest and pure in manner and deportment. She undoubtedly heard these same sentiments over and over again from her mother and from her teacher-governess, Mary Cassidy, as they tried to transform the "hurley-burley" young Katharine into a refined and dignified lady. However, the religious who has made the vow of chastity practices the virtue as an evangelical counsel dedicated to God out of love for him. Thus the virtue becomes supernatural in the life of the religious, especially graced as it is by the Holy Spirit and oriented toward her eschatological end in Christ. Rule 112, among others, of the Sisters of the Blessed Sacrament addresses how to persevere in the vow of chastity: "To preserve the angelic virtue more easily, the Sisters shall carefully restrain their senses, especially their eyes and imagination. They must be intolerant of idleness, prudent in their reading, and free of familiarity in speech and manner with anyone. They shall be constant in prayer, mortification, and penance, and devoted to humility and religious modesty." Indeed, these are recognizable as actions consistent with the practice of *kenosis*.

Poverty Again, through reinforcing the home as the first school of virtues, the Drexel household, though immensely wealthy, practiced spiritual poverty out of religious conviction. Katharine moved from spiritual poverty, a detachment from the goods of the earth, to practice actual material poverty as the founder of the Sisters of the Blessed Sacrament for Indians and Col-

---

59. MKD, *Directory and Customs of the Sisters of the Blessed Sacrament for Indians and Colored People: Maxims and Counsels and Excerpts from Conferences of Mother Mary Katharine* (Cornwells Heights, Pa.: Sisters of the Blessed Sacrament, 1961), pp. 30-33.

ored People. Poverty is the third evangelical counsel the religious vows to keep, and like both obedience and chastity, it, too, is practiced as an interior disposition made manifest in exterior action. It is a form of *kenosis.* In the sisterhood, spiritual poverty, or detachment from temporal goods, is the interior predisposition that makes it possible for sisters to give up voluntarily the goods of the created universe in joyful hope of the treasures in the world to come. It is, in fact, required before the actual poverty of consecrated life can be maintained in the proper spirit. Religious poverty does not mean abject poverty without basic needs being met. Necessary needs are to be met; it is the unnecessary goods that are to be redirected for the benefit of others. Katharine told her sisters to "desire little in this world: be not eager for what you desire, that is, live without desire: resign yourself most perfectly to the loving Providence of God your Father."[60] *Perfectae Caritatis* describes the person of Katharine Drexel when it posits that the "religious should diligently practice and if need be express also in new forms that voluntary poverty which is recognized and highly esteemed especially today as an expression of following Christ. By which they share in the poverty of Christ who for our sakes became poor, even though he was rich, so that by his poverty we might become rich [cf. 2 Cor. 8:9; Matt. 8:20]. With regard to religious poverty, it is not enough to use goods in a way subject to the superior's will, but members must be poor both in fact and in spirit, their treasures being in heaven [cf. Matt. 6:20]."[61]

One way that Mother Katharine kept the ideal of poverty before her spiritual daughters was through her example. An example of her desire to live in simple Christ-like poverty was the manner in which she refused to endow her order by holding back a portion of her annual income from her father's estate, thereby to create funds to keep the order fiscally sound after her death. Clerics and kin alike discussed with her the possibility of securing the future of the congregation. Her friend Monsignor Joseph Stephan, director of the Bureau of Catholic Indian Missions, wrote to her at the end of 1899, "Already in this one year you have given us $83,000, Mother. Don't you think that you should begin to think about your own congregation and set aside a permanent fund for them before giving to other missions?"[62] No, she did not.

---

60. MKD, *Conferences, Counsels, and Maxims of a Missionary Foundress,* p. 18.

61. *Perfectae Caritatis,* 13.

62. Quoted in Katherine Burton, *The Golden Door: The Life of Katharine Drexel* (New York: P. J. Kenedy and Sons, 1957), pp. 162-63.

She turned for advice to Fr. Dominic Pantanella, president of the College of the Sacred Heart in Denver, Colorado. He was a Jesuit who had fled his native Italy after an outbreak of anticlericalism turned into persecution. He eventually made his way to Old St. Joseph's in Philadelphia, where he met the Drexel family. He was known as an expert in canon law, and he was able to help her determine an appropriate financial arrangement of her funds for her congregation. Her income, though it came directly to her as per her father's will, was immediately signed over to the congregation. Though she was the superior of the order, it was not hers to dispose of at will. As the chief administrator for the congregation, she had the discretionary ability to allot sums up to five hundred dollars. An expenditure over that amount required her to consult with her council. In actual practice, she consulted with the council for sums over one hundred dollars.

At the time she was formulating the rule for the SBS, the Vatican did not allow congregations to be entirely mendicant. It was important to Rome that the sisters of orders be provided for and that they did not have to beg for their upkeep. Such would be a sin against mercy and justice and therefore a scandal for the Church. At the time of her letter to Fr. Pantanella in 1903, each sister in the SBS had an income of $250 from a small endowment. Katharine's question to the canon lawyer dealt with providing not for the sisters themselves, but for the work of their apostolate. She wanted to know if canon law required the congregation's works to be endowed. She was opposed to endowing future work when the entirety of her income went into present expenditures for missions and schools. The reasons for her opposition to endowing future works were at once spiritual and supremely practical. She wrote:

> What provision is there for the support of our works? <u>Answer</u>: The beneficent Providence of God. And why do I deem it best to trust to God for the support of our works? 1st: Because riches and treasures in Heaven are where neither moths nor rust can consume them. If we use our money in alms given to other Religious for carrying on works for the salvation of Indian and Colored — works for which we ourselves have not sufficient number of Sisters to carry out ourselves — if we judiciously give <u>the alms so as to insure</u> that the work be carried on well & not in a half hearted way by these other Religious — I hold that we will be doing a present good for the salvation of these souls which God will reward far, far beyond that which He would reward if with worldly prudence we were to store away immense sums of money to support our Institutes.

She explained to Fr. Pantanella that the four present missions of the SBS annually educated, fed, and clothed just over five hundred students, and that together the missions cost the congregation $51,640 per annum. She did not indicate how much the SBS gave to other orders of priests and nuns who worked with African Americans and Native Americans, but the amount was perhaps close to $300,000. Her portion of the interest from her father's estate ranged between $1,000 and $2,000 a day.[63] Most of what was given to other orders was done anonymously through the Catholic Mission Bureaus for African-Americans and Native-Americans. Being the banker's daughter that she was, she pointed out to the priest that it would take an endowment of $1,020,000, safely invested at a 5 percent rate of return, to yield an income of $51,000 a year.

> Now, whilst putting away such a sum as this [$1,020,000], think of the number of souls amongst the Colored and Indian that could be ministered to whilst hoarding up this money for endowment. Each soul that we might have come to rescue might in turn convert another soul & and think of the present good — the souls who may be lost while we are amassing a sum for future support of 4 Institutes containing 507 children. If these four Institutes of ours are good, God will provide for them if we on our part go forth to use all of our intelligence and means to bring the Indian & Colored to know, love & serve Him by all the ways in our power directly or indirectly. I firmly hold that it is the faithful who should be instrumental in maintaining for God His works. . . . [My] annual income [will] cease at my death. So, if I were to die to-morrow, there would be sufficient to support the Sisters; but as to our schools in Virginia, & the Navajos, God would have to support them or they would have to be sold and close. I feel, however, that if God wants them, He would support them or works in the future; if He does not, why should we?[64]

63. Lou Baldwin, *A Call to Sanctity: The Formation and Life of Mother Katharine Drexel* (Philadelphia: Catholic Standard and Times, 1999), p. 86. In the early years, the three Drexel sisters shared an annual income of approximately $750,000. Elizabeth died childless in 1890; her portion of the estate went to Katharine. When Louise died childless in 1943, her portion also reverted to Katharine. Unfortunately, the estate income by that time was reduced to only approximately $400,000 a year. Throughout the years, as SBS missions and schools increased in number and expense, the amounts given annually to other missionary orders of priests and nuns declined, but support never ceased entirely.

64. MKD to Pantanella, October 14, 1903.

In this last quotation from her letter to Fr. Pantanella, she merely states what the Second Vatican Council would later declare. First, she writes that the missions should be supported by the entire body of Christ, not just the institutes whose specific apostolate is missionary. The Decree on the Apostolate of the Laity states that by virtue of the great commandment of Christ to love God with one's whole heart and one's neighbor as oneself, the general laity "should make missionary activity their own by giving material or even personal assistance. It is a duty and honor for Christians to return to God a part of the good things that they have received from him."[65] Second, she makes the important point that the essence of her order is not self-perpetuation, but docility to the will of God and the evangelization of and service to the African American and native peoples. Such is characteristic of kenotic spirituality, to be empty of self in order to be receptive to the will of God, whatever it may be, and the will of God as expressed in his Church. The Church approves the rules of the congregations, receives the vows, and regulates the practice of the evangelical counsels. Therefore the Church decides the fate of orders that are floundering financially or in number of novices. "There may be communities and monasteries which the Holy See, after consulting the interested local ordinaries, will judge not to possess reasonable hope for further development. These should be forbidden to receive novices in the future. If it is possible, these should be combined with other more flourishing communities and monasteries whose scope and spirit is similar."[66] After all, she wrote her sisters, "Success is not the criterion of the spiritual life."[67]

Could there be a better example of the spirit of kenotic poverty than Katharine's utter sense of detachment from the goods of the temporal world and her willingness to put her entire order, the work of her life, into the hands of Providence? Fr. Pantanella agreed with her plans not to endow the works of her order and helped her write that part of her rule that dealt with poverty. In this very important way, she led her sisters in the spirit of poverty, setting the tone for the entire congregation. Her great income from her father's estate and the question whether or not to challenge her father's will, a course of action many were advising her to undertake, were a great burden to her. How liberating it must have been for her to have the question

---

65. *Apostolicam Actuositatem,* November 18, 1965, 10, in *The Sixteen Documents of Vatican II.*

66. *Perfectae Caritatis,* 21.

67. MKD, *Reflections on Religious Life,* p. 25.

settled. She wrote, "We are free when we practice voluntary poverty. We fly unimpeded to God."[68]

From a practical standpoint, because she was known as the "Millionaire Nun," she feared that if the congregation did not live in strict material poverty, the poor people it was formed to serve might not welcome the sisters. Additionally, others would not feel it their Christian duty financially to support the missions.

> I feel, dear Daughters, if we wish our works to be blessed we must be poor, confining ourselves to the necessary. The WORK we have to do is far beyond what our income will enable us to do — 10 millions, no 100 and 100 millions of souls cry to us for that bread of life — the knowledge and love of God. If others see that we are *really* poor, and that we bestow the most we can possibly afford in the works Our Lord had confided to us, they will be the more apt to help us in our work. If, on the contrary, they see us absorb alms on superfluities and enjoy these rather than enjoying aid for the salvation of souls, the poor even of this world are often animated with a more generous spirit of sacrifice, and we will chill the charity of those who otherwise might help us in our works for God. Even the aid of a poor working girl may be taken for this and God will bless her as He will the alms of this girl, May [Williams]; but He would not, I think, bless us in the accepting it except for a real necessity of ours or our work. (emphasis added)[69]

Evidently May Williams, out of gratitude to the sisters, wanted to give them something for their pleasure, so she enclosed in a letter a one dollar bill, along with twenty-five two-cent stamps. Her gesture seems innocuous and generous, but as the mother superior, Katharine used it as a teaching point on the evangelical counsel of poverty.

> It does not seem to me in accordance with the spirit of poverty for us Sisters of the Blessed Sacrament, who are a Missionary Congregation, to accept from a poor girl, earning her living, a superfluity of this kind. The money is not given for a <u>necessary</u> visit to St. Elizabeth's, but for one of mere gratification of the Sisters. The Catechism of the vows defines the second degree of Religious Poverty in its <u>practice</u> as "to be <u>satisfied</u> with

---

68. MKD, *Reflections on Religious Life*, p. 7.
69. MKD to the SBS at Our Lady of the Blessed Sacrament, 1913.

what is <u>necessary</u> (remark, '<u>necessary</u>'), to remove all irregular affectation, as well as all that <u>is superfluous</u> for our support (remark all that is
superfluous); this is the obligatory matter of the <u>virtue</u>." It jars on my
sense of what I would wish the spirit of our Congregation, to have it as a
gratification to us to be supplied with the superfluous — We who should
curtail all superfluities not only in accordance with the virtue of poverty
to which <u>all</u> religious, no matter of what Congregation, should incline;
but also because we are a Missionary Congregation and if anything what-
soever beyond the necessary is supplied, we should zealously wish that
that little even beyond the necessary should go towards saving souls, and
not towards supplying us with superfluities. . . . Now for us who have 10
millions of Colored in the U.S. and 250,000 Indians, not to speak of the
Colored and Indians in teeming masses in other parts of the world, we
should wish as much as possible to cut down on superfluities first in the
spirit of our vow for the Catechism of the Vow says: "A religious <u>who has
the spirit</u> of Poverty will accustom himself [or herself] to regard as consecrated to God, all that belongs to the community or is intended for its
use." Secondly, as ours is consecrated as much as possible to extending
the Kingdom of Christ, and as even a leaflet of the Sacred Heart Society
costs money, not to speak of the cost of maintaining children in schools,
in carfare for Sisters to attend the schools, in books for schools and libraries, clothing for the poor, diet for the poor, etc., etc., we should be most
conscientious in confining our <u>desires</u> to the necessary, as well as our
expenditures. . . . In the same Catechism we read with regard to a religious
who has the spirit of Poverty, "he will practice the <u>sacrifice</u> of all temporal
goods and <u>the conveniences</u> they procure, through a principle of mortification and penance, in expiation of sin; through contempt of <u>earthly</u>
goods and to secure to himself those of heaven; through love of Jesus
Christ his Divine King and the desire of resembling him in poverty, and
in order that all of his affections may be undividedly given to his Lord."[70]

Naturally, as one dedicated to poverty and a leader of others, she practiced personal poverty in every way possible, for the spirit of poverty obtains
in small things as well as in large ones. Katharine wore one pair of shoes for
over ten years, until there was nothing left of the original shoes except, like
Theseus's boat, their "shoeness."[71] Everything about them had been repaired

---

70. MKD to the SBS at Our Lady of the Blessed Sacrament, 1913.
71. Plutarch, *Lives of the Noble Greeks,* ed. Edmund Fuller (New York: Dell, 1971),

and replaced several times, including the tire-tread rubber on the soles. No doubt the soles had been leather at one time, but a woman who annually visited her fifty or so missions for more than forty years had a way of wearing out her shoes. She wore all her pencils down to their nubs. She used and re-used scraps of paper. She would write vertically and then horizontally across her letters to conserve paper. She knew that example is the best teacher. One of the Indian mission students said of her, "None of us knew she was the rich one. She did all of the dirty jobs."[72] Poverty and humility go hand in hand. In *Lumen Gentium, 42,* Vatican Council II addressed poverty and humility in the example of Christ.

> Jesus Christ . . . "emptied Himself, taking the nature of a slave . . . becoming obedient to death" [Phil. 2:7-8], and because of us, "being rich, he became poor" [2 Cor. 8:9]. Because the disciples must always offer an imitation of and a testimony to the charity and humility of Christ, Mother Church rejoices at finding within her bosom men and women who very closely follow their Savior who debased Himself to our comprehension. There are some who, in their freedom as sons [and daughters] of God, renounce their own wills and take upon themselves the state of poverty.

In the spirit of poverty and humility, Katharine could be found on her knees washing the convent floors, tending to garden and kitchen duties, taking on the classroom duties of an ill sister, or sitting at the sewing circle in the evenings repairing and reweaving or patching shoelaces and habits. She would never expect from her sisters that which she was unwilling to do, and apparently there was nothing she was unwilling to do. She sat up, sometimes all night long, with her sisters who were ill. She was nursing Sister Mary Patrick when the young novice died in the night of tuberculosis, the first of the Sisters of the Blessed Sacrament to die. The mother superior took it upon herself to wash the body, dress it in a fresh habit, and lay it in a bed of fresh linen. She wanted everything to be just right before the other sisters were called to pray at the bedside of their departed friend and sister. The superior then spent an hour alone praying for the soul of the young woman before the rest of the convent was notified of her death.

---

p. 27. Also see David Hume, *Treatise of Human Nature,* ed. L. A. Selby-Bigge (Oxford: Clarendon, 1967), p. 257.

72. Jeanette Rave, quoted in Anthony J. Costa, "The Spirituality of St. Katharine Drexel: Eucharistic Devotion Nourishing Apostolic Works" (Rome: Facultate S. Theologiae, Apud Pontificiam Universitatem S. Thomae, 2001), p. 131.

The Fourth Vow   In big things as in small ones, interior and exterior ones, as a religious woman, Katharine Drexel made her vows to obedience, chastity, and poverty. It was common in the nineteenth century for orders of nuns to add a so-called fourth vow that spoke directly to their specific apostolate. Therefore, in addition to vowing to uphold the practice of the evangelical counsels, Katharine vowed "to be the Mother and Servant of the Indian and Negro Races, according to the Rule and Constitutions of the Sisters of the Blessed Sacrament for Indians and Colored People; nor shall I undertake any work which may tend to the neglect or abandonment of the Indian and Colored Races." This resolution to be the mother and servant of African Americans and Native Americans was written into the sisters' constitutions, which the Church approved in 1907, and could not be changed without the express permission of the Holy See. The Sisters of Mercy had as their fourth vow "service of the poor, sick, and ignorant."[73] These types of vows helped the congregations keep their focus on their specific apostolate and protected them when they were tempted to assist other good causes not part of their original purpose. The Sisters of the Blessed Sacrament have kept their fourth vow to this day; though they have opened their missions and schools to all peoples in need, regardless of race, they stress the priority of Native Americans and African Americans. Without the maintenance of the evangelical counsels, the order could not hope to carry out its fourth vow.

In writing to her sisters on the virtue of poverty, Katharine turned, as she so often did, to the example of Christ. "Our Spouse was born poor and laid in a manger. 'The birds of the air have their nests; the Son of Man has nowhere to lay His head' (Matthew 8:20). He lived poor, died poor, and the last treasure He gave away was His mother."[74] Her discourse might have been on poverty, but in speaking of the gift of Mary, she also pointed the way to carry out the fourth vow to be the mother and servant of the African American and native populations. To her, Mary the mother of God was the perfect model of self-abandonment, with her simple "Fiat" to God's invitation to become the mother of his Son. She emptied herself of self-will to have her womb and life filled with Jesus. She was also the perfect example of what it means to be a mother. The Second Vatican Council echoes this theme of Mary's divine maternity and amplifies it: "By reason of the gift and role of divine maternity, by which she is united with her Son, the Redeemer, and

---

73. Lynch, *Sharing the Bread,* 1:48.
74. MKD, *Reflections on Religious Life,* p. 7.

with His singular graces and functions, the Blessed Virgin is also intimately united with the Church. As St. Ambrose taught, the Mother of God is a type of the Church in the order of faith, charity, and perfect union with Christ. For in the mystery of the Church, which is itself rightly called mother and virgin, the Blessed Virgin stands out in eminent and singular fashion as exemplar both of virgin and mother."[75]

More than an example, Mary is an active principal in fulfilling the work of her Son.

> This maternity of Mary in the order of grace began with the consent which she gave in faith at the Annunciation and which she sustained without wavering beneath the cross, and lasts until the eternal fulfillment of all the elect. Taken up to heaven she did not lay aside this salvific duty, but by her constant intercession continued to bring us the gifts of eternal salvation. By her maternal charity, she cares for the brethren of her Son, who still journey on earth surrounded by dangers and difficulties, until they are led into the happiness of their true home.[76]

In pointing her sisters to Mary, the "model of all virtues" and the "sure sign of hope and solace," Katharine told them how to carry out their apostolate as mothers to the African American and native peoples.[77] She said, "Earthly mothers, being imperfect, give way to their bad humor and sometimes scold their children; while Mary knows only how to console, to relieve, to purify."[78] According to the witness of Mother Mary Mercedes (d. 1940), who followed Katharine as mother general in 1937, Katharine learned the lessons of Mary's motherhood well and modeled them for her sisters as she guided the postulants and novices through their infancy in religion to the adulthood of the perpetually professed sister.

> While accessible at stated hours during the week, she took each Novice and Postulant for a spiritual talk, yet every evening from half past six until eight o'clock, Mother sat in the bay window of the parlor, which immediately joined the chapel. There one by one the different Novices and Postulants who wished to see her were seated outside the door. Every little

---

75. *Lumen Gentium*, 63.
76. *Lumen Gentium*, 62.
77. *Lumen Gentium*, 65 and 68.
78. MKD, *Reflections on Religious Life*, p. 28.

lapse of rule or little trouble, indisposition of soul or body was brought there. It just seemed as if you were going out of the invisible presence of God to His visible mouthpiece. Every little sorrow was soothed, every difficulty straightened out, everyone was encouraged to do everything for the love of God, that love of God which would do anything for the Spouse, that always walked in His presence with the greatest purity of intention and whose joy it was to do things for the Beloved. There was so much sweetness. So much sympathy, such keen understanding of everyone, such quickness to put her finger on the sore spot . . . each felt that Mother bore each one's individual trouble to the Feet of Our Lord and consulted Him alone about them.[79]

Katharine would never point to herself as an example. She desired that her sisters concentrate on Mary as the model of all motherly virtues. To remind them of their close association with the motherhood of Mary, all the sisters took Mary as their first name in religion. Hence there was a Sr. Mary Benedicta, a Sr. Mary Peter, and so forth. In following Mary, the virgin mothers of the SBS were to keep close to her Son and help to bring about the completion of his mission on earth. "It was the Father's Will that His Son be watched over and cared for by Mary, His Mother. So may we who regard her in a particular manner as our Mother and model, be confident that her intercession will enable us to fulfill the obligations of our Holy Institute and to implant Jesus Christ in the hearts of the Indians and Colored People."[80] In following Mary, they obey the command of Christ from the cross, "behold your mother" (John 19:27). "The Mother of Jesus obeyed as a servant and conducted herself as if she were inferior."[81] Mary was a type of mother and servant for the sisters to emulate as they lived out their missionary apostolate. Katharine prayed frequently to Mary and urged her sisters to do the same:

Think over the words of our Blessed Mother's "Magnificat." Let us say: I will take hold of the hand of my Mother whom God in His goodness and mercy and love gave to me. I will look up into her loving countenance and meet the encouraging gaze of her, the sinless one, looking upon one who is not sinless, yet seeing in me one who has been made by baptism

---

79. *Positio*, 1:515-16. Also in the Memoirs of MM Mercedes in the ASBS.
80. MKD to SBS, Christmas 1936, in ASBS.
81. MKD, *Reflections on Religious Life*, p. 28.

(through God's love and mercy) a child of God. Both of us can address her. "O sweet Spouse of the Holy Spirit. . . ." We can imagine her saying sentence by sentence, the "Magnificat" — then listening as we repeat back to her, "My soul magnifies the Lord!"[82]

In her vows to uphold the evangelical counsels and her fourth vow to be the mother and servant of the "Indian and Colored People," and in the mortification of her flesh, Katharine was practicing *kenosis*. Her *kenosis* was evident to those who knew her. Murray Lincoln, a Navajo, commented on her spirituality: "It was something that was beyond . . . something that was beyond mankind, something more powerful. . . . She really emptied herself . . . completely through the love of God."[83] *Kenosis* understands this way as both an action and an attitude. It is a recognition that the personal "I" must wane so that God may wax. One must make within oneself a negative space that Christ can fill. In 1881, Katharine wrote implicitly of the importance of *kenosis:* "Always try to approach the Holy Table with more and more love. Divest your heart of all love of the world and of yourself and then you will leave room for Jesus." After this entry into her spiritual journal, she continued, "Thank Our Lord for having redeemed your soul with His Most Precious Blood."[84] God's redeeming action needs a stage. In *kenosis,* one makes room for God to act, acknowledging one's dependence on God rather than on oneself. One leaves room for God so as to become an instrument of his will, which is salvation. At the age of twenty-three, she explicitly acknowledged that by herself and on her own she was nothing, could do nothing. "I here protest that of myself I can do nothing," and therefore she promised herself, "<u>Do not think of self</u> but of God in all things. To renounce self. By frequent offerings, by hastily stopping the least vain thought or thought of self."[85] Richard Cardinal Cushing, then bishop and director of the Society for the Preservation of the Faith in Boston, wrote of Katharine on the occasion of her golden jubilee in 1941, "What after all is the greatest contribution that Mother Katharine has made to the Church of God and neglected souls? . . . Her greatest contribution was the sacrifice of herself, *stripped of self,* to become part and parcel of God's plan to redeem the Negro and Indian of the

---

82. MKD, *Praying with Mother Katharine Drexel,* p. 14.

83. *Positio,* 2:345.

84. MKD, Meditation Slips, 4, 1881. Date according to Costa, "Spirituality of St. Katharine Drexel," p. 18.

85. MKD, Meditation Slips, 4, 1881.

United States."[86] She emptied herself so as to be filled with Christ, the same Christ who came to her most concretely in the Eucharist.

Eucharistic Spirituality

Kenotic spirituality is multivalent. Its various practices, from modesty of the eyes to the flailing of flesh, free the body and the mind for contemplation of the holy. Its aim is to bring to perfection the statement of St. Paul, "It is no longer I who live, but it is Christ who lives in me" (Gal. 2:20). Katharine emptied herself through prayer, penance, deprivation, and pain so that she could be filled with Christ. She said of herself, "I leave myself and give God my <u>nothing and my sins</u>."[87] More precisely, and most perfectly, she left herself, she emptied herself, so she could be filled with Christ in the Eucharist. Every single person whose interview was recorded in the *Positio* for Katharine's canonization made note of her deep eucharistic spirituality. It was her defining characteristic.

Her eucharistic spirituality was evident to those who knew her, even to those who only knew her casually. She was the founder of the Sisters of the Blessed Sacrament — how could it not? If nature abhors a vacuum, so does the spirit, making eucharistic spirituality the perfect complement to kenotic spirituality. The emptying out of self and the filling up with Christ are like lungs expiring and inspiring, creating, in effect, a single life-giving and sustaining action. Each action needs the other. The Eucharist was for Katharine, as it is for the Church, her font and summit.[88] It was the highest expression of Christ's love for her and her love for him. It was, moreover, the inexhaustible source of her spiritual strength.

The view of the Church of Vatican II, that the Eucharist was its source and summit, was proleptically captured in Katharine's meditations: "In Holy Communion the life of God in a particular way is imparted to my soul. It is there that God becomes the soul of my soul, to do, to suffer, all for the love of Him who died for me, and if Thou art for me, if Thou art within me, what can I fear, O my God."[89] She refers to Christ as the "Prisoner of Love" and

86. Sisters of the Blessed Sacrament, *Golden Jubilee Booklet, 1891-1941* (Cornwells Heights, Pa.: Sisters of the Blessed Sacrament, 1941), April 18, 1941, emphasis added.

87. MKD, Retreat Notes, December 28, 1889.

88. *Sacrosanctum Concilium,* December 4, 1963, 10, in *The Sixteen Documents of Vatican II.*

89. MKD, *Conferences, Counsels, and Maxims,* p. 92.

herself as the "Victim of Love." His unconditional eucharistic love for her overtook her soul and drove her to heroic works of charity because of her love for him, yet she was aware that she was constantly short of the goal of holiness required of her. Typically, she sought for what she needed in the Eucharist. In one of her private prayers, which she commonly wrote down in pencil on small scraps of paper she kept by her bedside, she noted: "By your dear call to me in Religious vocation, I must ever strive for sanctity and holiness and I shall do so only by participating in the holiness of God. Today's Holy Communion and every Holy Communion is the special means — every Holy Mass."[90] For Catholic Christians, the Eucharist is not just a memorial of Christ's Last Supper; it is a re-presentation of the sacrifice on Calvary almost two thousand years ago; it makes present that same priest and victim. Every partaking of the consecrated host is a present event that points to the eschatological future. The communicants, redeemed by Christ and nourished by his body and blood, become what they have consumed; according to the prayers of the priest, they become "one body, one spirit in Christ." As such, they are sent forward from the Mass "to love and serve the Lord."

One of the reasons Katharine chose to enter the convent with the Sisters of Mercy was because that order was one of the few that allowed the sisters daily Communion. It was a rule she would adopt for her own order. Mother M. Irenaeus, SBS, who joined Katharine as a novice in the Mercy convent, noted of her founder, "Throughout her Novitiate days and in later life, it seemed to me that when she attended Mass she was totally oblivious of everything . . . around her. The Blessed Sacrament was to her a living, vital reality."[91] Katharine exhorted her sisters, "We must hunger for this Bread of Life [the eucharistic Host] even as the 5,000 in the desert hungered for earthly bread."[92]

Yet even daily Communion was not enough for Katharine. She would spend hours kneeling, or even lying prostrate, in adoration of the Blessed Sacrament. "I adore you, my Eucharistic Lord. You are there exposed in the ostensorium. The rays are the rays of Your love for me, for each individual soul."[93] The need to consume the "Bread of Life" was to be complemented by adoration of the paschal victim in the consecrated host. Consequently, in addition to and as an extension of the Mass, her sisters were to spend at least one-half hour daily praying before the Blessed Sacrament, as well as

---

90. MKD, *Praying with Mother Katharine Drexel*, p. 8.

91. *Positio*, 2:110.

92. MKD, *Conferences, Counsels, and, Maxims*, p. 92.

93. MKD, *Praying with Mother Katharine Drexel*, p. 4.

visiting the Blessed Sacrament before and after their daily apostolic work. This was a way of gaining the necessary strength and grace for their very difficult work, but also of reminding the sisters that it was through Christ that the fruits of their labors would be born. It would be Christ, not they, who accomplished the Father's plan. Christ himself in his monstrance, or Christ in his Tabernacle, would send them forth and receive them home again. A vocation booklet from 1912, written by Mother Katharine, emphasized that her sisters received the privilege "accorded the motherhouse of having Exposition of the Blessed Sacrament daily from early morning until evening, and in the local houses the Blessed Sacrament is exposed for adoration two days each month."[94] This was a privilege not accorded to many other orders, and it was granted due to the insistence and personal influence of Katharine. The exposition of the Sacrament in the chapels of her missionary convents was extended throughout the years.

As if all the time she spent in the chapel were not enough, Katharine spent hours at night in bed in what she notated as "NA," for nocturnal adoration. "Oh my God, what things can I offer you for the permission to spend an hour of adoration in bed at night." Her meditation notes contain many entries like the following:

> It is now 1:15 A.M. I have been on this NA since 11:15, about two hours. I shall say the Morning Offering and retire for the night!

> One hour and forty minutes over the NA.

> I looked at my watch and to my great surprise the hands of the watch say 10 to 3. The meditation was supposed to be from 1:10 to 2:10. I must stop at once.

> It is now 36 minutes over the hour of my NA. See how slow I am in contemplation.[95]

She kept up this practice her entire life, but it was especially important after her third heart attack and retirement from active administration of the order in 1937.

---

94. MKD, *A Call from Jesus*, p. 17.
95. Sr. Consuela Duffy, SBS, *Katharine Drexel: A Biography* (Philadelphia: Reilly Co., 1966), p. 369.

The adoration of the Eucharist either exposed or in the Tabernacle arose over time out of the piety of the people. The late medieval Church saw adoration of the Sacrament during Holy Week: "Forty hours of prayer before the Blessed Sacrament during Holy Week, especially during the Triduum, possibly existed in the Croatian city of Zara in the twelfth century." Pope Urban IV promulgated the bull *Transiturus* in 1264 that established the Feast of Corpus Christi for the universal church. It was and remains a major feast day for the Church, bringing the attention of the faithful to the Real Presence of Christ in the Eucharist, thus making the consecrated Host itself worthy of adoration, for the Catholic Church teaches that it truly and substantially is the body, blood, soul, and divinity of Jesus Christ. "The Forty Hours devotion was established in Milan in 1537 with exposition throughout the year occurring in successive parishes."[96] St. Philip Neri introduced the practice of the forty hours devotion to Rome in the 1550s. Pope Paul III approved a petition soliciting indulgences for those who participated in the devotion; the devotion was officially approved by Pope Paul IV in 1560. St. John Neumann (d. 1860), archbishop of Philadelphia, introduced the Forty Hours Adoration of the Blessed Sacrament into the United States in the middle of the nineteenth century. Given the intimate relationships that the Drexel family enjoyed with the priests and bishops of the Diocese of Philadelphia, it is not surprising that Katharine would cling to the Mass and the adoration of the Blessed Sacrament as foundational to her apostolate and that of her order.

Mary Heimann points out that, after the Mass, benediction of the Blessed Sacrament was the most popular Catholic devotion in England in the late nineteenth century.[97] It was also an extremely important and popular devotion in the United States. At Old St. Joseph's, the church where the teenaged Drexel daughters had taught catechism classes for young black children, there was benediction monthly, if not weekly. Benediction was celebrated for all the novenas, and, most impressive of all, Old St. Joseph's celebrated a "triple Benediction," first at the Sacred Heart altar, then at the altar of Mary, and then at the main altar. According to Ann Taves, in the United States, "Benediction usually followed Vespers on Sundays and holy days. It was also celebrated during parish missions, sometimes as often as every day."[98] Old St. Joseph's followed the same order. It had vespers on

96. Costa, "Spirituality of St. Katharine Drexel," p. 111.

97. Mary Heimann, *Catholic Devotion in Victorian England* (Oxford: Clarendon, 1995), p. 58.

98. Ann Taves, *The Household of Faith: Roman Catholic Devotions in Mid-Nineteenth-Century America* (Notre Dame, Ind.: University of Notre Dame Press, 1986), p. 30.

Sunday evening and a parish mission once a year. The parish mission at Old St. Joseph's was held annually during Lent. "There were 'instructions' at the morning masses (beginning at 6:30 A.M., with two to three Masses throughout the day). There would be time for confessions." As was common, each night focused on a different topic. There would be two nights for men and two nights designed for women. The great culmination and success of the parish mission would be the increased number of communicants on Easter morning.[99] Parish missions were essential to Catholic revivalism in the nineteenth century in America, leading to an increase in personal piety and spiritualism of the type that can be seen in Katharine Drexel.[100] The core of the Catholic revival movement was the adoration of the Blessed Sacrament and its reception.

Partaking of and adoring the Blessed Sacrament were the sources of the sisters' love for African Americans and Native Americans. Sister Mary David Young, SBS, said of Mother Katharine, "I very often heard her say we really could not give what we didn't have and that it was very important that we become as deeply religious as we possibly could be and that our love for these people must emanate from our love of the Blessed Sacrament."[101]

The Eucharist was the source not only of Christ's love for the communicant and the communicant's love for Christ, but also of the communicant's love for others because of Christ. The Eucharist served a very practical function in the life of a missionary order of nuns and their founder. Katharine Drexel was always concerned for her sisters' spiritual health. She insisted that they spend a minimum of two hours a day attending to their spiritual needs, including time spent in eucharistic adoration.

> He in the Blessed Sacrament follows you with His loving eyes when you leave the chapel for your charges and in them He watches the interior glance of your souls' eyes lifted towards His dwelling there behind the little gold Tabernacle door — to see whether it begs sanctification for your labor for Him who is so full of eager desire to unite your labors to His so as to make them His very own. Where Christ lives in every action, is not the action by its participation become divine, holy? And our Lord's Heart

99. Bobbye Burke, archivist, Old St. Joseph's, Philadelphia, Pa., email to author, October 8, 2005.

100. See Jay P. Dolan, *Catholic Revivalism: The American Experience, 1830-1900* (Notre Dame, Ind.: University of Notre Dame Press, 1978), especially the chapter "The Revival Crusade."

101. *Positio*, 2:284.

in that Tabernacle is in one sense bound until you draw this union with Him to the labor, to thus sanctify it.[102]

When Katharine wrote her 1907 Christmas letter to her sisters at St. Michael's, she stressed the unifying quality of Christ in the Eucharist.

> There is a Bethlehem in your chapel, where Jesus dwells as 1907 years ago — a manger where He really lies — the Tabernacle, and from that manger the priest will place Him on your tongue. He will abide with you — your heart too will be the manger. Keep Him with you; find Him in the representatives of Himself, the children He has placed under your care, find Him in the grown-up dusky creatures who will come to your door at Christmas; find Him in the hearts of your Sisters, and in the hearts of those children whom you have been instrumental in bringing to Baptism and the Holy Table. Thus Jesus will be praised and served by you everywhere and in all. I too will find Him in your hearts at the Midnight Mass and you will find Him in mine — let us adore Him together, place our hearts in His and thus they will be altogether one with Him and we will beg Him to keep them together in Him in time, in eternity.[103]

In his remarks on the Catholic Church in the United States, Joseph P. Chinnici, OFM, wrote, "Frequent communion, nocturnal adoration, benediction, and visits to the Blessed Sacrament represented between 1895 and 1930 an ecclesiological vision. . . . The Prisoner in the Tabernacle was the one who made the Church, one, holy, catholic, and apostolic."[104]

It was more than an ecclesial vision for Katharine Drexel; it was a personal vision. This was the Church of which she would so happily proclaim of herself again and again, "Thank God . . . that I AM A CHILD OF THE CHURCH!"[105] The devotional revival movement that came to eucharistic flower at the very end of the nineteenth century had as one of its exemplars Katharine Drexel, who loved the Church through her love of the Prisoner in the Tabernacle, her Lord who condescended to come to her in the consecrated eucharistic Host. Katharine lived her life in Christ kenotically and

---

102. MKD, Letters to SBS, 678.

103. MKD, Letters to the Southwest Missions, 1907.

104. Joseph P. Chinnici, OFM, *Living Stones: The History and Structure of Catholic Life in the United States* (New York: Macmillan, 1989), p. 152.

105. MKD, *Praying with Mother Katharine Drexel*, February 12, 1941, p. 12.

eucharistically. Her deep spirituality nurtured her through a long and difficult vocation as a living gift of self.

Katharine's spirituality is the key to understanding both her mission and her strength. She assiduously practiced *kenosis*. She emptied herself through mortification of the flesh, denying herself sustenance and causing herself pain. She emptied herself through the evangelical counsels of obedience, poverty, and chastity. She lived her vow to be as a mother to African Americans and Native Americans in ministering to them in a way that mirrored the motherhood of the Virgin Mary. She created the emptiness within herself, spiritually obliterating herself, so she could be filled by God, particularly as he is in the Eucharist. She consumed him and adored him within the Blessed Sacrament. She wanted and needed nothing but Jesus in the Sacrament. It was this kenotic and eucharistic spirituality that sustained her throughout her life as the missionary founder of the Sisters of the Blessed Sacrament. The story of the development, growth, and recent decline of the order, as described in the previous chapter, serves as but a small part of her legacy. The next chapter will analyze what Pope John Paul II found compelling about Katharine Drexel, what he saw as the legacy of a remarkable woman, and why he upheld her as a beacon in the universal call to holiness.

CHAPTER 5

The Pope, the Times, and the Saint: "Be Not Afraid!"

Katharine Drexel's was a life of heroic virtue in service to others for the love of God. It was a saintly life, and others saw her in that light. The question remains, however, why was she recognized as a saint by the Catholic Church when others, perhaps equally worthy or even more so, are not canonized? Why this particular woman at this particular time? This question can only be answered by the pope who canonized Katharine Drexel.

Pope John Paul II began his long pontificate by telling the ecclesial and secular dignitaries assembled in St. Peter's for his coronation mass and the crowds waiting outside in St. Peter's Square, "Be not afraid!" These words would become a major theme of his pontificate. Be not afraid, because Christ is faithful. Be not afraid, because the things of this world will pass away, but Christ is eternal. "Open wide the doors for Christ. To his saving power open the boundaries of states, economic and political systems, the vast fields of culture, civilization, and development. Be not afraid. Christ knows 'what is in man.' He alone knows it." In his first homily as pope, the second new pope in one month, John Paul II asked for help and prayers for himself and for all who serve Christ, because to serve Christ is to serve "the human person and the whole of mankind."[1]

To serve "the human person and the whole of mankind" provides a direct link between John Paul II and Katharine Drexel. She served the human person and the whole of mankind by recognizing what others inside and outside the

---

1. Homily, October 22, 1978, online (accessed July 28, 2004). See the Vatican Web site for English translations of papal writings, homilies, and speeches, except where noted. The encyclicals of Pope John Paul II are also published in *The Encyclicals of John Paul II,* ed. J. Miller, CSB (Huntington, Ind.: Our Sunday Visitor, 2001).

Church did not, that African Americans and Native Americans were part of mankind and that the men, women, and children of those races deserved to be treated as individuals with the dignity befitting the human person. While the political and economic systems in the United States of Katharine's day degraded people of color and acted to their disadvantage, and the general Caucasian society viewed them and their cultures as inherently inferior, Katharine saw them as children of God who needed to be helped by education to claim their human dignity, to elevate themselves and their people in order to join the wider society, and to compete with whites for the benefits the country had to offer. Even while she was offering them a political and economic leg up, her ultimate goal was to bring them to know, love, and entrust themselves to Christ in the Catholic Church. She was not afraid to speak out or to do the unpopular thing. In Katharine, Pope John Paul II found someone whose life and works could inspire and benefit those of the twenty-first century.

If, as Father Stephan had written her, she and her sisters were the only ones interested in the plight of the Native Americans, and later when her personal money was needed to build almost twenty-five schools in rural Louisiana, which had the largest population of African American Catholics, it was because the American Catholic Church hierarchy, in general, and the laity, as well, mirrored the prejudices of the majority of the citizens of the United States.[2] But Katharine continued to seek ways to help Native Americans and African Americans to achieve their potential as individuals and as citizens. She believed that education had a circular and elevating power.

The educated person of color could elevate himself, participate in the education and leadership of others of his race, and thus benefit the race as a whole. Indeed, Xavier University in Louisiana produced graduates who fanned out across the state to staff the elementary and high schools funded by Katharine. The university also produced doctors, lawyers, judges, dentists, journalists, writers, artists, opera stars, priests, and bishops who worked to bring African Americans to an equal place in American society. Katharine was not afraid to swim against the tide, to "open the boundaries of states, political and economic systems, the vast fields of culture, civilization, and development," and to "open wide the doors for Christ," whom she believed was on her side. History has vindicated her, and Pope John Paul II has canonized her.[3]

2. Sydney E. Ahlstrom, *A Religious History of the American People* (New Haven: Yale University Press, 1973), p. 827.

3. John Paul II, Homily, October 22, 1978, online.

This chapter establishes why John Paul II chose to canonize America's millionaire nun. She is one of seven United States saints, and only the second born on its shores.[4] What was it about Katharine Drexel that merited her inclusion in the last canonization ceremony of 2000? The first half of this chapter looks at the ways in which the pope read the negative signs of the times for which Katharine might serve as an antidote. This entails a reading of his works covering what it means to be a Catholic Christian living out the faith in the modern world, and to know the truth about man and God. It also discloses John Paul's understanding of the essential place of love, *communio,* and the role of eucharistic spirituality. The eucharistic nature of the Church leads to a discussion of mission, which in turn leads to hope for the future. Of great importance are holiness and the prophetic place of the consecrated life in missionary activity. An exposition of John Paul's understanding of the place of saints and the communion of saints in the modern Roman Catholic Church is also paramount. After all, he streamlined the Church's archaic canonization process and beatified and canonized more people than any other pope, beatifying 1,338 individuals and canonizing 482 others.[5] The second half of this chapter brings Katharine into dialogue with the pope to demonstrate why she would become for the pontiff an antidote to the negative signs of the times, a saint to be emulated for the third Catholic millennium, especially in the United States, and a reason to "be not afraid."

Signs of the Times

Having versus Being

Times of crisis in the world and in the Church have always brought forth saints and prophets to help transform society and/or the Church, to call others to holiness, and to convince them of their sin and need for repentance. This happened during the time of the Babylonian exile of the Jews, the Roman persecutions of the early Christian church, the turbulence of the fourteenth century, and the periods of the Reformation and the Counter-

---

4. The other saints are St. Elizabeth Ann Seton, St. Mother Francis Xavier Cabrini, St. John Neumann, St. Mother Rose Duchesne, St. Mother Theodore Guerin, and St. Kateri Tekakwitha.

5. See the Vatican Web site for papal facts and statistics.

Reformation. The end of the twentieth century was, according to Pope John Paul II, such a time of need. The twentieth century saw bigger and bloodier wars and greater numbers of Christian martyrs than any previous century. It witnessed ideologies and structures of society that privileged science, technology, profits, and power over and against persons, individually and collectively as classes, races, and genders. Against this backdrop, and more than a half century after the Holocaust, John Paul called the West's culture one of death.[6] Death is literal in the case of the Western countries that have legalized abortion, euthanasia, and physician-assisted suicide, and that continue to use the death penalty for criminals. It is metaphorical in the case of worldwide degradation of the human person through racism, poverty, hunger, pornography, drugs, crime, and child exploitation. Death, or the fear of death or dislocation, also results from civil wars, wars of aggression, ethnic cleansing, tribalism, rogue states, worldwide and localized terrorism, and the activities of drug lords, drug cartels, and other international crime syndicates, not to mention the worldwide crisis of HIV/AIDS.

As a pilgrim pope, John Paul II traveled to more foreign countries than any of his predecessors and knew well the problems of the world, perhaps more intimately than any other world leader of his day. He made more than 120 pastoral visits outside of Italy during his pontificate, going to over 130 countries on every continent on the earth. He held almost 1,000 meetings with prime ministers and heads of state. He met regularly with scientists, philosophers, and artists, and his was certainly one of the most recognized faces in the world. For some he was a living saint, while for others he and his pontificate were highly controversial. His stated program of action on assuming the papacy in 1978 was to carry out the initiatives of the Second Vatican Council. He took as his pastoral initiative the universal call to holiness found in chapter 5, paragraph 39 of *Lumen Gentium.* Many Catholic liberals argue that he hijacked the Council and turned back the clock to a more authoritarian time by denying women the right to become priests, insisting on the right to life, opposing artificial birth control, upholding traditional morality, and opposing the democratization of the Church's governance. It is true that he upheld the all-male priesthood, the right to life, opposition to artificial birth control, traditional mores, and the hierarchical structure of the Church. However, many do not see these issues in the same light. Catholic traditionalists, or conservatives, supported the pope in these areas. On the other hand, more extreme conservatives complained that the pope

6. See Pope John Paul II's Encyclical *Evangelium Vitae,* March 25, 1995, 28.2.

was too liberal in giving more power to national bishops' conferences, in liturgical innovations and acculturations, and in his opposition to the death penalty and to the United States–led war in Iraq. Certainly there are those both inside the Church and without who believe that the Roman Catholic Church has outgrown the need for saints and miracles — all that is strictly medieval, and people today are much too sophisticated to believe in such things. In a church of one billion adherents, there is a wide range of attitudes and beliefs. The attitudes and beliefs important to this project are those of Pope John Paul II and St. Katharine Drexel.

Along with his predecessor, Pope Pius XII, who told a radio audience, "The sin of the century is the loss of the sense of sin [and] . . . the loss of a sense of God," John Paul II believed that the sorry state of man in the modern world was due to the loss of a sense of sin and the attendant loss of a sense of the reality of God.[7] In his Apostolic Exhortation *Reconciliatio et Paenitentia,* John Paul II wrote, "In fact God is the origin and supreme end of man, and man carries in himself a divine seed. Hence it is the reality of God that reveals and illustrates the mystery of man. It is therefore vain to hope that there will take root a sense of sin against man and against human values, if there is no sense of offence against God, namely the true sense of sin."[8] If sin were the problem, then conversion from sin would be the obvious answer to man's problems in the world. Indeed, the pope believed that "the grave challenges confronting the world at the start of this new Millennium lead us to think that only an intervention from on high, capable of guiding the hearts of those living in situations of conflict and those governing the destinies of nations, can give reason to hope for a brighter future."[9] It is the Holy Spirit in Roman Catholic belief that convicts and convinces an individual of sin. "And when [the Holy Spirit] comes, he will convince the world concerning sin and righteousness and judgment" (John 16:8). John Paul II expanded on this greatly in *Dominum et Vivificantem,* chapters 27–48.

Even the institutional Church needs to examine itself for the sins and the evil its leaders and members have inflicted on people and societies through-out the ages in the name of the Church of Christ. John Paul spent a good bit of his energy making apologies for the Church's past sins and seeking reconciliation with groups and individuals who were the targets of its sins.

---

7. Pius XII, Radio Address, October 26, 1946, quoted in John Paul II, *Dominum et Vivificantem,* May 18, 1986, 47.1.

8. John Paul II, December 2, 1984, 18.

9. John Paul II, Apostolic Letter, *Rosarium Virginis Mariae,* October 16, 2002 (Washington, D.C.: United States Conference of Catholic Bishops, February 2003), 40.

His statements about the Galileo case and the essential compatibility of the faith and reason and science,[10] along with his highly publicized apologies to various groups of Jews[11] and women,[12] are among the most well known of his public gestures and statements. John Paul led by exhortation and by example. He would have had men and women seek assistance from heaven at the prompting of the Holy Spirit to reawaken consciences and turn from sin. Following his logic in *Dominum et Vivificantem,* individuals, organizations, nations, and religions are all caught up in sin and sinful structures that do harm to others; all are therefore in need of conversion.

One of the main aspects of the pope's "personalism" is his interest in the concrete person — this person here, that person there — not humankind in the abstract sense, but each human person individually. The Church does not claim to be the expert in economic or political systems, science, or the arts. The Church claims her expertise in humanity, because through the incarnation Christ is united with each person.

> We cannot abandon man, for his "destiny," that is to say his election, calling, birth and death, salvation or perdition, is so closely and unbreakably linked with Christ. . . . Man in the full truth of his existence, of his personal being and also of his community and social being — in the sphere of his own family, in the sphere of society and very diverse contexts, in the sphere of his own nation (perhaps still only that of his clan or tribe), and in the sphere of the whole of mankind — this man is the primary route that the Church must travel in fulfilling her mission: *he is the primary and fundamental way for the Church,* the way traced out by Christ himself,

10. The pope's first reference to Galileo is in his address of November 10, 1979, to the Pontifical Academy of Sciences on the commemoration of Einstein's birth. "I wish that theologians, scholars and historians . . . might examine more deeply the Galileo case and, in an honest recognition of wrongs . . . [lead] to a fruitful concord between science and faith. . . . I give my entire support to this task."

11. As the cardinal of Krakow, Wojtyla visited the Krakow synagogue in 1968 during the Soviet pogrom in Poland, the first cardinal to ever visit. In April 1986, as pope, he visited the synagogue in Rome, where he addressed the assemblage as "My dear older brothers." The Jewish Anti-Defamation League recognized Pope John Paul II on the twenty-fifth anniversary of his pontificate, noting that "His deep commitment to reconciliation between the Catholic Church and the Jewish people has been fundamental to his papacy." ADL Press release, ADL Web site.

12. See *Mulieris Dignitatem,* August 15, 1988. *Mulieris Dignitatem* has not been universally well received. See Gerry McCarthy's interview with theologian Mary Malone at thesocialedge.com.

the way that leads invariably through the mystery of the Incarnation and the Redemption.[13]

The only creatures who are a problem for themselves, humans are aware of being threatened on all sides in the modern world. Men and women are under threat from the very production of their hands, minds, and wills. It is much more than the alienation of the worker from his product spoken of by Karl Marx; it is comprised of the created products, the means of production, and the attitudes of materialism and consumerism that are turned against man. In his encyclical *Redemptor Hominis,* sections 15 and 16, the pope mentioned several instances of legitimate concern. He began with the exploitation of the environment for industrial and military purposes, noting that man has become a destroyer rather than a steward of nature. While there has been great technological advancement, there has been no concomitant development of ethics and morality to guide the use of technology in a truly human manner. It is possible for those with advanced technology not only to exploit nature but also to exploit the nations and peoples of the less developed world and to do so with a shocking sense of entitlement. In Genesis, man is called upon to have dominion over the created world. However, according to the pope, "The essential meaning of this 'kingship' and 'dominion' of man over the visible world, which the Creator himself gave to man for this task, consists in the priority of ethics over technology, in the primacy of the person over things, and in the superiority of spirit over matter."[14] The Holy Father, in *Sollicitudo Rei Socialis,* points to two very common attitudes in people that oppose both God and neighbor: "the all-consuming desire for profit, and . . . the thirst for power. . . . In order to characterize better each of these attitudes, one can add the expression: 'at any price.' In other words, we are faced with the *absolutizing* of human attitudes with all of its possible consequences."[15] The question then becomes how to change such attitudes.

The concern here for profit and power through any means entails not just money and the ability to impose one's will on another, where other people become means rather than ends in themselves, objects not subjects; the threat, according to the pope, is at its base about atheistic materialism,

---

13. John Paul II, *Redemptor Hominis,* March 4, 1979, 14.1.

14. John Paul II, *Redemptor Hominis,* 16.1. Also see *Dives in Misericordia,* November 30, 1980, 11; *Dominum et Vivificantem,* 57; *Sollicitudo Rei Socialis,* December 39, 1987, 15.5-6.

15. John Paul II, *Sollicitudo Rei Socialis,* 37.1.

which is far removed from any objective moral order, sense of justice, or social solidarity. It is obvious that those who are exploited and have nothing suffer greatly from the iniquity of others. What may be less obvious is that those who have a superabundance of goods and services available to them also suffer. These people become enmeshed in "having" versus "being."

"Being" is used by Pope John Paul II to mean "human" with all the dignity in the manner that Christ "reveal[ed] man to himself" — human in the fullest sense of the word in the unity of body and soul.[16] Simply "having" need not necessarily be destructive of "being." "The evil does not consist in 'having' as such, but in possessing without regard for the *quality* and the *ordered hierarchy* of the goods one has. *Quality* and *hierarchy* arise from the subordination of goods and their availability to man's 'being' and his true vocation."[17] It is the mission of the Church to remind individuals of their true vocation to know, love, and serve God, and to become more human by becoming more and more conformed to Christ. For those in what the pontiff called the "superdeveloped" nations, quality of life issues become paramount, totally eclipsing any higher understanding of man, his transcendent reality, and his responsibility to himself or others. One is encouraged to have more goods, to be physically beautiful, to enjoy ever more pleasures — nothing is denied in the pursuit of pleasure. Indeed, the "pursuit of happiness" is enshrined in the United States Declaration of Independence as an inalienable right, along with life and liberty. No one would ever suggest that happiness is not a legitimate goal for humans, but when the definition of what makes one happy is put in terms of practical materialism, then the degradation of the human person is bound to follow.[18] The person becomes divided from his true self as reflected in Christ. He forgets his primary relationship with God and his proper telos in union with him. Solidarity with one's fellows and stewardship of the earth evanesce. Personal "choice" becomes the right that trumps all other rights, regardless of the thing or action chosen. Tol-

---

16. John Paul II, *Redemptor Hominis*, 10.1.

17. John Paul II, *Sollicitudo Rei Socialis*, 28.7. Also see *Evangelium Vitae*, 3-4, 10.4; *Redemptor Missio*, December 7, 1990, 58.2; John Paul II, Apostolic Letter, *Novo Millennio Ineunte* (Boston: St. Paul Books and Media, 2001), 51; John Paul II, Apostolic Exhortation, *Christifideles Laici* (Boston: St. Paul Books and Media, 1988), 34; John Paul II, Encyclical, *Ecclesia de Eucharistia* (Washington, D.C.: United States Conference of Catholic Bishops, 2003), 20; John Paul II, Apostolic Letter, *Tertio Millennio Adveniente*, November 10, 1984, 41-45; and Vatican Council II Pastoral Constitution on the Church in the Modern World, *Gaudium et Spes*, 35.

18. See John Paul II, *Evangelium Vitae*, 23.1.

eration becomes the trump virtue to the point that one may no longer call good and evil by their proper names.[19] In the name of toleration, religion and morality become internal and private, and are no longer welcome in the public square.

In his magisterial office, the pope taught that the way to ultimate and permanent happiness is the way of perfection, the perfection found only in Christ. "The Teacher from Nazareth invites the person He is addressing to *renounce* a program of life in which the first place is seen to be occupied by the category of possessing, of 'having,' and to *accept* in its place a program centered upon the value of the human person: upon personal 'being' with all the transcendence that is proper to it."[20] In response to the motto enshrined in the Rolling Stones' song "(I Can't Get No) Satisfaction," the Holy Father told two million youths gathered in Rome for World Youth Day 2000,

> It is Jesus in fact that you seek when you dream of happiness; he is waiting for you when nothing else satisfies you; he is the beauty to which you are so attracted; it is he who provokes you with that thirst for fullness that will not let you compromise; it is he who urges you to shed the masks of a false life; it is he who reads in your hearts your most genuine choices, the choices that others try to stifle. It is Jesus who stirs in you the desire to do something great with your lives, the will to follow the ideal, the refusal to allow yourselves to be ground down by mediocrity. . . . If you are what you should be, you will set the whole world ablaze.[21]

The pope believed that the invitation from Jesus was not merely a cry in the wind of stronger forces. The Christian faith teaches that, despite evidence to the contrary, God is still in charge and there will be ultimate victory. God is stronger than sin, stronger than death; his love will overcome all evil. One invitation to follow Jesus comes from the saints, of whom the pope said, "The saints took these words [of the Sermon on the Mount] of Jesus seriously. They believed they would find 'happiness' by putting them into practice in their lives, and they realized their truth in everyday experience: despite their trials and moments of darkness and failures, they already tasted here below the deep joy of communion with Christ. In him,

19. It is the fruit of the Holy Spirit that helps to form a conscience able to call good and evil by their right names. See John Paul II, *Dominum et Vivificantum*, 36.

20. John Paul II, Apostolic Exhortation, *Redemptionis Donum*, March 25, 1984, 4.

21. Quoted in George Weigel, *Witness to Hope: The Biography of Pope John Paul II* (New York: Cliff Street Books, 2001), p. 880.

they discovered the initial seed, already present in time, of the future glory of God's kingdom."[22]

John Paul II saw cause for hope in what he saw as positive signs of the times, for not all the signs were negative: "Despite the voices of the prophets of pessimism, I would like to repeat once again, with emphasis: as we approach the third millennium of Redemption, God is preparing a great Christian springtime, the beginnings of which can already be glimpsed."[23] The pope proclaimed, "Is it not one of the 'signs of the times' that in today's world, despite widespread secularization, there is a *widespread demand for spirituality?*"[24] Visit any commercial bookstore in North America to find shelf after shelf of books on spirituality. It is a commercial phenomenon in the publishing world, with titles on spirituality multiplying year after year. The pope detected "that the West is now experiencing a *renewed demand for meditation,* which at times leads to a keen interest in aspects of other religions. Some Christians, limited in their knowledge of the Christian contemplative traditions, are attracted by those forms of prayer. While the latter contain many elements which are positive and at times compatible with Christian experience, they are often based on ultimately unacceptable premises."[25] Because the pope did not delineate these "unacceptable premises," it is impossible to know to what he was referring. However, his main point seems to be that Christians are often unaware of the many sources and examples of Christian meditation. The crowded bookshelves on spirituality indicate that people in first-world countries are seeking meaning in their lives — something more beyond "more." Those in the developing world seek reassurance that their lives, too, are meaningful, even in the face of great suffering.

The Church calls humans beings to be themselves, their true selves, as revealed in Jesus Christ. Richard Gula tells an amusing anecdote about Rabbi Zusya that illustrates the importance of being one's true self. The rabbi says, "In the world to come, I shall not be asked, 'Why were you not Moses?' Instead I shall be asked, 'Why were you not Zusya?'"[26] The Church challenges

---

22. Homily, All Saints Day, November 1, 2000.

23. Quoted in Ralph Martin and Peter Williamson, eds., *Pope John Paul II and the New Evangelization: How You Can Bring the Good News to Others* (San Francisco: Ignatius, 1995), p. 87.

24. John Paul II, *Novo Millennio Inuente,* 33.

25. John Paul II, *Rosarium Virginis Mariae,* October 16, 2002, 28.

26. Bernard Hoose, ed., *Christian Ethics: An Introduction* (Collegeville, Minn.: Liturgical Press, 1998), p. 118.

men and women to find their greatness and dignity as human persons made in the image and likeness of God, their Creator — "male and female he made them" (Gen. 1:27), each sharing in the image of God, in his creative powers, and in the expressions of their intellects and wills.

The Truth about Man and God

In chapters 5 and 6 of *Dives in Misericordia,* Pope John Paul II analyzed the parable of the prodigal son as an example of how a father welcomes home a hitherto lost son who had squandered all he had received from the father in misdirected, sinful pursuit of happiness. What parent would not run out into the street in joy to intercept a child thought to have been lost? Whatever anger and disappointment one might feel at the wicked deeds of the child, having the child home again more than outweighs any demands of justice. In the Bible this parable is given along with similar parables of precious things lost and joyously recovered, but nothing is more precious than a person, a child of God, gathered once again into the loving arms of a father. Accordingly, the pope considered it imperative for man to reclaim his rightful dignity as a child of God and a brother of Jesus, redeemed by the incarnation, the cross, and the resurrection of Christ.

> Christ the Redeemer "fully reveals man to himself." If we may use the expression, this is the human dimension of the mystery of the Redemption. In this dimension man finds again the greatness, dignity, and value that belong to his humanity. In the mystery of the Redemption man becomes newly "expressed" and, in a way, is newly created. He is newly created! "There is neither Jew nor Greek, there is neither slave nor free, there is neither male nor female, for you are all one in Jesus Christ." The man who wishes to understand himself thoroughly — and not just in accordance with immediate, partial, often superficial, and even illusory standards and measures of his being — he must with his unrest, uncertainty and even his weakness and sinfulness, with his life and death, draw near to Christ. He must, so to speak, enter into him with all his own self, he must "appropriate" and assimilate the whole reality of Incarnation and Redemption in order to find himself. If this profound process takes place within him, he then bears fruit not only of adoration of God but also a deep wonder at himself. How precious must man be in the eyes of the Creator, if he "gained so great a Redeemer," and if God "gave his only begotten Son" in order that man "shall not perish but have eternal life."

In reality, the name for that deep amazement at man's worth and dignity is the Gospel, that is to say: the Good News. It is also called Christianity. This amazement determines the Church's mission in the world and, perhaps even more so, "in the modern world." This amazement, which is also a conviction and a certitude — at its deepest roots it is the certainty of faith, but in a hidden and mysterious way it vivifies every aspect of *authentic humanism* — is closely related to Christ. . . .

The Church's fundamental function in every age and particularly in ours is to direct man's gaze, to point the awareness and experience of the whole of humanity toward the mystery of Christ, to help all men to be familiar with the profundity of the Redemption taking place in Christ Jesus. At the same time man's deepest sphere is involved — we mean the sphere of human hearts, consciences and events. (emphasis added)[27]

To settle their restless souls, Pope John Paul called on men and women to reclaim their authentic dignity as human persons created, loved, and redeemed by God through Christ in the Holy Spirit. In a homily in Bern, Switzerland, the pope told the crowd assembled at Allmend Field,

"God's love has been poured into our hearts through the Holy Spirit" (Romans 5:5). It is not a merit of ours; it is a free gift. Despite the weight of our sins, God loves us and has redeemed us in the blood of Christ. His grace has healed our innermost being. Therefore, we can exclaim with the Psalmist: "How great, Lord, is your love over all the earth!" How great it is in me, in others, in every human being! This is the true source of man's greatness; this is the root of his indestructible dignity. The image of God is reflected in every human being. Here is the most profound "truth" of man, which can never be unknown or violated. Every outrage borne by man is revealed, in short, as an outrage to his Creator, who loves him with the love of a father.[28]

The pope here revealed that the dignity of men and women is based on divine love for humans. People may be outraged and may perpetrate outrage, but individual persons will always be loved by God and welcomed home joyously as was the prodigal son. According to the pope, it is this truth about the person that, once known, will set the person free — free to be his or her

---

27. John Paul II, *Redemptor Hominis,* 10.1-3.
28. June 7, 2004.

authentic self and free to help bring about a world more congruent with human dignity.

John Paul II emphasized that the church of Christ is responsible for upholding and proclaiming the truth about persons as revealed in Jesus Christ. "The Church thus appears before us as the social subject of responsibility for divine truth. With deep emotion we hear Christ himself saying: 'The word which you hear is not mine but the Father's who sent me.'"[29] In *Veritatis Splendor*, the pope continued the same theme. "This essential bond between truth, the good and freedom has been largely lost sight of by present-day culture. As a result, helping man to rediscover it represents nowadays one of the requirements of the Church's mission, for the salvation of the world. Pilate's question: 'What is truth?' reflects the distressing perplexity of a man who often no longer knows *who he is, whence* he comes and *where* he is going."[30] The pope clearly believed that without knowing the truth about themselves and the link between the truth and the good, people cannot make reasonable decisions even about their own good. They make decisions based on a disordered view of the good — decisions that ultimately work to their detriment and that of others; they become more concerned with making, having, consuming, and enjoying the so-called goods of the material world. They become more and more alienated from becoming or being their authentic selves.

In Nigeria in 1981, the pope warned his audience about the dangers of not knowing the truth: "Without spiritual values man is no longer true to himself, because without them he denies or ignores his essential relationship of dependence on the very source of his existence, on his Creator in Whose image he was made and continues to exist." But the pope relied on the greatness of humanity to bring men and women back into a right relationship with God. In Australia in 1986, he stated, "The great nobility of the human mind is based, above all, on its ability to know God and to search more and more deeply into the mystery of God's life, and then at that point to discover also man. Thus the truth of man leads us to the truth of God."[31] Because in Christian understanding truth is unitary, one can also say that the truth of God leads to the truth of man. But the truth cannot be forced on men and women. The pope wrote, "[Man] can be drawn toward the truth only by his

---

29. John Paul II, *Redemptor Hominis*, 19.1.

30. John Paul II, *Veritatis Splendor*, 84.3.

31. Both papal quotations found in Joseph Cardinal Cordeiro, "The Religious Sense of Man," in *John Paul II: A Panorama of His Teachings*, ed. Joseph Cardinal Bernardin (Brooklyn: New City Press, 1989), pp. 72-73; hereafter *Panorama*.

own nature, that is, by his own freedom, which commits him to search sincerely for truth, and when he finds it, to adhere to it both in his convictions and in his behavior."[32] However haphazardly, human intellect always seeks truth, and human will always seeks the good. If man perseveres in seeking the truth, it will be revealed to him.[33]

The pope believed that part of the problem faced by modern men and women was philosophical. In the postmodern world, the very concept of objective truth is under assault. The pervasiveness of subjective existentialism in the West is exemplified by the joint opinion by Justices O'Connor, Souter, and Kennedy in the 1992 Supreme Court case *Planned Parenthood v. Casey,* in which they wrote in support of a virtually unlimited constitutional abortion right: "At the heart of liberty is the right to define one's own concept of existence, of the meaning of the universe and the mystery of human life." Such self-definition of meaning, of truth, flies in the face of a Christian's firm belief in absolute truth, as the pope understood it. Speaking before the Pontifical Academy of Sciences, the pope said, "Truth cannot contradict truth."[34] The Bible warns, "There is a way that seems right to a man, but in the end it leads to death" (Prov. 14:12). According to Christian understanding, man does not create truth; truth is ultimately revealed to him as the truth of God through Christ, who is Truth. "I am the way, the truth, and the life" (John 14:6). Pilate's question "What is truth?" should have been "Who is truth?" It is this Christ, the Truth, who said, "The Son of Man came not to be served but to serve" (Matt. 20:28). The church of Christ is responsible for protecting and handing down divine truth; the church has continued his service and ministry across the ages into the third millennium: "As the Father has sent me, even so I send you" (John 20:21). The Father sent the Son and the Son sent his disciples out to the ends of the earth. Why? To proclaim the truth, the good news. What is the basis for the truth? According to Catholic Christianity, it is in the love of God who desires the ultimate good for all human persons — their communion with him in heaven for eternity.

Christianity teaches humans that Christ is the source of love, reflecting the love of the Father; Christ is love's model and its measure. God made each man and woman for love. The commandment to love — love God, love self, and love neighbor — is the foundation and summation of

---

32. John Paul II, *Crossing the Threshold of Hope* (New York: Knopf, 1995), p. 190.
33. See Weigel, *Witness to Hope,* p. 802.
34. *L'Osservatore Romano,* English ed., November 24, 1986, p. 22.

the Decalogue.[35] The Church believes that the human person is "the only creature that God has wanted for its own sake."[36] People were created to be in loving relationship with God and their neighbors. If "God is love," as proclaimed in 1 John 4:8, his love is not a mere attribute attached to his person, but it is of his essence as God, in the same way that God is holy or that God is Truth. According to traditional Christian teaching, an individual possessed of the truth about God looks to Christ as the model of love. Possessed of great dignity and created in the image and likeness of God, each person is able to love because God first loved her or him. One cannot love one's neighbor without loving God, nor can one love God without loving one's neighbor. The pope taught that one cannot love either neighbor or God without first loving one's true self and not the socially constructed, egocentric, pleasure-seeking, acquisitive, power-seeking self so prevalent in modern culture.

But of what does the command to love consist? What must one do or not do? Following Kantian ethics, one must not treat another human being as an object of pleasure. Pope John Paul II points out that this negative imperative does not begin to exhaust the meaning of love. Love "requires the affirmation of the person as person." This is his personalistic principle based on the inherent dignity of each individual person. The person becomes most human and more Christ-like when he or she loves and is loved by another. Indeed, "The person is realized through love."[37] This is accomplished, in the model of Christ, in making what Vatican II called "a sincere gift of self."[38] The pope emphasizes that *"man affirms himself most completely by giving of himself.* This is the fulfillment of the commandment of love. This is the full truth about man.... *If we cannot accept the prospect of giving ourselves as a gift, then the danger of a selfish freedom will always be present."*[39] Christian love seeks no rewards and includes even enemies and persecutors.

Love, Communio, *and Eucharistic Spirituality*

Drawn by human nature to love and be loved, to search for truth and the good, men and women are led by Christ to look in the right places and in the right manner to find them. Christians believe that it is the Christian

35. John Paul II, *Veritatis Splendor,* 13.2.

36. *Gaudium et Spes,* 24.

37. Bernardin, *Panorama,* pp. 201, 202.

38. *Gaudium et Spes,* 24.

39. Bernardin, *Panorama,* p. 202.

church that, since Pentecost, has in the fullest sense led the individual in the ways of God, for Christian love is not a mere emotion but an assurance and a program of action. Within the body of Christ, there are many ways of performing the actions required by love. All are called to love, and everyone loves and acts within the spheres of individual vocations. The Church nourishes love in all of its true manifestations: "The reason is that the Church . . . believes in man. She *thinks of man,* and addresses herself to him *not only* in the light of historical experience, not only with the aid of the many methods of scientific knowledge, but in the first place in the light of the revealed word of the living God. Relating herself to man, she seeks *to express* the eternal *designs* and transcendent *destiny* which *the Living God,* the Creator and Redeemer, has linked with him."[40] To repeat, "The Church cannot abandon man."[41] Made up of the body of Christ, she is in service to all in imitation of, conformity to, and at the commandment of her founder. The Church serves the person in his or her unity of body and soul. She welcomes each one into a *communio* of love, nourishing above all by the Eucharist. *Communio* is deeper in meaning than a community; it "denotes a union of persons that is proper to them alone; and it indicates the good that they do to one another, giving and receiving in a mutual relationship."[42] *Communio* in the Church is best likened to the *communio* that belongs to the Holy Trinity: three distinct persons in one Godhead held together in love. The *communio* of the Church is begotten in the water of baptism and the bread of the Eucharist. It is not familial or tribal and not based on blood. One must choose to be part of the *communio* of the Church.

The Church is a *communio* such that once one becomes a member of the body of Christ, one is inalterably changed. The moment one enters into full communion with the Church, one becomes a different person suffused with grace and divinized as a sister or brother to Christ the Lord. The faithful become what they consume in the Eucharist.[43] This is what Jean-François Lyotard would have referred to as *le différend. Le différend* makes a sudden, unpredictable, and what may seem like an unaccountable difference in dis-

---

40. John Paul II, Encyclical Letter, *Laborem Exercens,* 4.1.

41. John Paul II, *Redemptor Hominis,* 14.1.

42. Karol Wojtyla [John Paul II], *Sources of Renewal,* trans. P. S. Falla (San Francisco: Harper and Row, 1980), p. 61.

43. "Our sharing in the body and blood of Christ leads to no other end than that of transforming us into that which we receive." St. Leo the Great, quoted in Congregation of the Doctrine of the Faith, *Some Aspects of the Church Understood as Communion* (Boston: St. Paul Books and Media, 1992), note 20.

course with others.[44] It is a life-changing event; one views the world differently afterward. To borrow further from critical theory, Alain Badiou would use the term *l'évènement* to describe what Lyotard means by *le différend*.[45] To use a mundane example of *l'évènement,* imagine a proposal of marriage given and accepted. That event has immediate and unpredictable repercussions for the couple involved. They will be previously separate individuals who are now viewed by themselves and everyone else as a "couple." They have new rights and new responsibilities. Lyotard and Badiou, although non-Christian, express here a usage and a style of language and argumentation that are at home with the Christian understanding of *metanoia,* the complete conversion and change of heart that take place within the *communio* of the Church. One enters into a unique love relationship with God, self, and others proper only to the members of the mystical Body of Christ, which is the Church.

According to John Paul II, the Church is the home and school of this *communio,* or "communion," the more commonly used word. The pope recommended the promotion of a spirituality of communion in order to properly carry out the demands of *communio:*

> A spirituality of communion indicates above all the heart's contemplation of the mystery of the Trinity dwelling in us, and whose light we must also be able to see shining on the faces of the brothers and sisters around us. A spirituality of communion also means an ability to think of our brothers and sisters in faith within the profound unity of the Mystical Body, and therefore as "those who are part of me." This makes us able to share their joys and sufferings, to sense their desires and attend to their needs, to offer them deep and genuine friendship. A spirituality of communion implies also the ability to see what is positive in others, to welcome it and prize it as a gift from God: not only as a gift for the brother or sister who has received it directly, but also as a "gift for me." A spirituality of communion means, finally, to know how to "make room" for our brothers and sisters, bearing "each other's burdens" (Galatians 6:2) and resisting the selfish temptations which constantly beset us and provoke competition, careerism, distrust, and jealousy. Let us have no illusions: unless we follow this spiritual path, external structures of communion will serve little purpose.

---

44. See Jean-François Lyotard, *The Differend: Phrases in Dispute,* trans. George Van Den Abbeele (Minneapolis: University of Minnesota Press, 1988).

45. See Alain Badiou, *Ethics: An Essay on the Understanding of Evil,* trans. Peter Hallward (London: Verso, 2001).

They would become mechanisms without souls, "masks" of communion rather than its means of expression and growth.[46]

It is no coincidence that the Church's main sacrament, which most expresses her very nature, by which she lives and has her being, her very "source and summit," is called Communion. The sacrament of Communion, or the Eucharist, is for Roman Catholics not the mere memorial, in the modern sense, of Christ's Last Supper. It is not just an action performed in the present that calls to mind a similar action two thousand years ago. It is actually the same event as Christ's offering himself to his Father on the cross for the remission of the sins of humankind. It is a memorial sacrifice in the Hebraic understanding of the term — a *re-presentation* of a past event that actually takes place in the present. Christ, the High Priest, offers himself, the spotless Victim, as an oblation in praise and glory to the Father, in perfect expiation of the sins of man, and uniting communicants to the Father and one another in the bond of communion. "In this gift Jesus Christ entrusted to his Church the perennial making present of the paschal mystery. With it he brought about a mysterious 'oneness in time' between that Triduum and the passage of the centuries."[47] This oneness of time is a cause of amazement and wonder.

It was the pope's express desire to rekindle this eucharistic amazement in the faithful. He wrote,

> The Church is called during her earthly pilgrimage to maintain and promote communion with the Triune God and communion among the faithful. For this purpose she possesses the word and the sacraments, particularly the Eucharist, by which she "constantly lives and grows" and in which she expresses her very nature. . . . The Eucharist thus appears as the culmination of all the sacraments in perfecting our communion with God the Father by identification with his only-begotten Son through the working of the Holy Spirit. . . . In the Eucharist "unlike any other sacrament, the mystery [of communion] is so perfect that it brings us to the heights of every good thing: here is the ultimate goal of every human desire, because here we attain God and God joins himself to us in the most perfect union." Precisely for this reason it is good to cultivate in our hearts a constant desire for the sacrament of the Eucharist.[48]

46. John Paul II, *Novo Millennio Ineunte*, 43.
47. John Paul II, *Ecclesia de Eucharistia*, 5.
48. John Paul II, *Ecclesia de Eucharistia*, 34.

This desire for the Eucharist can become a "spiritual communion." Such spiritual communion is endorsed by the pope, who wrote that spiritual communion was "recommended by the saints who were the masters of the Spiritual Life."[49] So important is the Eucharist, the "sacrament of love," in the life of the Roman Catholic Church, that the pope called it "the most precious possession which the Church can have in her journey through history." He continued, "The Church draws her life from the Eucharist. This truth does not simply express a daily experience of faith, but recapitulates *the heart of the mystery of the Church.*"[50]

Pope John Paul II Comes into Dialogue with Katharine Drexel

Eucharistic Spirituality

Pope John Paul II came into dialogue with St. Katharine Drexel precisely at the point of their shared eucharistic spirituality. Each one believed that the spiritual benefits of the Eucharist are continued beyond the immediate consumption of the Host. There is the spiritual communion of desire, as mentioned above, which precedes its reception. Adoration of the Blessed Sacrament prolongs the last Eucharist and anticipates the next. "The Church and the world have a great need of Eucharistic worship. Jesus waits near us in this sacrament of love. Let us be generous with our time in going to meet Him in adoration and contemplation that is full of faith and ready to make reparation for the great faults and crimes of the world. May our adoration never cease."[51] John Paul II, like Katharine Drexel before him, punctuated his day with time spent in adoration of the Blessed Sacrament.

> To live the Eucharist it is necessary, as well, to spend much time in adoration in front of the Blessed Sacrament, something which I myself experience every day drawing from it strength, consolation, and assistance.... The bread and wine, fruit of human hands, transformed by the power of the Holy Spirit into the Body and Blood of Christ, become the pledge of the "new heaven and new earth" (Rev. 21:1) announced by the Church

49. John Paul II, *Ecclesia de Eucharistia*, 34.

50. Pope John Paul II, Letter to All the Bishops of the Church, *Dominicae Coenae* (Boston: Daughters of Saint Paul, February 4, 1980), 1, 5, and 9.

51. John Paul II, *Dominicae Coenae*, 3.

in her daily mission. In Christ whom we adore present in the mystery of the Eucharist, the Father uttered his final word with regard to humanity and human history. How could the Church fulfill her vocation without cultivating a constant relationship with the Eucharist, without nourishing herself with this food which sanctifies, without founding her missionary activity on this indispensable support? To evangelize the world there is need of apostles who are "experts" in the celebration, adoration and contemplation of the Eucharist. . . . It is the "bread of life" which sustains those who, in turn, become "bread broken" for others, paying at times with martyrdom their fidelity to the Gospel.[52]

Katharine Drexel, who shared a similar eucharistic spirituality with Pope John Paul II, taught her Sisters of the Blessed Sacrament that eucharistic spirituality was to be the center of their lives, the same source and summit as the Church's. The 1913 Constitutions of the order stated the rule unequivocally:

As the congregation is, in a special manner dedicated to Jesus Christ really present in the Holy Eucharist, the Sisters shall make this Mystery the principal object of their love and devotion, especially by frequent visits to the Blessed Sacrament and by inculcation in those for whom they labor, respect, and love for Jesus in the Blessed Sacrament. To animate their zeal and fervor by the example of their Divine Master, they shall endeavor to study this Mystery, all the mysteries and virtues of His life, death, and resurrection and by this means render more sensible the commemoration of what it is daily renewed in the Holy Eucharist. All the Sisters shall every day make a visit of one-half hour to the Blessed Sacrament.[53]

This is not just one rule among many; it expresses the very centrality of the Eucharist in the life of the order. Eucharistic devotion is at the center of true Catholic spirituality. "Even apart from the time of the actual celebration of the Eucharist great saints and poor sinners in the Catholic Church have prayed, worshipped, wept, and rejoiced before the Blessed Sacrament. Since the time of Saint Francis and Saint Thomas Aquinas in the thirteenth century there has not been a single Catholic saint for whom this devotion to the Eucharist has not been an integral part of spiritual

---

52. John Paul II, Homily, April 29, 2004.
53. SBS Holy Rule 124.

life."[54] The pope wrote that the adoration of the Blessed Sacrament "becomes an inexhaustible source of holiness."[55] Katharine noted that to be before the Blessed Sacrament was her "sweetest joy," for "the religious needs strength. Near the Tabernacle the soul finds strength, consolation and resignation. The religious needs virtue. Jesus is the model of virtues in the Blessed Sacrament. The religious needs hope. In the Blessed Sacrament we possess the most precious pledge of our hope. The Host contains the germ of future life."[56] Like Pope John Paul II, Katharine and her sisters found "strength, consolation, and assistance" from eucharistic devotion. She prayed that it would transform her soul.[57] As Joseph Cardinal Ratzinger, later Pope Benedict XVI, pointed out, the eucharistic "adoration is an intensification of communion. It is not 'individualistic' piety: it is a prolonging of, or a preparation for, the community element."[58]

The eucharistic spirituality of John Paul II and Katharine Drexel yields a *communio* that has both a vertical and a horizontal reality and a visible and an invisible reality. Partaking of the Eucharist unites the communicant with God. It also unites the communicant with others who share in the divine nature, the anonymous and named saints in the communion of saints, the faithfully departed who enjoy the Beatific Vision no longer through a glass darkly as on earth, but face-to-face in heaven, and those who "will be incorporated in her [the heavenly church] after having been fully purified."[59] The horizontal reality of the Eucharist is that it unites the faithful into the Body of Christ. Each one becomes then an *alter Christus,* another Christ. To repeat the pope's words, those who receive the broken bread become "the bread broken for others." Through receiving Christ,

54. Benedict Groeschel and James Monti, *In the Presence of Our Lord: The History, Theology, and Psychology of Eucharistic Devotion* (Huntington, Ind.: Our Sunday Visitor, 1997), p. 15.

55. John Paul II, *Ecclesia de Eucharistia*, 10.

56. MKD, *Reflections on Religious Life* (Bensalem, Pa.: Sisters of the Blessed Sacrament, 1983), p. 21.

57. MKD: "O Jesus, I adore you in the Host of exposition. This act of adoration is no trivial act, but will certainly sanctify and transform my soul. I adore your heart, which desires me to unite myself to your sufferings." Ellen Tarry, *Saint Katharine Drexel: Friend of the Oppressed* (Boston: Pauline Books and Media, 2000), p. 148.

58. Joseph Ratzinger, *The Ratzinger Report: An Exclusive Interview on the State of the Church,* with Vittorio Messori, trans. Salvator Attanasio and Graham Harrison (San Francisco: Ignatius, 1986), p. 133.

59. Congregation for the Doctrine of the Faith, *Some Aspects of the Church Understood as Communion* (Boston: St. Paul Books and Media, 1992), p. 5.

one becomes another Christ with the commandment to do unto others according to Christ's teaching and example. Thus, in participating in the Eucharist, one claims Christ and is compelled to proclaim him to others. In this way, "the Church is not a reality closed in on herself. Rather she is permanently open to missionary and ecumenical endeavor, for she is sent to the world to announce and witness, to make present and spread the mystery of communion which is essential to her, and to gather together all people and all things into Christ."[60] It is this fundamental link between a necessary eucharistic faith and a life of charity, or love, that Pope John Paul II makes so clear in his doctoral work on St. John of the Cross. Using one definition of faith as union with God, the young Karol Wojtyla wrote, "Love increases the union [achieved in the Eucharist], and it is likewise love which determines the degree of transformation."[61] It is the life lived in complete charity that is the most full measure of the quality of the individual's faith.

It was not an arbitrarily used rhetorical tactic for St. Paul to teach that, of faith, hope, and charity, "the greatest of these is charity" (1 Cor. 13:13). The Gospel of John describes how Jesus washed the feet of his disciples in preparation for the Passover meal that was to be his last. Pope John Paul II, in his homily of March 3, 2002, taught:

> As he finishes the washing of the feet, he again invites us to imitate him: "For I have given you an example, that you should do as I have done to you" (John 13:15). In this way he establishes an intimate connection between the Eucharist as the sacrament of his sacrificial gift, and the commandment to love that commits us to welcoming and serving our brothers and sisters. Partaking of the Lord's table cannot be separated from the duty of loving our neighbor. Each time we partake of the Eucharist, we too say our "Amen" before the Body and Blood of our Lord. In doing so we commit ourselves to doing what Christ has done, to "washing the feet" of our brothers and sisters, becoming a real and visible image of the One who "emptied himself, taking the form of a servant" (Philippians 2:7). . . . The Eucharist is a great gift, but also a great responsibility for those who receive it.[62]

60. Congregation, *Some Aspects of the Church*, p. 4.

61. Karol Wojtyla, *Faith according to St. John of the Cross* (San Francisco: Ignatius, 1981), p. 50.

62. Vatican Web site.

Jesus said, "He who does not gather with me scatters" (Matt. 12:30), and "Each branch of mine that bears no fruit, he [the Father] takes away" (John 15:2). The love inherent in the Eucharist must bear fruit. The person who does not bear fruit does not remain in the sacred communion, but becomes attenuated from the Body of Christ, and even lost to eternal life. But, "communion begets communion: essentially it is likened to a mission on behalf of communion. In fact, Jesus said to his disciples: 'You did not choose me, but I chose you and *appointed you that you should go and bear fruit* and that your fruit should abide' (John 15:16). Communion and mission are profoundly connected with another, they interpenetrate and mutually imply each other to the point that *communion represents both the source and the fruit of mission: communion gives rise to mission and mission is accomplished in communion.*"[63]

Mission and Hope

Communion leads naturally to mission. To be in communion means to share in the imperative of evangelization. According to the pope, "Eucharist and Mission are inseparable."[64] While mission does not necessarily imply the mission of the missionary who goes to foreign territories and distant lands, the missionary life is perhaps the fullest expression of gathering and bearing fruit. The pope wrote that *"the Church is missionary by her very nature";*[65] "It is the primary service the Church can render to every individual and to all humanity in the modern world";[66] "It is the primary task of the *missio ad gentes* to announce that it is in Christ, 'the Way, and the Truth, and the Life' (John 14:6), that people find salvation."[67] The philosopher and systematic theologian Paul Tillich described the importance of missionary activity to the church as "an element of a living being without which he must finally die." According to Tillich, the success of missions is proof for the universality of Christ's message:

> Missionary work is that work in which the potential universality of Christianity becomes evident day by day, in which universality is actualized with every new success of the missionary endeavor. The action of missions

63. John Paul II, *Christifideles Laici,* 32.
64. John Paul II, Homily, April 4, 2004.
65. John Paul II, *Redemptor Missio,* 62.1, emphasis mine.
66. John Paul II, *Redemptor Missio,* 2.4.
67. John Paul II, *Novo Millennio Ineunte,* 56.

gives the *pragmatic* proof of the universality of Christianity. . . . Missions [also] bear witness on behalf of the Church as the agency of the conquering Kingdom of God. Only missions can prove that the Church is the agent through which the Kingdom of God continuously actualizes itself in history. Missionaries come to a country in which the Church is still in latency. In this situation the manifest Church opens up what is potentially given in the different religions and cultures outside Christianity.[68]

Mission is a multifaceted endeavor. The Church is about salvation and the building of the kingdom of God. Evangelization brings salvation to both the evangelizer and the evangelized. Mission and evangelization are primary forms of obedience to Christ's commandment to love and to carry the good news to all nations. Pope John Paul II believed that all peoples are in need of evangelization — those in the Church who may only imperfectly know and understand the fullness of the gospel, those who have fallen away from Christianity due to the lure of secularity or the pull of other faiths, and those who have never heard the gospel. Katharine Drexel's mission was to those who were not secure in their faith and to those who had never heard the gospel, the African Americans and Native Americans of the United States.

The pope wrote that the mandate for Christians to become missionaries stems not only from Christ's commandment to "make disciples of all nations" (Matt. 28:19), but also "from the profound demands of God's life within us."[69] Christians *must* share the gifts and blessings they have received from God. God clearly intends for all to be invited to the heavenly banquet: "The Church, and every individual Christian within her, may not keep hidden or monopolize this newness and richness which has been received from God's bounty in order to be communicated to all mankind."[70] In the pope's analysis of faith in the works of St. John of the Cross, one's charity is the measure of one's faith and, as charity, builds one's faith. Both Katharine and the pope who would canonize her held in common the belief that there is no more precious gift to share with others than one's faith through missionary activity, and to them, it was a privilege and a duty. John Paul II saw missionary activity as essential to the Church.

---

68. Paul Tillich, "The Theology of Missions," *Christianity and Crisis,* March 4, 1955, online.

69. John Paul II, *Redemptor Missio,* 11.5.

70. John Paul II, *Redemptor Missio,* 11.4.

From the beginning of his pontificate, he preached and taught in anticipation of the third millennium of Christianity. His essential rhetoric was always future-oriented. When he did recall the past, it was often to bring to mind the virtues of saints and the conversions of nations, such as when he recollected Clovis for the people in Rheims or St. Augustine in Canterbury. In his message for Mission Sunday 2001, the pope used the story of Christ's direction to Peter to put out to sea to cast his nets once again after a fruitless night of fishing to direct the faithful to take part in and sustain the Church's mission. He believed that people must always "remember the past with gratitude, live the present with passion, and look forward to the future with confidence. This tending towards the future, illuminated by hope, must be the basis of all Church activity in the third millennium. . . . It is time, indeed, to look forward, keeping our eyes on the face of Jesus. . . . Contemplation of the face of the Lord leads the disciples to 'contemplate' the faces of men and women of today: the Lord identifies himself in fact with 'the least of my brothers' (Matthew 25:40 & 45)."[71]

The pope's thoughts extended to the future with a palpable sense of urgency. He shared the Evangelist Matthew's sense of urgency: "Go quickly and tell his disciples he has risen" (Matt. 28:7). Indeed, in the pope's 1987 encyclical *Redemptoris Missio,* in talking about the need for missions, he employed the word "urgent" and variations of "urgent" ten times. The language the pope used in this encyclical is one indication of the great importance he placed on missions, for it is full of exhortatory and emphatic language; such words as "must," "must not," "necessary," "demand," "mandate," "commit," and "need" are used over and over again. In speaking of the importance of missions, he wrote in 1995, "As the year 2000 approaches, our world feels an urgent need for the Gospel."[72] In the 2004 papal message on World Mission Sunday, he returned to this theme of urgency as he looked to the future. His first sentences read, "The Church's missionary activity is an urgency also at the beginning of the third millennium. Mission . . . is still only beginning and we must commit ourselves wholeheartedly to its service."[73]

Here is a man with an eschatological sense of time, for he considers that something continuing for two thousand years is "only beginning." He could think this way because on his pilgrim journeys he read the many negative signs of the times and knew just how much needed to be done to recon-

71. June 5, 2001.
72. John Paul II, *Crossing the Threshold,* p. 114.
73. April 4, 2004, 1.

cile the world to Christ. As he entered into the third millennium, the pope sensed that the day of the Lord's return was getting closer and closer. This was all the more reason to hold up Katharine Drexel for emulation. If the Church is "built [to be] as a new Jerusalem, [and] principle of unity in Christ between different peoples and nations," then there is yet much to be done to achieve its ideal.[74] If the parousia, the second coming of Christ, is drawing near, there is both great need and great urgency in the missionary field, yet the pope was always confident of ultimate success because it is Christ and the Holy Spirit who work through the missionary.

> Let us go forward in hope! A new millennium is opening before the Church like a vast ocean upon which we shall venture, relying on the help of Christ. The Son of God, who became incarnate two thousand years ago out of love for humanity, is at work even today: we need discerning eyes to see this and, above all, a generous heart to become the instruments of his work. . . . Now, the Christ whom we have contemplated and loved bids us to set out once more on our journey: "Go therefore and make disciples of all nations, baptizing them in the name of the Father, the Son, and the Holy Spirit" (*Mt* 28:19). The missionary mandate accompanies us into the Third Millennium and urges us to share the enthusiasm of the very first Christians: we can count on the power of the same Spirit who poured out at Pentecost and who impels us still today to start out anew, sustained by the hope "which does not disappoint" (*Rom* 5:5).[75]

One way the pope encouraged missionary work and the vocation to the missions was to canonize and commemorate great missionaries of the past. For example, on the day that St. Katharine Drexel was raised to the altar, or canonized, the pope canonized not only three nuns, but also thirty-three foreign missionaries to China who gave their lives along with eighty-seven of their converts. The encyclical of John Paul II *Slavorum Apostoli* commemorated the eleven-hundredth anniversary of the evangelization of the Slavs by the missionary brothers Saints Cyril and Methodius. In an address to the European Ecumenical Symposium, October 12, 1985, the first Slavic pope gave his intentions in writing the encyclical: "I endeavored to portray the admirable charism and work of the two great evangelizers, convinced as I was that the entire Church, and especially those involved

---

74. John Paul II, Homily on the Feast of Corpus Christi, June 10, 2004.
75. John Paul II, *Novo Millennio Ineunte*, 58.

in evangelization today, can draw great profit from the example of their life, of their ecclesial sense, and their apostolic method."[76] Here the pope's backward glance, in fact, looks forward. He held up examples from the past as inspiration for present and future Christian living and for carrying out the mission of Christ.

John Paul II explicitly turned to consecrated women as the ideal missionaries. In speaking to a large group of religiously vowed women in Buenos Aires, on April 10, 1987, the pope said:

> Those who are called to this consecration, and who take their places within the Church's dynamic action, are *par excellence* people who have volunteered to leave all and to go spread the gospel to the ends of the earth. You were called ... to experience within yourselves and to live out in all its consequences the motto of St. Paul which becomes a daily examination of conscience: "Woe to me if I do not preach the gospel!" Yes, woe to me, woe to us if we today do not preach the gospel to a world which, in spite of appearances, still hungers for God.[77]

He pointed out that theirs is a unique vocation that involves "a total commitment to evangelization, a commitment which involves the missionary's whole person and life, and demands a self-giving without limits of energy or time."[78] By the Code of Canon Law, the body of positive church law that guides, among other issues, the rights and responsibilities of the clergy and the laity, consecrated men and women "have a special obligation to play a special part in missionary activity."[79] The pope wrote that "the Church needs to make known the great Gospel values of which she is the bearer. No one witnesses more effectively to these values than those who profess the consecrated life in chastity, poverty, and obedience, in total gift of self to God and in complete readiness to serve humanity and society after the example of Christ."[80] The pope went on in words that could have described Katharine Drexel and her sisters, who vowed to be as mothers to Native American and African American people:

76. *The Encyclicals of John Paul II*, ed. J. Miller, CSB (Huntington, Ind.: Our Sunday Visitor, 2001), p. 195.

77. Bernardin, *Panorama*, pp. 95-96.

78. John Paul II, *Redemptoris Missio*, 65.3.

79. *The Code of Canon Law*, trans. the Canon Law Society of Great Britain and Ireland (London: Canon Law Society Trust, 1983), p. 783.

80. John Paul II, *Redemptoris Missio*, 69.3.

I extend a special word of appreciation to the missionary Religious Sisters, in whom virginity for the sake of the Kingdom is transformed into a motherhood in the spirit that is rich and fruitful. It is precisely the mission *ad gentes* that offers them vast scope for "the gift of self with love in total and undivided manner." The example and activity of women who through virginity are consecrated to love of God and neighbor, especially the very poor, are an indispensable evangelical sign among those peoples and cultures where women still have far to go on the way toward human promotion and liberation. It is my hope that many young Christian women will be attracted to giving themselves generously to Christ, and will draw strength and joy from their consecration in order to bear witness to him among the peoples who do not know him.[81]

Yet the pope and Katharine both knew that the life of a missionary was extremely difficult and demanding. John Paul II remarked of Saints Cyril and Methodius, "They undertook among these people [the Slavs] that mission to which both of them devoted the rest of their lives, spent amidst journeys, privations, sufferings, hostility and persecutions."[82] Katharine, too, spoke often of the hardships encountered in the missionary field. She instructed her sisters: "How do we get accustomed to seeing God in the neighbor? By repeated acts. Even in this life we shall have reward for we shall have Peace. True love of Our Lord does not shrink back from ugliness, dirt, misery, and sin. Such children should remind us of Our Little Lord Jesus, Who became a 'leper' for our sins. Let us do everything for the poor, in the Name of Jesus. Let us look upon them with the eyes of the soul, or put on saintly spectacles, that we may see in them the living image of Jesus."[83]

Katharine personally visited each of her missions at least once every year, and between visits she wrote to them constantly, giving directions and succor. In a letter dated October 4, 1913, she wrote to her sisters in the Omaha, Nebraska, mission:

It is [Jesus] you serve in them [the poor and the unlovely]. You will do everything for them if you, your own selves are holy and united to God. If you give them good example by your patience with them, your acts of charity, by teaching them reverence to Our Lord in the Blessed Sacra-

81. John Paul II, *Redemptoris Missio*, 70.1.
82. John Paul II, *Slavorum Apostoli*, 52.
83. ASBS, vol. 25, p. 1 (conference of January 3, 1928).

ment by your reverence, and careful bow before the Tabernacle, by your own work perfectly done in <u>each</u> department — so that in you they see that perfection consists in not doing extraordinary things but in doing extraordinarily well what each has to do, in fine by teaching as Our Lord, "And Jesus began to <u>Do</u> and teach."[84]

Above all, the missionary must rely on God. Acknowledging this, Katharine wrote, "A missionary is one sent with the power of Christ. . . . We are incapable of bringing even one person to God. . . . It is God alone who has given each one. Thank Him. Bless Him."[85] The pope called the Holy Spirit "the principal agent of mission."[86] He also said those with a missionary vocation are "sent" as Christ was sent, that he will be present to them as they carry out his work, for "Christ . . . is with [the missionary] at every moment of life — 'Do not be Afraid . . . for I am with you' (Acts 18:9-10) — and [Christ] awaits [the missionary] in the heart of every person" she evangelizes.[87]

Holiness

What type of person is called to the special vocation of the missionary? In his encyclical *Redemptoris Missio,* the pope wrote, "The call to mission derives, of its nature, from the call to holiness. A missionary is really such only if he commits himself to the way of holiness: 'holiness must be called the fundamental presupposition and an irreplaceable condition for everyone fulfilling the mission of salvation in the Church.' "[88] The missionary is to be marked by obedience to the Holy Spirit, and must have a chaste, intimate communion with Christ, for "we cannot understand or carry out the mission unless we refer it to Christ as the one who is sent to evangelize."[89] The missionary is to embrace poverty, in spirit and in actuality. "The missionary is required to 'renounce himself and everything that up to this point he considered as his own, and to make himself everything to everyone.' This he does by a poverty that sets him free for the Gospel, overcoming attachment to people and things about him, so that he may become a brother to those to whom he

---

84. ASBS, vol. 15, pp. 157-58.

85. MKD, *Reflections on Religious Life,* p. 4.

86. John Paul II, *Redemptoris Missio,* 30.1.

87. John Paul II, *Redemptoris Missio,* 88.4.

88. John Paul II, *Redemptoris Missio,* 90.1.

89. John Paul II, *Redemptoris Missio,* 88.1.

is sent and thus bring them Christ the Savior."[90] The missionary must be a person of charity. If she is to proclaim the love of God to others and to convince them of their own loveliness, she must first show genuine love herself. The pope wrote that the missionary is to be a "contemplative in action" who must be able to say with the apostle John, "that which we have looked upon ... concerning the word of life ... we have also proclaimed to you" (1 John 1:1-3).[91] The missionary finally "is a person of the Beatitudes ... poverty, meekness, acceptance of suffering and persecution, the desire for justice and peace, charity. ... By living out the Beatitudes, the missionary experiences and shows concretely that the Kingdom of God has already come, and that he has accepted it. The characteristic of every authentic missionary is the inner joy that comes with faith. In a world tormented and oppressed by so many problems, a world tempted by pessimism, the one who proclaims the 'Good News' must be a person who has found true hope in Christ."[92]

In her vows of poverty, chastity, and obedience and in the fourth vow to be a mother to the Native American and African American peoples, Katharine lived her life being receptive to the Holy Spirit and in hope of the world to come. After a series of heart attacks when she could no longer be a "contemplative in action," she gave up her position as superior general and retired to two rooms of the second floor of the motherhouse to spend the rest of her days in quiet suffering and prayer. She wrote of her pain from a Christian's perspective: "My nature is terrified by the bitter sufferings of crucifixion, by the bloody furrows which my sins have traced on the Sacred Body of Jesus. Sufferings exhaust me; sometimes I can no longer endure them when my heart is afflicted; and yet I could not suffer too much in order to prepare myself for such a blessing as Holy Communion."[93] In awareness of her own mortality, she wrote, "Let us contemplate Jesus Our Lord on His last journey. He bids me follow Him. There is no other way to heaven."[94] Her original desire upon entering the convent had been to join a contemplative order, and she would spend the last twenty years of her life in contemplation. Mass was celebrated for her daily in her room, except for Sundays and holy days. When she was able to get about by herself or in a wheelchair, she spent most of her time in the tribune, a small balcony overlooking the sanctuary of

90. John Paul II, *Redemptoris Missio*, 88.3.

91. John Paul II, *Redemptoris Missio*, 91.2.

92. John Paul II, *Redemptoris Missio*, 91.3.

93. MKD, no date, 3202.

94. MKD, *Praying with Mother Katharine Drexel* (Bensalem, Pa.: Sisters of the Blessed Sacrament, 1986), p. 29.

the chapel below. In her last years when she was completely bedridden, the Blessed Sacrament was in her room twenty-four hours a day. The sisters reported that she slept very little and prayed continuously. Her face was turned to heaven through Calvary. Like Pope John Paul II, she was not afraid: "In Holy Communion the life of God in a particular way is imparted to my soul. It is there that God becomes the soul of my soul, to do, to suffer, all for love of Him who died for me, and If Thou art for me, if Thou art within me, what can I fear, O my God?"[95] Her contemplation of God brought her into a complete unitive and loving relationship with him so that there was nothing for her to fear, not even death. As she wrote in one of her meditations, "My dying is eternal life with Christ."[96]

Great throngs of the public came to Katharine Drexel's wake; police were required to direct traffic. The sisters held back the mourners who wanted to touch the body. However, they would make relics of religious articles for people by touching them gently to her body. One man held up a book to be touched to her body, and another held up his child, saying, "Take a look at the nun, son. Some day you can say that you looked upon a saint."[97] At her concelebrated funeral mass with 250 prelates, priests, and brothers participating, Joseph McShea, archbishop of Philadelphia, gave the homily.

> First and foremost, in youth and old age, in health and in sickness, with friend and with strangers, the beloved soul of Mother Katharine was activated, inspired, and impelled by an insatiable love of God and a complete subjection to His adorable Will. Hers was not a humanitarianism that stoops where love should begin. She was not a mere social reformer, educator, or philanthropist striving to better the conditions of her fellow man while permitting him to ignore God. Hers was a love primarily of God, practiced with her whole heart, her whole soul and her whole mind....
>
> It was this same love of God that inspired her to place herself and her religious family under the protective mantle of Jesus, ever living, ever loving and ever nourishing the souls of men in the ineffable Sacrament of the Holy Eucharist. Nor is it unfitting to mention that her last years of venerable old age, when a mind fatigued and exhausted had lost the resilience and perception of youth, she awakened each morning with a renewed

95. Meditation Slips, 12, p. 72.

96. Quoted in Baldwin, *St. Katharine Drexel: Apostle to the Oppressed,* ed. Rev. Paul S. Quinter, Elena Bucciarelli, and Frank Coyne (Philadelphia: Catholic Standard and Times, 2000), p. 194.

97. *Positio,* 2:373.

brightness of spirit when witnessing the Holy Sacrifice of the Mass and in receiving the Body and Blood of Jesus Christ in Holy Communion.[98]

The day after her death, an editorial in the *Catholic Standard and Times* stated: "One of the most remarkable women in the history of America was called home to God yesterday. The priests and people of the Archdiocese of Philadelphia have been proud to claim her as their own, and yet she belonged truly to all America, but especially to the forgotten people of America — our Indians and Negroes. Reverend Mother Katharine Drexel belonged to Philadelphia and to America, but one cannot help seeing in the story of her life that she belonged to God."[99] One who belongs to God is a saint. According to the memoirs of Sister Mary Gabriella, SBS, one of the mourners at Katharine's wake brought his entire family, stating, "We came to look upon a saint. She surely was a saint to live the life she did."[100]

Sainthood: Past and Present

After years of wending its way through the Vatican bureaucracy, Katharine Drexel's cause for sainthood eventually came to the desk of Pope John Paul II. One of the most visible expressions of the pope's continuous call to universal holiness had been the great number of saints and blesseds he recognized. In Catholic belief, it is not the pope, but God, who creates saints. The Church, in the person of the pope, simply recognizes that which God has done. While many more anonymous saints than named individuals have been "raised to the altar," it is the named and officially canonized saints that are held up for veneration and emulation. Everyone is called to be holy, to be a saint. One must be a saint to enter heaven. Official sainthood in no way conflicts with the idea of universal holiness. Recognized saints are in themselves models and beacons of holiness. By their examples, they inspire holiness in others. Vatican II recognized the great plurality in the forms of holiness, and following the council, Pope John Paul II went out of his way to canonize a large number and variety of saints. To recognize saints of the Church is a way of teaching the faithful what individuals can do in response to the divine call and divine grace. One reason the pope was able to canonize

98. *Catholic Standard and Times,* March 11, 1955, in the SBS Annals.
99. Quoted in Sr. Consuela Duffy, SBS, *Katharine Drexel: A Biography* (Philadelphia: Reilly Co., 1966), p. 389.
100. ASBS, 1955.

and beatify so many people is that he greatly changed and streamlined the canonization process.

Aside from the apostles, John the Baptist, and Mary the mother of Jesus, who were universally recognized as saints in the early church, the first saints were the martyrs of the Roman persecutions. St. Stephen, whose martyrdom was overseen by Saul of Tarsus, was the church's first recorded martyr. Martyrs were considered perfect Christians because they had made the ultimate and supreme sacrifice of their lives out of love for God. Their martyr deaths were acts of perfect *kenosis,* as they emptied themselves of life to be joined to God in heaven.[101] From the earliest times, their bones were treated with special reverence and their places of interment became the foci of public prayer and veneration. These earliest martyrs were spontaneously accepted by their friends, neighbors, and acquaintances as saints. Their prayers and intercessions were sought first by those who knew them personally and later by those who knew them only by reputation. Altars were built at their tombs.[102]

As time went on, the phenomenon of veneration was extended to other Christians, called confessors of the faith, who had not died a martyr's death but had defended and suffered for the faith. After having admitted their Christian faith to the Roman officials, St. Macrina and her husband were forced from their home and into the forests for seven years to escape the Christian persecutions of the early fourth century in Asia Minor. While in the forest, she and her husband and children lived on wild plants, tree bark, and small game. Among her grandchildren, to whom she passed on the Christian faith, are the saints Gregory of Nyssa, Basil the Great, and Macrina the Younger. St. Macrina is an example of a confessor of the faith, though St. Martin of Tours is a better-known confessor. Eventually, the veneration and reverence paid the martyrs and the confessors spread to those deceased who had a reputation for having lived exemplary Christian lives, often in great austerity and penitence.

Popular, but strictly local, cults sprang up quite spontaneously and unofficially to venerate the saints. There were no official proceedings to declare a person a saint in the early church. The people, recognizing the apparent holiness of a deceased person, simply began to pray to him or her for inter-

101. In *Redemptoris Mater,* 18 and 19, Pope John Paul II links *kenosis* and Christ's sacrifice on the cross.

102. For a good discussion of the history and development of canonization, see Kenneth L. Woodward, *Making Saints: How the Catholic Church Determines Who Becomes a Saint, Who Doesn't, and Why* (New York: Simon and Schuster, 1990).

cessory favors. Answered prayers, cures, and apparent miracles spread the popularity of the local saint. The faithful began to come from farther away to pray to the saint. Bishops helped to promote the popularity of local saints and to encourage pilgrimage to their shrines. Pilgrimages to the shrines of the saints became a major economic force in medieval Europe, for communities and churches depended on the money brought in by visiting pilgrims. One did not need the entire saint's body before which to pray. Soon bones, skulls, and other relics began to circulate throughout the Christian world. Saints became widely known for their exemplary Christian lives and for their thaumaturgic powers. The cult of saints remains an important element of Roman Catholic spiritual life. The Church has always stressed the difference between *latria,* worship due Christ alone, and *doulia,* veneration due the saints. This has been a point of no little confusion down through the years. Strictly speaking, the saints are not worshiped; they are venerated. Worship is for God alone.

A saint was first a saint by the belief of the people, but over time it became the practice for a person's sainthood to be officially recognized and approved by the local bishop. Officially recognized saints' names were placed on a canon, or a list, to be read out during various liturgies of the Church. There were many such lists down through the centuries. It was not until after the Protestant Reformation that the Catholic Church developed a complete canon of saints for the universal church. However, long before the Reformation, Catholic bishops were beginning to formalize the process of canonization.

Some bishops required a *vita,* a written account of a proposed saint's life and works, before recognition of sainthood. Others questioned eyewitnesses or examined miracle stories. By the end of the tenth century, a movement had arisen to reserve to the pope in Rome the naming of important saints. The first written record of a papal canonization is from 993, when Pope John XV recognized Archbishop Udalricus (d. 973) of Augsburg as a saint during a Lateran synod of cardinals and bishops. St. Udalricus was credited not only with personal holiness, but also with saving southern Germany from the Magyars. Pope Alexander III (1159-1181) decreed that no saint was to be venerated in the Church without pontifical approval. However, the Church was not so centrally governed in medieval Europe as it is today. In 1234, Pope Gregory IX published a series of laws for the universal church that asserted, among other things, papal control over the process of saint-making throughout the Church. It was a papal prerogative that would have to be asserted over and over again. In 1588, Pope Sixtus V created the Congregation for Rites, which had the charge of preparing documents on persons to be considered by the pope for canonization and beatification.[103]

It was not until the bull of Pope Urban VIII in 1634 that the canonization process became firmly fixed and placed in the exclusive hands of the Vatican. Canonization became a juridical process, rather than the spontaneous voice of the people proclaiming a saint. Lawyers within the Congregation of Rites would put cases for beatification and canonization before judges. Witnesses would be examined, and the Promoter of the Faith, the so-called Devil's Advocate, would argue against the case for the cause of sainthood. Until Pope John Paul II reformed the process of making saints, the Church followed the eighteenth-century norms established by Pope Benedict XIV, who had been a canon lawyer in the Congregation for Rites before becoming pope. The process was modified somewhat and formally included in the 1917 Code of Canon Law and continued until 1982. In all cases, then as now, the decision of the pope as to who becomes a saint is binding on the Church.

Before 1917, fifty years had to elapse between a person's death and when that person's cause for canonization could be heard. During that time, initiators began the preliminary investigations and tried to interest the local bishop in the cause. After the appointed time, a petition was put to the bishop to begin his investigation and find out if there was enough evidence of holiness to proceed. If so, the bishop certified to Rome that there was no present cult of veneration for the proposed saint. The bishop concurrently collected the writings of the individual and secured for them a *nihil obstat*, certifying that nothing heretical was contained within them.[104] All the documents and testimony were collected at the local level and then sent to the Vatican in a dossier. The cause for the individual was then assigned to a postulator. A defense attorney, who argued on behalf of the candidate, aided the postulator. The petitioners paid the postulator and the defense attorney, unless it was a *pro bono* cause.[105] The lawyer for the cause exchanged briefs with the Promoter of the Faith (the Devil's Advocate) until differences between them were resolved. This process could take years, even decades or

---

103. In beatification a pope declares that a deceased member of the Church has lived a life of heroic virtue and is worthy of the title "Blessed." It is preliminary to canonization, whereby the pope declares an individual a saint.

104. A declaration of *nihil obstat* certifies that a writing or body of writings contains nothing that is contrary to official Church doctrine.

105. *Pro bono* is a cause done for reduced fee, or no fee, due to the poverty of the claimant.

centuries. Eventually all the material was gathered together into a *positio*.[106] The *positio* had to be read and accepted by all the appropriate people in the Congregation for Rites.

Next, purported miracles were rigorously examined as the Church looked for divine signs that could confirm its judgment concerning a particular candidate. It is the miracles that define the saint. This means that without miracles, canonization will not occur. A holy life, service to the Church, devotion to God, and proper motivation were, and are, important, but they are insufficient criteria upon which to base canonization. Prior to the reform of the process by Pope John Paul II, two miracles were required for beatification and two more for canonization. First, a panel of medical doctors had to find that the cure did not occur and could not have occurred naturally. Then, a panel of theologians studied the cures to ascertain whether or not they were, in fact, the result of the intercession of the proposed candidate. If the answers were all in the affirmative, the pope met with the cardinals of the Congregation to decide whether or not to go forward with the beatification or canonization of the candidate. Beatification identifies the individual as "Blessed" and is the last step before canonization.

While the meeting between the Congregation and the pope may be *pro forma,* it also addresses real questions, often political. Pope Paul VI (1963-1978) delayed the canonization of the martyrs of the Spanish Civil War so as not to appear to favor the Franco regime and the Spanish government. He also delayed the cause for the canonization of the Mexican martyrs of the 1920 Cristero rebellion to avoid provoking further persecutions by the anti-clerical Mexican government of his day. The 120 Chinese martyrs canonized with Katharine Drexel caused the Chinese government to protest to the Vatican. The Beijing Foreign Affairs Ministry complained that the canonization would "have a grave negative impact on the process of normalization of the relations between the Vatican and Beijing," which had been broken off in 1951. A bishop of the state-controlled so-called Patriotic Catholic Church in China also condemned the canonizations, especially since they took place on the fifty-first anniversary of the birth of the People's Republic: "To choose today's date to canonize those so-called saints is a clear insult and humiliation. Today is a great holiday that celebrates the liberation of the Chinese nation from the invader and from the violent robbery of the imperialists and

---

106. The *positio,* similar to a law brief, puts forward the evidence, precedents, testimonies of witnesses and experts both for and against the cause of canonization for the proposed saint; it also includes a religious biography of the candidate.

colonialists."[107] One can be sure that the significance of the date was not lost on the pope or the Vatican officials who planned the ceremony.

The recent beatification (1987) and canonization (1998) of Edith Stein, Sr. Teresa Benedicta of the Cross, caused quite a controversy and tension in Catholic-Jewish relations. Many Jewish people were insulted that the Catholic Church would co-opt one of their own and proclaim her a Christian saint. Pope John Paul did not ignore Edith Stein's Jewish heritage. Rather, he addressed it directly as an honor:

> Today we greet in profound honor and holy joy a daughter of the Jewish people, rich in wisdom and courage, among these blessed men and women. Having grown up in the strict tradition of Israel, and having lived a life of virtue and self-denial in a religious order, she demonstrated her heroic character on the way to the extermination camp. United with our crucified Lord, she gave her life for genuine peace and for the people.... For Edith Stein, baptism as a Christian was by no means a break with her Jewish heritage. Quite on the contrary she said: "I had given up my practice of the Jewish religion as a girl of fourteen. My return to God made me feel Jewish again." She was always mindful of the fact that she was related to Christ not only in a spiritual sense, but also in blood terms.... She died as a daughter of Israel for the glory of the Most Holy Name and at the same time as Sister Teresa Benedicta of the Cross, literally, blessed by the Cross.[108]

In raising Edith Stein to the altar, Pope John Paul II made both a religious and a political statement. He indicated that in remembering St. Teresa Benedicta, one honors a saint who gave her life willingly for her people and one recalls the horror of the Holocaust and all the lesser lies perpetrated by mankind in service to evil or misguided ends. In following her example, people are called to seek the truth, and as she wrote, "Whoever seeks the truth is seeking God, whether consciously or unconsciously."[109]

Politics have often been a factor in deciding who is and who is not a saint. From the Baroque era onward, the process itself became time consuming and expensive. As times have changed, so have the saints recognized in the times changed. According to Stephen Wilson,

107. October 1, 2000.
108. Homily, Cologne, Germany, May 1, 1987, quoted in Weigel, *Witness to Hope,* pp. 541-42.
109. Quoted by Pope John Paul II in his homily at her canonization, October 14, 1998.

Those who have examined the sociology of saints are agreed that they reflect the structure of the societies which produce and honor them. This is true of the medieval saints, of the canonized saints of the West, of the saints of Byzantium and of Russia; and two features stand out. First, saints are of overwhelmingly aristocratic or upper-class origin, and hagiographers place great emphasis on this, if only by pointing to their subject's renunciation of the privileges of high status. . . . Secondly, saints are also overwhelmingly male. The "canon" of Russian saints includes fewer than a dozen women, while among saints canonized in the West, the proportion of women, as Delooz demonstrates, never rose above 20 percent until [the twentieth century] and was often considerably below this. . . . A further feature is also revealing. In the Western Church . . . female saints are nearly always virgins and not married women with children.[110]

Donald Weinstein and Rudolph Bell recognized that while hagiographers and historians may pay a great deal of attention to a saint's aristocratic rank or high status, the common people tend to view saints as classless: "Except at the two extremes of the social scale, kings and peasants, whose class was usually germane to the perception of their holy lives, saints, especially if they had taken monastic or clerical vows, tended to be seen as classless — which is to say that the perception of their saintly activities did not give prominence to whether they bore a title or came from a good family."[111] It matters not that rank-and-file believers view saints as classless, for that is after the fact of canonization. In the making of saints, those whose backers have influence, sufficient resources, and time are the most successful. Thus, there are indeed many kings, queens, and aristocrats among the canon of saints. If a candidate for sainthood is a female, if she cannot be a queen, it is best that she be a nun; and more specifically, it is best if she is the founder of an order. There are many founders of religious orders on the roll of the saints. Religious orders have the motivation to see their founders canonized; they have the resources to sustain the project through; and they have long institutional memories. When the Second Vatican Council recommended that religious orders remain close to the charisms of their founders, many orders began to file petitions for the canonization of founders.[112] The cause for the canon-

110. Stephen Wilson, ed., *Saints and Their Cults: Studies in Religious Sociology, Folklore, and History* (Cambridge: Cambridge University Press, 1983), pp. 37-38.

111. Donald Weinstein and Rudolph M. Bell, *Saints and Society: The Two Worlds of Western Christendom, 1000-1700* (Chicago: University of Chicago Press, 1982), p. 205.

112. See *Lumen Gentium*, 46, and *Perfectae Caritatis*, October 28, 1965, 2b.

ization of Katharine Drexel began in 1964. On the day she was canonized, she shared the ceremony with St. Maria Josefa of the Sacred Heart of Jesus Sancho de Guerra, the founder of the Servants of Jesus. Father Redemptus Valabek of the Congregation for the Causes of Saints is quoted by Woodward as saying, "Once one group of nuns decides to get their foundress beatified, they all want their foundresses beatified."[113]

The Saints of Pope John Paul II

The approach of John Paul II toward saint-making appears to have been pastoral and evangelical. Even though the Second Vatican Council made a universal call to holiness, it recognized that holiness is not a singular quality. There are at least as many paths to holiness as there are saints, for each saint, indeed each individual, is unique. Each saint responds to God's grace within the confluence of his or her time and place. Saints provide Christians with unending sources of inspiration for lives lived in holiness. Indeed, the cult of saints is so pervasive in the Catholic Church that every church altar contains the relics of a saint. An altar is defined by canon law as "a tomb containing the relics of a saint." And where his relics are, the saint is said to be present. The tomb of St. Martin of Tours has an inscription that reads,

> Here lies Martin the bishop, of Holy memory,
> Whose soul is in the hands of God, but he is fully here,
> Present and made plain in miracles of every kind.[114]

The process for making saints was so long and involved that there was a backlog of more than one thousand when John Paul II became pope. As the pilgrim pope who traveled the world over, he loved to present new blesseds or saints to the countries he visited. Pope Paul VI had divided the Congregation for Rites into two congregations, one being the Congregation for the Causes of Saints. On January 25, 1983, John Paul II officially changed the canonization process by his Apostolic Constitution *Divinus Perfectionis Magister.* His goal was to make the process "simpler . . . while maintaining the soundness of the investigation in matters of such great import." In effect, the process became more streamlined, less cumbersome, faster, and cheaper. The new regulations do away with the adversarial model that had

---

113. Woodward, *Making Saints,* p. 108.
114. Quoted in Woodward, *Making Saints,* p. 57.

been the norm for four hundred years. No longer is there a Devil's Advocate who attempts to defeat a particular cause for sainthood. Under the new rules, there are still tribunals where eyewitness testimony is taken, but instead of dealing with unending court briefs written by lawyers, the Congregation now relies mainly on accounts by relators that "respond more adequately to the dictates of historical criticism."[115] Local bishops assume the responsibility of collecting proof of holiness, or heroic virtue, as well as assembling all the writings of the proposed saint. The material is sent to Rome where the writings still require a *nihil obstat,* and the locally gathered testimony is turned over to a relator, who may or may not be trained in historical-critical methodology, but who writes a *positio* outlining the life and virtues of the individual. With the writing of the *positio,* the relator's job is complete. The relator for Katharine Drexel was Fr. P. Peter Gumpel, a German Jesuit and university historian; Joseph Martino, former bishop of Scranton, Pennsylvania, was the vice relator, who actually wrote the biographical section of the *positio.* The postulator was the Italian Jesuit Fr. Paul Molinari.

The postulator's task is to see the cause for sainthood through to its completion. He or she turns the completed *positio* over to a panel of eight theologians. If six of the eight approve of the candidate, the cause is passed on to the Congregation's board of cardinals and bishops for their judgment. Miracles are judged, as before, by panels of medical doctors and theologians, though the number of miracles required has been halved. One miracle is required for beatification of a nonmartyr (martyrs need no miracles for beatification), and an additional miracle is required for canonization. The pope has final approval of who becomes a blessed or a saint. To create more blesseds, Pope John Paul II was known to dispense with proven miracles, as he did for Blessed Kateri Tekakwitha, a Native American of the Mohawk tribe who died in 1680, and Blessed Rupert Mayer, a German Jesuit priest who died in 1945.

The pope believed that God talks to his people in and through the saints, and that the saints present the face of God. As the chief pastor of a church of over one billion people, the pope's task is to lead the Church's mission of holiness. The saints and blesseds are the manifestation of the success of that mission. The saints are looked upon as friends of God and friends of mankind. It is God who makes saints; the Church simply holds them up for all to see.

---

115. *Divinus Perfectionis Magister,* introduction.

They are valuable examples for the Church: Blesseds and Saints show us practical ways to holiness. Their lives are lives of witnessing to Christ. Today they are held up to the people of the new evangelization and to the people of our times. The Church presents the riches of the patrimony of their holiness and witness to new generations and the times to come and this heritage serves as a reference point in their human and Christian formation. In the life of the Church [saints] also serve as a contribution to the mission of evangelizing the world. Since they constitute a heritage, the Saints are also a programme, that is, they show us what we need to do. They are an example for us to follow of how, or in what way, we should fulfill our commitment to being human and Christian.[116]

The pope wrote in his encyclical *Novo Millennio Ineunte,* that in the saints one sees "holiness, a message that convinces without the need of words . . . the living reflection of the face of Christ."[117] Here he reiterated the line in *Lumen Gentium,* "God shows to men, in a vivid way, his presence and his face in the lives of those companions of ours in the human condition who are most perfectly transformed into the image of Christ. He speaks to us in them, and offers us a sign of his kingdom, to which we are so powerfully attracted, so great a cloud of witnesses is there given."[118]

Early in his pontificate, John Paul II asked the Congregation for the Causes of Saints to bring him candidates from around the world who represented all walks of life. Martyrdom is still the most direct route to sainthood. Of the 482 saints he canonized, 411 were martyred. Of the 1,338 blesseds beatified by the pope, 1,030 were martyred. The next surest path to sainthood is still found in the consecrated life. However, the pope tried to raise the number of the laity represented in the canons of saints and blesseds, and he recognized more than 500 of them. One example is Blessed Pierre Toussaint, the New York barber-philanthropist who was born into Haitian slavery.

To those who complained that the Vatican had become a "saint factory," the pope responded directly: "It is sometimes said that there are too many beatifications today. However, in reflecting reality, which by God's grace is what it is, it also responds to the desire expressed by the [Vatican] Council [II]. The Gospel is so wide spread in the world and its message has sunk

116. An interview with Archbishop Edward Nowak, secretary of the Congregation for the Causes of Saints, in "New Evangelization with the Saints," *L'Osservatore Romano,* weekly English ed., November 28, 2001, online (accessed October 1, 2004).

117. John Paul II, *Novo Millennio Ineunte,* 7.

118. *Lumen Gentium,* 50.

such deep roots that the great number of beatifications vividly reflects the action of the Holy Spirit and the vitality flowing from Him in the Church's most essential sphere, that of holiness. Indeed, it was the Council that put particular emphasis on the universal call to holiness."[119]

The increased number of saints and blesseds shows the vitality of the Church and reflects also the huge size and diversity of the universal church. Pope John Paul II emphasized that "the greatest homage which all the Churches can give to Christ on the threshold of the third millennium will be to manifest the Redeemer's all-powerful presence through the fruits of faith, hope, and charity, present in men and women of many different tongues and races who have followed Christ in the various forms of Christian vocation."[120] The greatest historical figures for the Church are not kings, conquerors, or popes, but the saints, for they hold the keys to holiness. "The main task of the Church is to lead Christians along the path of holiness. . . . The Church is the 'home of holiness,' and the Charity of Christ, poured out by the Holy Spirit, is her soul."[121] As long as he was pope, John Paul II continued to raise to the altar new blesseds and new saints for the faithful. For "the saints [are] . . . unique figures in whom is found not a theory nor even merely a moral, but a plan of life to be recounted, to be discovered through study, to be loved with devotion, to be put into practice with imitation."[122]

While Pope John Paul II beatified and canonized more holy men and women than his predecessors, and more from wider walks of life, the majority of the canonizations he presided over were male clerics. Of the women he canonized, most were religious nuns and sisters. Additionally, the majority of all his canonizations were Europeans. These statistics ought not to detract from the fact that John Paul II went out of his way to beatify and canonize candidates from Africa, Asia, and the Americas and to increase the number of women and laity among the saints. In part, the statistics speak to how little control a pope has over the canonization processes, and in part they testify to how difficult it is to break traditional modes of thought. Even though the pope makes the last decision of approval, with the initiation for sainthood in the hands of local bishops, ultimately the bishops say who does and does

119. Address to the Extraordinary Consistory in Preparation for Jubilee Year 2000, June 13-14, 1994, *L'Osservatore Romano*, weekly English ed., June 22, 1994, online.

120. John Paul II, *Novo Millennnio Ineunte*, 37.

121. Pope John Paul II, Message for the 39th World Day of Prayer for Vocations, April 21, 2002, online, www.vatican.va, 1.

122. Cardinal Jose Saraiva Martins, CMF, *L'Osservatore Romano*, weekly English ed., April 16, 2003, 8, online.

not become a saint in the Roman Catholic Church. However, it is the papal pronouncement that makes it ecclesiastically certain that the named saint is in heaven. As part of his teaching office, the pope proclaims: "We solemnly decide and define that [name] is a saint and inscribe him [or her] in the catalog of saints, stating that his memory shall be kept with pious devotion by the universal Church." This is a solemn pronouncement and carries the weight of the authority of the pope's teaching office.

The Cause for the Sainthood of Katharine Drexel

As a founder of an order of nuns, St. Katharine Drexel was a very traditional candidate for canonization. That she was from the United States made her somewhat unusual. What is remarkable about her canonization process is that hers was the first *positio* written in English, and hers was the first petition for sainthood to go through the process as reformed by Pope John Paul II in 1983. That her cause was actually initiated in 1964 and not taken up until 1983 indicates how complex and lengthy was the old juridical process. Under the new process, she was beatified in 1988 and canonized on October 1, 2000. The length of time between her beatification and her canonization was due to the need to authenticate a second miraculous cure. The Sisters of the Blessed Sacrament received thousands of letters from people claiming miracles wrought by the intervention and intercession of Katharine Drexel. One miracle was needed for her beatification and a second one for her canonization. The first authenticated miraculous cure was of Robert Guntherman, who, at the age of fourteen, in 1974, was hospitalized with a very high fever and serious ear infection. It was a life-threatening illness that left him completely deaf in one ear. His inner ear bones were surgically scraped to no effect. He remained deaf. One of the Sisters of the Blessed Sacrament suggested that his family pray directly and exclusively to Katharine Drexel. The ear bones were regenerated and Robert's hearing was restored. The Philadelphia doctors could not explain his complete and sudden cure. In 1987, the Vatican medical review board found that Robert's cure was medically inexplicable; thus it was miraculous. In 1988, a board of theologians found that the miracle was due to the intervention of Katharine Drexel. Seven months later Katharine Drexel became the Blessed Katharine Drexel.

A second miracle was sought by the supporters of her cause. Hundreds of incidents were investigated, but none proved to be, in fact, miraculous. Finally, little Amanda Wall, a seventeen-month-old toddler who was born deaf, suddenly began to hear after her family prayed to Blessed Katharine Drexel. Again, the Philadelphia doctors could find no natural cause for the sudden onset of Amanda's hearing. It took two years for the case to be heard by the Vatican's medical examiners. In 1999, the medical review board proclaimed that Amanda Wall's sudden ability to hear had no known medical explanation. It was a miracle. In January 2000, the board of theologians ascribed the miracle to the direct intervention of Katharine Drexel. The way was cleared for her canonization. The father of Amanda Wall was a non-Catholic; he was a nondenominational Protestant who converted to Catholicism after his daughter's miracle. He explained what he saw as the reason behind the two hearing miracles attributed to Katharine Drexel's intercession: "I think this is her way of telling us we should listen to the Word of God."[123] That explanation may be as good as any other in explaining what the miracles mean, but just what did Pope John Paul II intend when he canonized St. Katharine Drexel?

If canonization is part of a pope's teaching office, what lessons should be learned from St. Katharine Drexel and her life of holiness? At the mass for her canonization, the pope said:

> "See what you have stored up for yourselves against the last days!" (James 5:3). In the second reading of today's liturgy, the Apostle James rebukes the rich who trust in their wealth and treat the poor unjustly. Mother Katharine Drexel was born into wealth in Philadelphia in the United States. But from her parents she learned that her family's possessions were not for them alone, but were meant to be shared with the less fortunate. As a young woman, she was deeply distressed by the poverty and hopeless conditions endured by many Native-Americans and Afro-Americans. She began to devote her fortune to missionary and educational work among the poorest members of society. Later, she understood that more was needed. With great courage and confidence in God's grace, she chose to give not just her fortune but her whole life totally to the Lord.[124]

The pope was upholding her holy poverty as an example for others to follow.

As stated earlier, the pope was interested in concrete individuals. While saints are saints for the universal church, John Paul II was careful to raise

---

123. Archdiocese of Philadelphia news release, March 10, 2000.
124. October 1, 2000, online at the Vatican Web site.

to the altar specific saints for specific peoples and regions of the world. In St. Katharine Drexel, he was designating a specific saint who had virtues that deserved to be imitated by a specific people, the Catholics living in the United States; but he was also holding her up as a Catholic exemplar for American non-Catholics. To see what he intended with this particular saint, it is necessary to return to what the pope saw as the negative signs of the times. One of his ongoing emphases was the devastating effects of atheistic materialism and a culture that privileges "having" over "being." He was concerned with both the exploited and the exploiter in such a culture. The United States of America qualifies as one of the pope's so-called super-developed countries. In the hedonistic pursuit of happiness that creates vast wealth for some at the degradation and exploitation of others, having more has often meant that others have less, and those with little means are judged as inferior. Everyone is a true loser in such a system. All are degraded and alienated from their true selves as children of God. To share with Katharine Drexel in the communion of saints is to have as a close companion one who gave up wealth, social power, and position to make a holy gift of herself in service to others. "Having" was not important to Katharine Drexel. "Being" the face and hands of Christ in service to others was everything. Katharine's holy poverty is a virtue to be admired and imitated in an avowed consumer society. On the day after her canonization, Pope John Paul II said of her, "St. Katharine Drexel took to heart the words of Jesus to the young man in the Gospel: 'If you seek perfection, go and sell your possessions, and give to the poor. You will then have treasure in heaven'" (Matt. 19:21).[125] When one has nothing else to give, one gives oneself. When one has nothing, in fact or in spirit, humility is the one virtue closely associated with holy poverty.

When important visitors came to the convent of the Sisters of the Blessed Sacrament, Katharine Drexel would often have someone else meet them at the station, preferring to continue her eucharistic adoration, her prayers, or simply her work, rather than to put herself forward. At the opening ceremony for Xavier University, she did not join the bishops, clergy, and secular political leaders of Louisiana on the platform. She watched the ceremony from an upper-story window seated alone. When in her later years the president of Haiti wanted to present her with a presidential decoration and citation in thanksgiving for the work of her sisters in Haiti, she had to be persuaded to accept the awards. She never liked to be the center of attention. Even in her youth she described her lavish debutante ball as a "little party."

125. Homily, October 2, 2000, online.

Though she undoubtedly knew her social graces, she must have been Philadelphia society's most reluctant debutante. Her humility is a virtue to be imitated by those grown arrogant in prosperity. The Catholic Church teaches that it is in weakness, not in strength, that grace works best.

Katharine Drexel's holy chastity is a model for all men and women to follow both inside and outside of marriage. In a society where "having it all" includes sexual license, the pope feared for the souls of those exploited by the sexual revolution that resulted in one in two marriages ending in divorce and skyrocketing out-of-wedlock births with 34 percent of babies born outside of marriage in the United States (68 percent of African American babies are born to single mothers), thereby pushing more women and children into poverty. Of the 48 percent of unintended pregnancies that occur each year in the United States, one-half end in abortion. In 2000 alone, 1.31 million abortions were performed in the United States. African American women are three times more likely to have an abortion than are Caucasian women.[126] Due to the sexual revolution in the United States, men are becoming superfluous as fathers and breadwinners; they are losing a sense of responsibility and taking on an attitude of sexual entitlement that threatens both men and women. Katharine Drexel's obedience to Christ and his church is a model for a society that has raised individualism to iconic status, where the individual is a god, creating his or her own meaning and directing life to suit only himself or herself. According to the late pope, such autonomy quickly and easily leads to the selfish pursuit of happiness and slavery to sin. Obedience to God brings true liberation and the freedom to do as one ought in conformation to Christ.

"Poverty, chastity, and obedience," Pope John Paul II wrote, "are distinctive features of the redeemed person, inwardly set free from the slavery of egotism. *Free to love. Free to serve*. . . . Following in the footsteps of the crucified and risen Christ, they live this *freedom of solidarity,* taking on the spiritual and material burdens of their brothers and sisters."[127] He could have used the term *kenosis* here. *Kenosis* is a distinctive feature of the redeemed person. An African American, Georgetown University theologian Diana L. Hayes, who is not married, has taken a vow of celibacy. She claims her vow has set her free to be of service to others and to have a wide selection of

---

126. These statistics are widely used and are derived from the National Center for Health Statistics, and the Alan Guttmacher Institute. Also see Luther Keith, "Blacks Must Address Number of Out-of-Wedlock Births," *Detroit News,* October 30, 2003, online.

127. Homily, February 11, 2003, online.

intimate friends and family with whom she feels more "present." She is able to give to them her undivided self. "For me, the celibate state provides, not a selfish freedom of self-indulgence and irresponsibility, but a responsible freedom to live a life of service to God."[128] By elevating St. Katharine Drexel, John Paul II did not say that all women should be nuns of consecrated virginity, because clearly they should not. In the total gift of self, which is the mark of true love, men and women may practice a kind of chastity in marriage as well as outside of it. It is the love of God that led Katharine Drexel to make the gift of herself in order to become a mother to African American and Native American peoples in the United States. She emptied herself to be filled with the love of her eucharistic God, whom she then shared with his brothers and sisters.

Her canonization directly calls attention to her particular charism, her mission to the least of Christ's brothers and sisters in the United States. In holding up Katharine Drexel, the pope proclaimed that her canonization "served to raise awareness of the continuing need, even in our own day, to fight racism in all its manifestations."[129] Pope John Paul II opposed racism in all its forms. The ideal *communio* in the Church precludes racism: "Perfect communion in love preserves the Church from all forms of particularism, ethnic exclusivism or racial prejudice, and from national arrogance. This communion must elevate and sublimate every purely natural legitimate sentiment of the human heart."[130] While the Church as a divine institution and the body of Christ may be protected from racism and particularism, as a human institution, the Church's members, even its hierarchy, have not always been untarnished by these sins.

The Belgian missionary Father Joseph Anciaux, SSJ, was so alarmed at the indifference of the U.S. Catholic clergy toward the needs of African Americans that he wrote directly to Pope Pius X in Rome. His 1903 letter has come to be known by the title "The Miserable Conditions of Black Catholics in America." In it, he wrote, "Nearly all priests, even the most pious, fear reproach of white citizens so much they scarcely dare to make the slightest effort on behalf of blacks; others are so imbued with prejudice that they say: 'The care of blacks is not my concern. They do not belong to my flock.'" He noted that one callously indifferent priest responded to Anciaux's efforts to

128. Diana L. Hayes, "A Sexual Ethic of Singleness — Built upon the Foundation of Celibacy," *Witness Magazine,* April 2000, online.

129. Homily, February 11, 2003, online.

130. John Paul II, *Slavorum Apostoli,* 11.3.

minister to African Americans by saying, "One wastes time and money in ministering to blacks. . . . What reason can there be that you are so solicitous of the Negro?"[131] The first ordained priests of African American descent were the three Healy brothers, born in America of an Irish father and a slave mother. It is telling that they chose to pass for Caucasian throughout their lives. As late as 1954, when the bishop of Raleigh, North Carolina, put an end to segregated Catholic churches in his diocese, the editor of the Catholic magazine *Commonweal* observed, "The American Catholic Church was about as interested in blacks in America as it was in American Indians, which was not very much."[132] From these types of statements, it is easy to see why Katharine Drexel's charismatic and prophetic love for African American and Native American people was so revolutionary in her time and such an appropriate mirror to hold up to a people still enveloped in a residually racist society. She taught her sisters: "Have a cordial respect for others in heart and mind; if there is any prejudice in the mind we must uproot it, or it will pull us down."[133] Racism destroys both its object and its subject. In the homily at her canonization, Pope John Paul II proclaimed that

> Katharine Drexel is an excellent example of that practical charity and generous solidarity with the less fortunate which has long been the distinguishing mark of American Catholics. To her religious community, the Sisters of the Blessed Sacrament, she taught a spirituality based on prayerful union with the Eucharistic Lord and zealous service of the poor and the victims of racial discrimination. Her apostolate helped to bring about a growing awareness of the need to combat all forms of racism through education and social services. May her example help young people in particular to appreciate that no greater treasure can be found in this world than in following Christ with an undivided heart and in using generously the gifts we have received for the service of others and for the building of a more just and fraternal world.[134]

That there are saints like Katharine Drexel is one of the signs of the times that gave Pope John Paul II hope for the third millennium. Its dawn was a time pregnant with possibilities for the now deceased pope. For John Paul II,

---

131. Quoted in Tim Unsworth, "Racism and Religion: Partners in Crime?" *Salt of the Earth Magazine*, January 1994, online.

132. Quoted in Unsworth, "Racism and Religion."

133. MKD, *Reflections on Religious Life*, p. 36.

134. October 1, 2000, online.

who led the Roman Catholic Church for more than twenty-five years, it was a time of great expectations. He believed that saints are a sign that the economy of Christ's salvation of mankind is coming to fruition. Despite moral decay, death, famine, and war, he would preach, "Be not afraid to welcome Christ and accept his power. . . . Open wide the doors for Christ. To his saving power open the boundaries of states, economic and political systems, the vast fields of culture, civilization, and development. Be not afraid. Christ knows 'what is in man.' He alone knows it. . . . Be confident in his love."[135] He preached, especially, "Do not be afraid to be saints!"[136]

135. Homily, All Saints' Day, November 1, 2000. Repeated by Pope John Paul II in his homily at the mass to celebrate his twenty-fifth anniversary as pope, online.
136. Pope John Paul II, quoted in Weigel, *Witness to Hope,* p. 588.

CHAPTER 6

A Coda: The Mystery Revealed

The previous chapters have revealed Katharine Drexel in bits and pieces in a manner not unlike the blind men describing an elephant by the parts on to which each held. This project has proceeded much the same way. Chapter 1 discussed Drexel's early life, portraying her as a rather serious young girl, but still full of humor and fun, who learned philanthropy at her mother's knee. It showed her as preoccupied with the development of her virtues, especially purity and humility, and the diminution of her vices, particularly pride, vanity, and scrupulosity. Chapter 2 covered the process of her discernment as she argued with Bishop O'Connor about the shape of her future life, disclosing her as strong-willed and courageous. She and her spiritual adviser were continually at odds over her eating habits, clothing, and entertainments, as well as her sacramental and prayer life. She saw herself drawn to the convent; he wanted her in the world. It was a heroic struggle on her part, which culminated in her defiance of the bishop. He capitulated on the matter of her vocation, but then proposed that she found a new order of sisters to serve as missionaries to the African American and Native American peoples. She had wanted to join a contemplative order. She saw herself withdrawing from the world, and not rushing out to change it in a dramatic fashion. However, it became an idea that she fully embraced. Chapter 3 described the development of her order, a process that required her to be encouraging and forceful, tactful and forthright. Chapter 4 delved deeply into her spiritual life, uncovering a wellspring of depth in her great devotion to the Eucharist and her unending self-emptying. Chapter 5 viewed her through the lens of Pope John Paul II, who claimed her as a daughter of the Church whose virtues and views mirrored his own. Throughout this project, Katharine Drexel has been revealed as one who gave her fortune and her life to bring Christ and the Catholic Church to the Native

Americans and African Americans of the United States. Yet somehow, through all this exposition, she remains something of a mystery.

One of the things a writer does when in the midst of a project such as this is to talk endlessly to as many people as possible who are even tangentially connected to the subject or who show the slightest interest in it. I have found myself talking to complete strangers on planes and trains about kenotic spirituality. I have queried priests, bishops, and nuns about the Catholic Church and civil rights, about the Church among blacks and Indians, about home missions, and directly about Katharine Drexel. Everyone I have ever asked why Drexel should be a saint has given me a different answer; they are like the blind men describing the elephant.

Some have commented on her dedication to uplifting the Native American and African American peoples. They see her as a Catholic Martin Luther King Jr. in her dedication to civil rights. She was his forerunner by two generations and in her seventies when he was born. Sister Mary John Soulliard, SBS, sees her work for civil rights as reason enough for her sainthood. She recalled walking with Mother Katharine one afternoon when the founder said, "Sisters, we will do this work until the conscience of America is awakened." Sister Mary John went on to remark, "I used to think that someday I wouldn't have a job."[1] For Sister Mary John and many others, Katharine Drexel is a saint because of her work to uplift the downtrodden.

Others see Katharine in opposition to discrimination and prejudice, so that her sainthood comes not only from what she did but also from how and why she did it. Sister Patricia Suchalski, president of the SBS, put it this way:

> At the time Katharine was growing up and when she founded our congregation the social climate regarding African-Americans and Native-Americans was deplorable. Discrimination and prejudice were rampant and literally allowed through the laws of our government. In many ways, I believe Katharine Drexel was the Mother Teresa of her day. Unlike Mother Teresa however the media was not what it is now so the sharing of her work and what she believed was very limited. The work Katharine Drexel embarked upon was also very distasteful to much of white American society. She faced much opposition. Why did she do what she did? Where did she get the "wisdom" to see the African-American and Native-American peoples with such different eyes than most of her contemporaries? I think the response to that flows from her deep relationship with God from her

1. Email to author, December 6, 2005.

early years. It was because of that ever deepening relationship which allowed her soul . . . her heart . . . her very being to be open to the slightest movement of God within her. God shared God's wisdom of the equality of all peoples with Katharine and because of her openness she was able to grasp what few others of her time were able to. Her love of the Eucharist . . . the Body and Blood of Jesus . . . enabled her to understand that call for . . . ALL to take and eat . . . and once we have eaten together around that table are we not all united as one no matter who we are? Her sainthood I believe flows from this . . . she received God's word and she responded to it as a prophet does. Like all prophets her words and actions caused many to wince. Katharine believed in the equality of all united through Jesus in the Eucharist. She went about making sure that those who others did not count as equal were invited to the table and given all the opportunities to recognize the dignity of their person that was theirs by right from God. Her sainthood I believe is a way of saying to the universal Church that Katharine's beliefs of the equalities of all peoples are what we are called to believe and act out in our lives and Katharine's belief that this equality stems from the "invitation" that must be issued to all to sit and partake together around the table of the Eucharist is what the last Supper was/is all about. I think as we look at our world and society today that message is primary for us as a global community. Her canonization for the Church and society in America and across the globe seems to be a message we continue to need at this time of our histories.[2]

To Bobbye Burke, the archivist at Old St. Joseph's Church in Philadelphia, Katharine Drexel is a saint for two reasons: her love of the Eucharist and her ability to be a powerful woman in a church led by men. "She was a daughter of the Church," Burke said.[3] It was the churchmen who made her a saint, according to Burke. Her far-flung missions for Native Americans and African Americans were in more than twenty-two dioceses across the nation. Each of those dioceses is headed by a bishop or, in some cases, a cardinal archbishop. Even though she resided in the Philadelphia Archdiocese, every bishop in whose diocese she had established a mission or a school had a stake in her sainthood. She could be the saint for each of them. She was an important part of the history of at least twenty-six dioceses, and, as a saint, she had something to teach the people.

2. Email to author, November 4, 2005.
3. Interview with author, November 19, 2005.

The Vatican Web site on saints says the following about Katharine Drexel:

> Katharine left a four-fold dynamic legacy to her Sisters of the Blessed Sacrament, who continue her apostolate today, and indeed to all peoples:
> - her love for the Eucharist, her spirit of prayer, and her Eucharistic perspective on the unity of all peoples;
> - her undaunted spirit of courageous initiative in addressing social iniquities among minorities — one hundred years before such concern aroused public interest in the United States;
> - her belief in the importance of quality education for all, and her efforts to achieve it;
> - her total giving of self, of her inheritance and all material goods in selfless service of the victims of injustice.

These are the official reasons for her canonization. This legacy that she leaves behind, not only for the Sisters of the Blessed Sacrament but for all men and women, is what the Catholic Church holds up for all to see, to be inspired by, to be emulated. Katharine Drexel, as a saint, is a role model, a companion in the communion of saints, and an intercessor.

Saints are role models in virtue, and Katharine's virtues are many, as has been amply demonstrated. Saints are also role models for Christian action in the world. Her work in "addressing social iniquities among minorities" is yet to be completed. Many iniquities still exist, though many, thanks to Katharine and others like her, are eradicated. There is plenty yet to be done by those inspired by Katharine. Saints are role models in spirituality. Katharine's great love of the Eucharist and her lifelong self-emptying gift of self for others set the standard very high for those who look to her for spiritual and practical guidance. Yet as one reads her journals, letters, and meditations, it all seems very easy. She was in constant companionship with Jesus. She wrote to him, about him, and for him in a most familiar manner, as to an intimate friend or, indeed, a lover. It is this intimacy that seems at once so astonishing and so mundane. To be a companion of St. Katharine, according to the Church, is to be a companion of Jesus — and not just sometimes, but all the time. Finally, saints act as intercessors. St. Katharine Drexel is believed to have been the intercessor for the miraculous cures of Robert Guntherman and Amanda Wall. Prayers for her intercession are believed to be efficacious.

One Sister of the Blessed Sacrament with whom I spoke about Katharine Drexel thought that everyone was trying to make sainthood too hard.

According to her, sainthood is really very ordinary. After all, every Christian hopes to become a saint, because only saints go to heaven. Most Christians will tell you that they expect to go to heaven, and yet most fall far short of the standard set by a Katharine Drexel. So, is heaven full of ordinary individuals, or need only the extraordinary apply? Not knowing the answer to that important question, the Christian churches tell stories about people of extraordinary virtue and witness in hopes of inspiring everyone to live up to a higher standard. In the words of Kenneth Woodward, in the process of saint-making, "A life is transformed into a text," a story.[4] But texts and stories are limited. The more one learns about another person, even a saint, the more it becomes clear that there is much that can never be known. Each person is ultimately a mystery. Why was Katharine Drexel more open to God's call than one of her sisters, cousins, or friends? I know very few who experience the easy intimacy that Katharine experienced with Christ, but I know many who desire such intimacy. She was very direct with Christ, and she believed that he was very direct with her. How did that happen? After spending six years studying Katharine Drexel, there is still much about her that I do not understand. There are thousands of letters, prayers, and meditations by her that describe what she did throughout her life, and why she did it, but even after considering all that, questions remain. This is a mystery to be pondered and respected.

Despite this mystery, what has been revealed about Katharine Drexel is still important. Her self-emptying kenotic spirituality perfectly balanced her eucharistic spirituality. It was from her spiritual core that she was able to go forth to do battle with the iniquities of her day, to fight for the rights and education of Native Americans and African Americans. At the same time, her main goal was to bring Native Americans and African Americans to Christ in the Catholic Church. Her great wealth became her great poverty of spirit that allowed her to see Christ in Native Americans and African Americans, where most Americans simply saw "the other." She was, for the Catholic Church in America, the right person at the right time. Pope John Paul II canonized her as St. Katharine Drexel, a role model, companion, and intercessor for Catholics in the twenty-first century.

---

4. Kenneth L. Woodward, *Making Saints: How the Catholic Church Determines Who Becomes a Saint, Who Doesn't, and Why* (New York: Simon and Schuster, 1990), p. 18.

Acknowledgments

How was one to know that a graduate school project would turn into a labor of love? It was a love that went both ways. The more I learned about St. Katharine Drexel, the more I fell in love with my subject. However much I strived for scholarly objectivity, I am sure there are many places in the book where my clear sympathy and affection for Katharine Drexel and her mission come through. Astute readers will notice those places and, I hope, not be distracted by them.

What I did not expect from such an undertaking were the love and support I received from family, friends, colleagues, and even complete strangers throughout the long process. My children, Christine, Robert, and Alexander Hughes, were supportive from the very germ of an idea. They read some of my drafts and made critical suggestions, but it was their enthusiasm for my complete success that was so gratifying and energizing. My husband, William Hughes, has been my constant helpmate, companion, sometimes editor, and fabulous gourmet cook. My brother, Bill Dempsey, and sister, Katherine Lomax, always let me know how proud they were of my accomplishment. It was my brilliant friend Margaret Lee who gave me the idea of pursuing an English university degree, as she was pursuing an Australian doctoral degree. We are conspicuous now in a sea of black as we both wear the red robes of doctors of theology at our community college's annual graduation ceremonies. It was the constant goading of Martin Letcher and Linda Frazier that kept the idea of such a project alive and before me. So great was the support of my dear friend Martin, that she even traveled to England with me twice. After my family, the first person I wanted to tell of my book contract was Martin, but her life's thread had been cut short. She would have been so happy for me and I am sad that she will never hold the published book in her hands.

Acknowledgments

The Sisters of the Blessed Sacrament were unfailingly helpful in answering my inquiries, making their archives open to me, and granting interviews. Their archivist, Stephanie Morris, was most kind in helping to navigate all the materials there, especially the personal letters of St. Katharine Drexel, her family, and others. The Sisters of the Holy Family of Jerusalem, down the street from the SBS motherhouse in Bensalem, provided me with a week's hospitality while I worked in the SBS archives. Sister Claire Spellman, SND, my high school principal, mentor, and friend, shared some reminiscences of her novitiate days in the 1940s. Bobbye Burke, who began as a total stranger and ended up a valued friend, provided me with documents and information about nineteenth-century Catholicism in Philadelphia at Old St. Joseph's Church. Fr. Anthony J. Costa, of the Archdiocese of Philadelphia, lent me his thesis on St. Katharine Drexel. Bishop Joseph Martino of Scranton, at the intervention and request of Bishop Edward Slattery of Tulsa, lent me his personal, typewritten copy of the *positio* for St. Katharine Drexel, which I was able to study under the watchful eyes of Fr. James White in the Diocese of Tulsa archives. Friends Carol Kealiher and Mary Hittinger provided their eagle-eyed editing skills. Dr. Ann Loades and Dr. Sheridan Gilley, my advisers, and Dr. V. Alan McClellan and Dr. Russell Hittinger, my readers, were essential to my success at Durham University in Durham, England. It was really Ann Loades's enthusiasm for a project on Katharine Drexel that set the entire study in motion; before she signed on, it was just a good idea. Msgr. Gregory Gier has been a booster, along with George Schnetzer, Mary Lhevine, Monica Skrzypczak, Margaret Lee, Russell Hittinger, Mary Hittinger, Steven Wilson, and my entire academic division who were there at the end with toasts and congratulations. And, providentially, who should come along after the fact but the charming Mr. William B. Eerdmans, who saw the possibilities of a book on St. Katharine. He put me into the hands of the capable and ever-patient editor Linda Bieze.

Thank you one and all. Thank you, thank you, thank you!

Selected Bibliography

Primary Materials

The following Katharine Drexel collections, correspondence, and publications are in the archives of the motherhouse of the Sisters of the Blessed Sacrament, Bensalem, Pennsylvania:

———. *A Call from Jesus Dwelling in the Blessed Sacrament.* Bensalem, Pa.: Sisters of the Blessed Sacrament, 1912.

———. Christmas Thoughts.

———. Collected Journals.

———. *Conferences, Counsels, and Maxims of a Missionary Foundress.*

———. Conferences of Mother Katharine Drexel.

———. *Directory and Customs of the Sisters of the Blessed Sacrament for Indians and Colored People: Maxims and Counsels and Excerpts from Conferences of Mother Mary Katharine.* Cornwells Heights, Pa.: Sisters of the Blessed Sacrament, 1961.

———. *An Hour with St. Katharine Drexel.* Edited by Anthony F. Chiffolo. Liguori, Mo.: Liguorian Press, 1999.

———. Letters, Volumes I and II.

———. Letters to the Southwest Missions.

———. Meditation Slips.

———. Memoirs.

———. Notebooks.

———. *Praying with Mother Katharine Drexel.* Bensalem, Pa.: Sisters of the Blessed Sacrament, 1986.

———. *Reflections on Life in the Vine.* Bensalem, Pa.: Sisters of the Blessed Sacrament, 1982.

————. *Reflections on Religious Life*. Bensalem, Pa.: Sisters of the Blessed Sacrament, 1983.

————. Retreat Notes.

————. School Notebooks and Exercises.

————. Sisters of the Blessed Sacrament Holy Rule.

————. Sisters of the Blessed Sacrament. Annals.

————. Spiritual Conferences.

————. Old Annals.

Secondary Materials

Accattoli, Luigi. *When a Pope Asks Forgiveness: The Mea Culpa's of John Paul II*. Translated by Jordan Aumann. New York: Alba House, 1998.

Ahlstrom, Sydney E. *A Religious History of the American People*. New Haven: Yale University Press, 1973.

————. *A Religious History of the American People*. 2 vols. Garden City, N.Y.: Image Books, 1975.

Aumann, Jordan, OP. *Christian Spirituality in the Catholic Tradition*. San Francisco: Ignatius, 1985.

Bacik, James J. *Catholic Spirituality: Its History and Challenge*. New York: Paulist, 2002.

Badiou, Alain. *Ethics: An Essay on the Understanding of Evil*. Translated by Peter Hallward. London: Verso, 2001.

Baldwin, Lou. *A Call to Sanctity: The Formation and Life of Mother Katharine Drexel*. Philadelphia: Catholic Standard and Times, 1999.

————. *St. Katharine Drexel: Apostle to the Oppressed*. Edited by Rev. Paul S. Quinter, Elena Bucciarelli, and Frank Coyne. Philadelphia: Catholic Standard and Times, 2000.

Balthasar, Hans Urs von, SJ. *Christian Meditation*. Translated by Sr. Mary Thereselde Skerry. San Francisco: Ignatius, 1989.

————. *Thérèse of Lisieux: The Story of a Mission*. Translated by Donald Nicholl. New York: Sheed and Ward, 1954.

Baym, Nina, et al., eds. *Norton Anthology of American Literature*. 3rd shorter ed. New York: Norton, 1979.

Berkhof, Louis. *Systematic Theology*. Grand Rapids: Eerdmans, 1941.

Bernardin, Joseph Cardinal, ed. *John Paul II: A Panorama of His Teachings*. New York: New City Press, 1989.

Bodo, Murray, OFM. *Tales of an Endishodi: Father Bernard Haile and the Navajos, 1900-1961.* Albuquerque: University of New Mexico Press, 1998.

Bonaventure. *The Journey of the Mind to God.* Translated by Boehner Philotheus. Indianapolis: Hackett, 1993.

———. *The Mind's Road to God.* Translated by George Boas. Upper Saddle River, N.J.: Library of Liberal Arts, 1953.

Boyer, Louis. *The Christian Mystery from Pagan Myth to Christian Mysticism.* Translated by Illtyd Trethowam. Petersham, Mass.: St. Bede's Publications, 1995.

———. *History of Christian Spirituality.* 3 vols. New York: Seabury Press, 1969.

Boyer, Peter J. "Hollywood Heresy." *New Yorker,* May 22, 2006.

Brown, David. *Through the Eyes of the Saints: A Pilgrimage through History.* New York: Continuum, 2005.

Brown, Dee. *Bury My Heart at Wounded Knee: An Indian History of the American West.* New York: Henry Holt, 1990.

Brown, Peter. *The Cult of the Saints: Its Rise and Function in Latin Christianity.* Chicago: University of Chicago Press, 1981.

Burton, Katherine. *The Golden Door: The Life of Katharine Drexel.* New York: P. J. Kenedy and Sons, 1957.

Butler, Anne M. "Mother Katharine Drexel: Spiritual Visionary for the West." In *By Grit and by Grace: Eleven Women Who Shaped the American West,* edited by Glenda Riley and Richard Etulain. Golden, Colo.: Fulcrum, 1997.

Catechism of the Catholic Church. Washington, D.C.: United States Conference of Catholic Bishops, 1994.

Chinnici, Joseph P., OFM. *Living Stones: The History and Structure of Catholic Life in the United States.* New York: Macmillan, 1989.

Chinnici, Joseph P., OFM, and Angela Dries, OSF. *Prayer and Practice in the American Catholic Community.* Maryknoll, N.Y.: Orbis, 2000.

Coakley, Sarah. "Kenosis and Subversion: On the Repression of 'Vulnerability' in Christian Feminist Writing." In *Swallowing the Fishbone? Feminist Theologians Debate Christianity,* edited by Daphne Hampson. London: SPCK, 1996.

———. *Powers and Submissions: Spirituality, Philosophy, and Gender.* Oxford: Blackwell, 2002.

Coburn, Carol, and Martha Smith. *Spirited Lives: How Nuns Shaped Catholic Culture and American Lives, 1836-1920.* Chapel Hill: University of North Carolina Press, 1999.

Code of Canon Law, The. Translated by the Canon Law Society of Great Britain and Ireland. London: Canon Law Society Trust, 1983.

Conference of England and Wales, Bishops' Conference of Ireland, and Bishops' Conference of Scotland. *One Bread, One Body.* London: Veritas, 1998.

Congregation for the Causes of Saints. *Canonizationis Servae Dei Catherinae Drexel, Fundatricis Congregationis Sororum A SS. Sacramento Pro Indis et Colrata Gente, (1858-1955): Positio super virtutibus.* 3 vols. Rome, 1986. Vol. 1 written by Rev. Joseph Martino.

Congregation for the Doctrine of the Faith. *Instructions on Christian Freedom and Liberation.* Boston: Daughters of St. Paul, 1986.

————. *Some Aspects of the Church Understood as Communion.* Boston: St. Paul Books and Media, 1992.

Congregation for the Institutes of Consecrated Life and Societies of Apostolic Life. *Directives on Formation in Religious Institutes.* Boston: St. Paul Books and Media, 1994.

————. *Fraternal Life in Community.* Boston: St. Paul Books and Media, 1994.

————. *Instruction on the Contemplative Life and on the Enclosure of Nuns.* Boston: St. Paul Books and Media, 1999.

————. *Starting Afresh from Christ: A Renewed Commitment to Consecrated Life in the Third Millennium.* Boston: St. Paul Books and Media, 2002.

Cronin, Kevin M., OFM. *Kenosis: Emptying Self and the Path of Christian Service.* Rockport, Mass.: Element Books, 1992.

Cunningham, Lawrence S. *The Catholic Experience.* New York: Crossroad, 1986.

————. "Saints and Martyrs: Some Contemporary Considerations." *Theological Studies* 60, no. 3 (September 1999): 529.

Curran, Patricia, SND. *Grace Before Meals: Food Ritual and Body Discipline in Convent Culture.* Chicago: University of Illinois Press, 1989.

Daly, Mary. *Beyond God the Father: Towards a Philosophy of Women's Liberation.* Boston: Beacon Press, 1973.

————. *The Church and the Second Sex.* London: Geoffrey Chapman, 1968.

Davis, Cyprian. *The History of Black Catholics in the United States.* New York: Crossroad, 1990.

Davis, John H. *The Bouviers: Portrait of an American Family.* New York: Farrar, Straus and Giroux, 1969.

De Sales, St. Francis. *Introduction to the Devout Life.* Translated and edited by John K. Ryan. New York: Image Books, 1989.

Dolan, Jay P. *The American Catholic Experience: A History from Colonial Times to the Present.* Garden City, N.Y.: Doubleday, 1985.

————. *Catholic Revivalism: The American Experience, 1830-1900.* Notre Dame, Ind.: University of Notre Dame Press, 1978.

Downey, Michael. *Altogether Gift: A Trinitarian Spirituality.* Maryknoll, N.Y.: Orbis, 2000.

Drexel, Ellen Katharine. *St. Katharine Drexel: Friend of the Oppressed.* Boston: Paulist, 2000.

Duffy, Sr. Consuela, SBS. *Katharine Drexel: A Biography.* Philadelphia: Reilly Co., 1966. (This is the official biography of Drexel.)

Eliade, Mircea. *Rites and Symbols of Initiation: The Mysteries of Birth and Rebirth.* New York: Harper Torchbooks, 1958.

Ellis, John Tracy. *American Catholicism.* 2nd ed. rev. Chicago: University of Chicago Press, 1969.

————. *Documents of American Catholic History, 1493-1986.* 3 vols. Wilmington, Del.: Michael Glazier, 1991.

Faber, Frederick William. *The Precious Blood.* Rockford, Ill.: TAN Books, 1979.

————. *Spiritual Growth: The Progress of the Spiritual Life.* 15th ed. Baltimore: John Murphy, n.d.

Ferrero, Mario. "Competition for Sainthood and the Millennial Church." *Kyklos* 55 (2002): fasc. 3, 335-60.

Finke, Roger, and Rodney Stark. *The Churching of America, 1776-1990.* New Brunswick, N.J.: Rutgers University Press, 1992.

Flynn, Maureen. "The Spiritual Uses of Pain in Spanish Mysticism." *Journal of the American Academy of Religion* 65 (1995).

Frascati-Lochhead, Marta. *Kenosis and Feminist Theology: The Challenge of Gianni Vattimo.* Albany: State University of New York Press, 1998.

Garrigou-LaGrange, Reginald, OP. *Christian Perfection and Contemplation.* Translated by Sr. M. Timothea Doyle, OP. St. Louis: Herder, 1937.

————. *The Three Ages of the Interior Life.* Translated by Sr. M. Timothea Doyle, OP. St. Louis: Herder, 1948.

Glucklich, Ariel. "Sacred Pain and the Phenomenal Self." *Harvard Theological Review* 19, no. 4 (October 1998): 391-92.

Groeschel, Benedict, and James Monti. *In the Presence of Our Lord: The History, Theology, and Psychology of Eucharistic Devotion.* Huntington, Ind.: Our Sunday Visitor, 1997.

Groppe, Elizabeth Teresa. "The Contribution of Yves Congar's Theology of the Holy Spirit." *Theological Studies* 62, no. 3 (September 2001): 451.

Gunn, Robert Jingen. *Journey into Emptiness: Dogen, Merton, Jung, and the Quest for Transformation.* New York: Paulist, 2000.

Hampson, Daphne. *Theology and Feminism.* Oxford: Basil Blackwell, 1990.

Hayes, Diana. "A Sexual Ethic of Singleness — Built upon the Foundation of Celibacy." *Witness Magazine Online,* April 2000.

———. "Strong, Faith-filled Black Women Enrich U.S. Catholic Church." *National Catholic Reporter Online,* October 25, 2004.

———. "We've Come This Far by Faith: Black Catholics and Their Church." *U.S. Catholic Historian* 2 (Fall 2001): 15.

Hayes, Diana, and Cyprian Davis, OSB. *Taking Down Our Harps: Black Catholics in the United States.* New York: Orbis, 1998.

Hayes, Michael A., ed. *Mission and Evangelization.* London: Burns and Oates, 2004.

Heimann, Mary. *Catholic Devotion in Victorian England.* Oxford: Clarendon, 1995.

Hoose, Bernard, ed. *Christian Ethics: An Introduction.* Collegeville, Minn.: Liturgical Press, 1998.

Hoover, Rose. "The Communion of Saints: Lest the Journey Be Too Long." *The Way: Contemporary Christian Spirituality* 30 (July 1990): 216.

Hume, David. *Treatise of Human Nature.* Edited by L. A. Selby-Bigge. Oxford: Clarendon, 1967.

Jackson, Helen Hunt. *A Century of Dishonor.* New York: Harper and Brothers, 1881.

Jantzen, Grace M. *Power, Gender, and Christian Mysticism.* Cambridge: Cambridge University Press, 1995.

John XXIII. Opening Speech to Vatican Council II. October 11, 1962.

John of the Cross. "Ascent of Mount Carmel." In *The Collected Works of St. John of the Cross,* translated by Kiernan Kavanaugh, OCD, and Otilio Rodriguez, OCD. Washington, D.C.: ICS Publications, 1979.

John Paul II. *Christifideles Laici.* Boston: St. Paul Books and Media, n.d.

———. *Crossing the Threshold of Hope.* New York: Knopf, 1995.

———. *Dominicae Coenae.* Boston: St. Paul Books and Media, 1980.

———. *Ecclesia de Eucharistia.* Washington, D.C.: United States Conference of Catholic Bishops, May 2003.

———. *Ecclesia in America.* Boston: St. Paul Books and Media, 1999.

———. *Encyclicals of John Paul II, The.* Edited by J. Miller, CSB. Huntington, Ind.: Our Sunday Visitor, 2001.

——— [Karol Wojtyla]. *Faith according to St. John of the Cross.* San Francisco: Ignatius, 1981.

———. *Novo Millennio Ineunte.* Boston: St. Paul Books and Media, 2001.

———. *Original Unity of Man and Woman: Catechesis on the Book of Genesis.* Boston: St. Paul Books and Media, 1981.

———. *Redemptionis Donum.* Boston: St. Paul Books and Media, 1984.

———. *Rosarium Virginis Mariae.* Washington, D.C.: United States Conference of Catholic Bishops, February 2003.

————. *Salvifici Doloris.* Boston: St. Paul Books and Media, n.d.

———— [Karol Wojtyla]. *Sources of Renewal.* Translated by P. S. Falla. San Francisco: Harper and Row, 1980.

————. *Tertio Millennio Adveniente.* Boston: St. Paul Books and Media, 1994.

————. *Vita Consecrata.* Boston: St. Paul Books and Media, 1996.

Johnson, Elizabeth. "A Community of Holy People in a Sacred World." *New Theological Review* 12 (May 1999): 17.

————. *Friends of God and Prophets: A Feminist Theological Reading of the Communion of Saints.* New York: Continuum, 1998.

————. "Mary, Mary, Quite Contrary." *U.S. Catholic* 68, no. 12 (December 2003).

Johnson, Vernon. *Spiritual Childhood.* London: Sheed and Ward, 1977.

Keating, James, and David M. McCarthy. "Moral Theology with the Saints." *Modern Theology* 19, no. 2 (April 2003): 203ff.

"The K.K.K. Lives On." *Interracial Review* 19, no. 4 (April 1946): 52.

Koenig, Elizabeth. "Keeping Company with Jesus and the Saints." *Theology Today* 56 (April 1999): 18ff.

Koerner, Brendan. "Saint Makers." *U.S. News and World Report,* January 11, 1999, p. 53.

Lawrence, Brother. *The Practice of the Presence of God.* White Plains, N.Y.: Peter Pauper Press, 1963.

Legrande, Roland. "A Contemporary Pilgrimage; Personal Testimony of Blessed Katharine Drexel's Charism." *U.S. Catholic Historian* 8, no. 1 and 2 (Winter/Spring 1989): 48.

Lehmijoki-Gardner, Maiju, ed. and trans. *Dominican Penitent Women.* New York: Paulist, 2005.

Letterhouse, Sr. M. Dolores, SBS. *The Francis A. Drexel Family.* Cornwells Heights, Pa.: Sisters of the Blessed Sacrament, 1939.

Lincoln, Bruce. *Emerging from the Chrysalis: Studies in Rituals of Women's Initiation.* Cambridge: Harvard University Press, 1981.

Lounibos, John B. "Self-Emptying in Christian and Buddhist Spirituality." *Journal of Pastoral Counseling* 35, pp. 30-41. From a paper presented at the College Theology Society, Section on Spirituality, 46th Annual Convention, Villanova University, June 2, 2000.

Lynch, Sr. Patricia, SBS. *Sharing the Bread in Service: Sisters of the Blessed Sacrament, 1891-1991.* 2 vols. Bensalem, Pa.: Sisters of the Blessed Sacrament, 1998.

Lyotard, Jean-François. *The Differend: Phrases in Dispute.* Translated by George Van Den Abbeele. Minneapolis: University of Minnesota Press, 1988.

MacGregor, Geddes. *He Who Lets Us Be: A Theology of Love.* New York: Paragon House, 1987.

Malcolm, Lois. "An Interview with David Tracy." *Christian Century,* February 24-30, 2002, p. 24.

Mardock, Robert Winston. *The Reformers and the American Indian.* St. Louis: University of Missouri Press, 1971.

Martin, Ralph, and Peter Williamson, eds. *Pope John Paul II and the New Evangelization: How You Can Bring the Good News to Others.* San Francisco: Ignatius, 1995.

Martins, Cardinal Jose Saraiva, CMF. "Lives of the Saints Show the World the Divine in the Human." *L'Osservatore Romano,* weekly English ed., April 16, 2003, p. 9.

McCormack, Bruce L. "Karl Barth's Christology as a Resource for a Reformed Version of Kenoticism." *International Journal of Systematic Theology* 8, no. 3 (July 2006).

McNeill, John Thomas, and Helena M. Gamer, eds. *Medieval Handbook of Penance.* New York: Columbia University Press, 1938.

Merton, Rev. Thomas. *Spiritual Direction and Meditation.* Collegeville, Minn.: Liturgical Press, 1960.

Mitchell, Donald W. *Spirituality and Emptiness: The Dynamics of Spiritual Life in Buddhism and Christianity.* New York: Paulist, 1991.

Morris, Charles R. *American Catholic: The Saints and Sinners Who Built America's Most Powerful Church.* New York: Times Books, 1997.

Morrow, Diane Batts. *Persons of Color and Religious at the Same Time: Oblate Sisters of Providence, 1828-1860.* Chapel Hill: University of North Carolina Press, 2002.

Nolan, Bruce. "Xavier Nun Reaches Sainthood: Katharine Drexel Helped Minorities." *Times Picayune,* October 1, 2000, p. 1.

Nowak, Archbishop Edward. "New Evangelization with the Saints." *L'Osservatore Romano,* weekly English ed., November 28, 2001.

———. "Saints Prove That Christ Appeals to All Hearts." *L'Osservatore Romano,* weekly English ed., November 28, 2001, p. 3.

Oates, Mary J. *The Catholic Philanthropic Tradition in America.* Bloomington: Indiana University Press, 1995.

Oepke, Albrecht. "Kenoō." In *Theological Dictionary of the New Testament,* edited by Gerhard Kittel. 8th ed. Vol. 3. Grand Rapids: Eerdmans, 1981.

Packard, Jerrold M. *American Nightmare: The History of Jim Crow.* New York: St. Martin's Press, 2002.

Plessy v. Ferguson. Judgement, Decided May 18, 1886. *Records of the Supreme*

Court of the United States. Record Group 267, 163, #15248, National Archives, Washington, D.C.

Plutarch. *Lives of Noble Greeks.* Edited by Edmund Fuller. New York: Dell, 1971.

Podimattam, Felix M., OFM Cap. *Kenosis Spirituality: Paschal Path to Holiness.* Malleswaram, Bangalore, India: Claritian Publications, 2002.

Polkinghorne, John, ed. *The Work of Love.* Grand Rapids: Eerdmans, 2001.

Prucha, Francis Paul. *American Indian Policy in Crisis: Christian Reformers and the Indian, 1865-1900.* Norman: University of Oklahoma Press, 1976.

————, ed. *Americanizing the American Indians: Writings by the "Friends of the Indians," 1880-1900.* Cambridge: Harvard University Press, 1973.

Rahner, Karl. "The Church of the Saints." In *Theological Investigations,* vol. 3, translated by Karl H. Kruger and Boniface Kruger, pp. 91ff. Baltimore: Helicon Press, 1966.

————. *Theological Investigations.* Vol. 3, *Theology of the Spiritual Life.* Translated by Karl H. Kruger and Boniface Kruger. New York: Crossroad, 1982.

Ranjith, Malcolm. "The Eucharistic Spirituality of the Church." *L'Osservatore Romano,* weekly English ed., July 21, 2004, p. 8.

Ratzinger, Joseph Cardinal. "Letter to the Bishops of the Catholic Church on the Collaboration of Men and Women in the Church and in the World." July 31, 2004.

————. *The Ratzinger Report: An Exclusive Interview on the State of the Church,* with Vittorio Messori. Translated by Salvator Attanasio and Graham Harrison. San Francisco: Ignatius, 1986.

Reeves, Thomas C. *Twentieth Century America: A Brief History.* New York: Oxford University Press, 2000.

Regan, Margaret. "A Saint among Us: St. Katharine Drexel." *Tucson Weekly,* October 5, 2000.

Richard, Lucien, OMI. *Christ: The Self-Emptying God.* New York: Paulist, 1997.

Rottenberg, Dan. *The Man Who Made Wall Street: Anthony J. Drexel and the Rise of Modern Finance.* Philadelphia: University of Pennsylvania Press, 2001.

Ruether, Rosemary Radford. *Sexism and God-Talk.* London: SCM, 1983.

Russell, Letty M. *Becoming Human.* Philadelphia: Westminster, 1982.

————. *Human Liberation in a Feminist Perspective: A Theology.* Philadelphia: Westminster, 1974.

Ryan, Thomas, ed. *Reclaiming the Body in Christian Spirituality.* New York: Paulist, 2004.

Scarry, Elaine. *The Body in Pain: The Making and Unmaking of the World.* New York: Oxford University Press, 1985.

Schneiders, Sandra. "Religious Life: The Dialectic between Marginality and Transformation." *Theology Today* 40 (Winter 1988): 59ff.

Schüssler Fiorenza, Elisabeth. *In Memory of Her: A Feminist Reconstruction of Christian Origins.* London: SCM, 1983.

Shakespeare, William. *Hamlet.* In *The Complete Works of Shakespeare,* edited by Hardin Craig. Chicago: Scott, Foresman, 1961.

Sheldrake, Philip. *Spirituality and History: Questions of Interpretation and Method.* London: SPCK, 1991.

Sisters of the Blessed Sacrament. *Golden Jubilee Booklet, 1891-1941.* Cornwells Heights, Pa.: Sisters of the Blessed Sacrament, 1941.

Sixteen Documents of Vatican II, The. Introduced by Douglas Bushman. General editor, Marianne Lorraine Trouvé. Boston: Pauline Books and Media, 1999.

Sorokin, Pitirim A. *Altruistic Love: A Study of American "Good Neighbors" and Christian Saints.* Boston: Beacon Press, 1950.

Stewart, George C., Jr. *Marvels of Charity: History of American Sisters and Nuns.* Huntington, Ind.: Our Sunday Visitor, 1994.

Sullivan, Lawrence P. *Icanchu's Drum: An Orientation to Meaning in South American Religions.* New York: Macmillan, 1988.

Tarry, Ellen. *Katharine Drexel: Friend of the Neglected.* Nashville: Winston-Derek Publishers, 1990.

————. *Saint Katharine Drexel: Friend of the Oppressed.* Boston: Pauline Books and Media, 2000.

Taves, Ann. *The Household of Faith: Roman Catholic Devotions in Mid-Nineteenth-Century America.* Notre Dame, Ind.: University of Notre Dame Press, 1986.

Teresa of Avila. *Interior Castle.* Translated by E. Allison Peers. New York: Image Books, 1989.

Thomasius, Gottfried. "Against Dorner." In *God and Incarnation in Mid-Nineteenth-Century German Theology: G. Thomasius, I. A. Dorner, A. E. Biedermann,* translated and edited by Claude Welch. New York: Oxford University Press, 1965.

Tilley, Maureen. "The Ascetic Body and the (Un)Making of the World." *Journal of the American Academy of Religion* 59 (1990).

Tillich, Paul. "The Theology of Missions." *Christianity and Crisis,* March 4, 1955.

Tracy, David. *The Analogical Imagination: Christian Theology and the Culture of Pluralism.* New York: Crossroad, 1981.

Unsworth, Tim. "Racism and Religion: Partners in Crime?" *Salt of the Earth,* March 1994.

Vance-Trembath, Sally M. "John Paul II's *Ut Unum Sint* and Conversations with Women." *Theological Studies* 40, no. 2 (March 1999).

Weigel, George. "A Century of Saints." *Wall Street Journal,* Eastern ed., October 4, 2000, p. A26.

————. *Witness to Hope: The Biography of Pope John Paul II.* New York: Cliff Street Books, 2001.

Weinstein, Donald, and Rudolph M. Bell. *Saints and Society: The Two Worlds of Western Christendom, 1000-1700.* Chicago: University of Chicago Press, 1982.

White, James D. *Getting Sense: The Osages and Their Missionaries.* Tulsa: Sarto Press, 1997.

————. *This Far by Faith: 1875-2000, 125 Years of Catholic Life in Oklahoma.* Tulsa: Sarto Press, 2000.

————, ed. *Diary of a Frontier Bishop.* Tulsa: Sarto Press, 1996.

Williams, Lee E., and Lee E. Williams II. *Anatomy of Four Race Riots: Racial Conflict in Knoxville, Elaine (Arkansas), Tulsa, and Chicago, 1919-1921.* Oxford: University and College Press of Mississippi, 1972.

Wilson, Stephen, ed. *Saints and Their Cults: Studies in Religious Sociology, Folklore, and History.* Cambridge: Cambridge University Press, 1983.

Woodward, Kenneth L. *Making Saints: How the Catholic Church Determines Who Becomes a Saint, Who Doesn't, and Why.* New York: Simon and Schuster, 1990.

Zaleski, Philip. "The Saints of John Paul II." *First Things,* no. 161 (March 2006): 28.

Unpublished Dissertations

Costa, Anthony J. "The Spirituality of St. Katharine Drexel: Eucharistic Devotion Nourishing Apostolic Works." Rome: Facultate S. Theologiae, Apud Pontificiam Universitatem S. Thomae, 2001.

Web sites

Sisters of the Blessed Sacrament: http://www.katharinedrexel.org/home.html.

The Vatican: http://www.vatican.va/.

Index